PAP$4.47

P9-DGL-404

STAINED GLASS
LAMPS
Construction and Design

Construction and Design

ANITA AND SEYMOUR ISENBERG
are also the authors of
How to Work in Stained Glass,
published by Chilton Book Company in 1972

STAINED GLASS LAMPS

LAMPS

Anita and Seymour Isenberg

CHILTON BOOK COMPANY

Radnor, Pennsylvania

Copyright © 1974 by Anita and Seymour Isenberg

All rights reserved
Published in Radnor, Pa. by Chilton Book Company
and simultaneously in Ontario, Canada,
by Thomas Nelson & Sons, Ltd.
Designed by William E. Lickfield
Manufactured in the United States of America

LIBRARY OF CONGRESS CATALOGING IN PUBLICATION DATA

Isenberg, Anita.
   Stained glass lamps.
   (Chilton's creative crafts series)
   Includes bibliographies.
   1. Glass craft.   2. Glass painting and staining.
3. Lampshades, Glass.   I. Isenberg, Seymour,
joint author.   II. Title.
TT298.I84   745.59'32   73-16084
ISBN 0-8019-5839-3
ISBN 0-8019-5840-7 (pbk.)

4567890   43210987

To ARTHUR—
who still hasn't gotten his lamp

Foreword

The enthusiasm accorded our previous book (*How to Work in Stained Glass*, Chilton Book Company) indicated a widespread, active audience which would eventually require more specific information than a survey volume could provide. Judging from the letters crossing our desk, interest was most insistently directed toward stained glass lampshades—designs, procedures, patterns, calculations and examples.

If you want to make a stained glass shade, you can do so guided by the information in this book. We suggest that you may find the going easier if you acquire some further background about working with stained glass from our previous book. This volume, however, is meant to be self-sustaining and, as such, will give you the basic essentials of working with glass before taking you into more sophisticated projects. Of necessity we have had to cover briefly some of the material dwelt on at length in our prior book; for this we ask the indulgence of the reader of our former work while feeling at the same time that the review will do him no harm.

Our original intent regarding the patterns you will find here was to publish them to exact size. This proved infeasible, but you can bring them up to size without much difficulty by the use of either graph paper or a pantograph or an enlarging projector.

We have broken down the lamps into an arbitrary classification strictly for teaching purposes. We have attempted a number of different methods of placing shades in different "classes" for descriptive purposes, and the listing we have selected here seems to work the best. For the purist who may insist that what we describe as a square or rectangular shade is really pyramidal, we have no argument. The criteria for our classifications have been the techniques needed for working on the lamp. Our classification is based more on this than on the outward shape of any project.

Although we have attempted to categorize the various types of lamps available, individual experimentation and flair cannot be bound in pockets of convenience. When is a lamp not a lamp? (See Fig. 1.) We would take the broad definition here and describe any sculptured object that gives off light as a

Fig. 1 Stained glass "shield" light. The curvature of this piece just allows for light from behind it to flow gracefully over its surface and illuminate a space in front of it. Not a lamp? We disagree.

stained glass lamp. A few of the best we have seen are pictured on these pages. Whatever your own definition is, hopefully this, as well as the following chapters, will encompass it.

A word as to the photographs. Of all subject matter, stained glass is probably the most frustrating to get on film. If you use a flash, you will get a certain amount of "bounce back," and if you don't, you will probably not capture the image you want. We take all our pictures under studio conditions—well lighted with photo floods and a white background with minimum shadow. A lot of experimentation was necessary to achieve the correct lighting balance. We used two cameras—a 35mm Leica® and a Rolleiflex® 120mm. While the larger Rolleiflex negative is more gratifying enlargement-wise and the camera superb for still-life shots, it is a little awkward for shooting over someone's shoulder for a sequential procedure. Here the flexibility of the 35mm comes into play. It is a good idea to get a camera for your studio no matter how small your output of stained glass and to learn to photograph all your work. The camera makes no excuses; your eyes well may. Looked at through a camera's lens, your craft is given the most objective criticism possible. But then, that's probably a book in itself.

Northvale, New Jersey, 1973

Acknowledgments

It is likely that the only people who read this section are those who presume their names will be mentioned. Yet the majority of individuals who helped bring this book into being must go nameless. They are the ones whose encouraging letters and telegrams regarding our earlier book provided the stimulus for us to go ahead with another. To list all of you by name would add another chapter to a work which has already run something more than originally calculated. What matter? You know who you are—and so do we. Our thanks.

More specifically our thanks to Leah Burger for her line drawings and collating, to Greta Vardi for getting many of the patterns into final form, to Albert Burger for his mold experiments, to Clemence Stanley and Gertrude Clark for taking on their shoulders a lot of Stained Glass Club business so as to give us some much needed extra time, to Ed Ferman for his patient teaching of camera technique, and to the Hobby Industry Association of America for their very effective public relations.

All illustrations are by the authors as are the works demonstrated unless otherwise noted.

Contents

Foreword   vii

Acknowledgments   ix

PART I
PRELIMINARIES   *Chapter 1*   INTRODUCTION   1

The Fascination of Stained Glass Lampshades   1
A Brief History   2
Plastic Versus Stained Glass   4
Opalescent or Transparent Glass?   4
Types of Stained Glass   5
Advantages of Doing It Yourself   6
Artistry Is a Matter of Degree   7

Chapter 2   GETTING DOWN TO BASICS   8

The Workspace   8
Necessary Tools and Supplies   10
Cutting Glass   13
Working with Lead   16
Soldering Procedure   18
The Sketch—Initial Idea to Final Design   19
Making the Pattern   20
Think in 3-D   22
The Final Design—Function and Decor   23

Chapter 3   FABRICATING YOUR LAMP   25

Crowns and Skirts   25
Calculating Your Space   31
The Cardboard Mock-Up   33
Kitchen, Hallway, Bedroom or Bath?   37
Foil or Came?   37
Beginning and Advanced Productions   39
Mixing Different Glasses   41

Chapter 4   WIRING AND HANGING   42

    A Lamp Must Be Sturdy   42
    Types of Chains and Fixtures   47
    Swagging or Capping?   49
    Placing Your Lamp—How High or How Low?   50
    Hanging Versus Table Lamps   51
    Bases   53
    The Antique Shop   56
    A Fixture Need Not Be Fixed   59

PART II
PROCEDURES   Chapter 5   THE LANTERN   61

    Designs and Constructions   62
    Odd and Even Panels   72
    Getting the Right Angle Even   72
    Designing the Metal Top   75
    Choice of Bulbs   79
    Sconces   79
    Candleholders   80

Chapter 6   THE STRAIGHT PANEL LAMP   86

    Pyramid Style with Added Skirt   86
    The Tiered Pyramidal Shade   92
    The Multi-Pieced Pyramid   100
    Tiered Pyramid Style with Ornate Skirt   103
    The Inverted Pyramid   106

Chapter 7   TUBULAR SHADES   108

    Calculating the Design   108
    Rolling the Tubular Shade   109
    Molding the Tubular Shade   110
    Closed Tubular Shades   111

Chapter 8   SQUARE AND RECTANGULAR SHADES   114

    Getting the Sides Even   114
    Reinforcing the Sides   116
    Inlays and Offsets   117
    Skirting the Edges   118
    Brass Came—A Specific Use   120
    Ornamental Lead Effects   122
    Casting Your Own Designs in Lead   122

Chapter 9   THE GLOBE SHADE   134

    Making the Globe from a Form   134
    Use of an Existing Globe   140

Chapter 10   THE STORY LAMPS   142

What Is a Story Lamp?   142
Straight Panel Lamp with a Story Skirt   143
The Fruited Skirt   144
The Bent Panel Lamp with a Story Skirt   150
The Tiffany Style Small-Pieced Lamp   151
   Creating Your Form   154
   Getting Your Design on the Mold   157
   Cutting the Glass to Fit Your Pattern 159
   Using Copper Foil   160
   Soldering the Pieces on the Mold   164
   The Grozing Pliers   166

Chapter 11   THE BENT PANEL LAMP   170

Calculating the Dimensions   170
Designing the Mold   174
Heating the Mold   176
Using the Kiln   178
Putting the Lamp Together   180

PART III
POSTSCRIPT   *Chapter 12*   SELLING YOUR WORK   185

Advertising   185
   Talking to Groups   185
   Craft Magazine Displays   186
Dealing with Clients   188
Lamp Kits   188
Consignments   189

Chapter 13   TEACHING   190

Advantages of Teaching   190
Where to Teach   190
A Basic Curriculum   191
Acquiring Self-Confidence   192
Outlining Your Course   192
How Not to Teach a Class   193
Helpful Teaching Techniques   193

Chapter 14   REPAIRS   195

A Quick Survey   195
   Straight Panel Lamps   196
   Bent Panel Lamps   198
   Small-Pieced Lamps   203
   Pricing   205

PART IV
POTPOURRI   *Afterword*   207

Magazines Dealing With Stained Glass   208

Lamp Mathematics   209

Suppliers   214

Glossary   215

Bibliography   219

Index   220

PART I
Preliminaries

CLAUDIUS: Give me some light—away!
ALL: Lights, lights, lights!
Hamlet, Act III, Sc. ii.

Chapter 1

Introduction

If you prefer lighting one candle to cursing the darkness, the shades provided here may turn *you* on. The vibrant colors of stained glass glowing in a darkened room set off their surroundings and add an electricity to their precincts out of all proportion to the current supplying them. Lampshades made of this material become, in fact, stained glass lightboxes. Such a shade, three-dimensional as it is, becomes the central focus of the room in which it is placed and, depending on its style and positioning, may overwhelm any other decor, so potent and individualistic is its character.

Part of the ever-growing interest in stained glass lampshades is due to the tremendous surge of excitement growing out of the rediscovery of stained glass as an art form adaptable to the interests of hobbyist and professional alike. While the homes of most individuals have limited space for the planning and installation of a stained glass window, fireplace screen or room divider, almost any home can readily accommodate a stained glass lampshade. In fact, a number of the homes for which the authors have designed such shades have six or seven. It is small wonder then that the beginning student should desire to make a lamp as his first project in stained glass (an ambition to be deplored) and that his teacher, though knowing better, should succumb to his blandishments. As will be described in a later chapter, such an allowance accounts for a good many of the poor lamps hanging around. The fact of the matter is that the production of these items represents a specialty within a craft form that is itself particularized to a high degree. The assumption is erroneously made that just because one has had an introductory lesson or two in the craft as a whole, or even if one has not, a lamp is the logical place to proceed simply because it may be the most practical thing to make. The notion that a teaching session must immediately turn out a utilitarian end product is a contradiction in terms. It is part of the fascination with this art form that students want their products as soon as possible. With suncatchers, pendants or even small panels, this is possible; with lampshades, it is possible only by compromising the original intent to a crippling degree. The lack of any workbook on lamp making per se has contributed

Fig. 1.1 A bevy of lamps in flight, various styles.

greatly to the present hit or miss methodology. Hopefully this book will provide a guide to this rather exacting craft form that, while not limiting enthusiasm, will channel it into more productive ends.

A Brief History

Unlike windows of stained glass, lampshades have a fairly brief history. While the idea was not Louis C. Tiffany's alone, he is pretty much recognized as the father of the stained glass shade and its most productive designer. The turn of the century in this country saw a turn toward "the arts," and by the 1920s "art nouveau" was in full swing. Tiffany's delicate, lacelike creations were never really mass-produced by machine, but machines were developed by other companies to bend glass on molds of Swedish steel and stamp them out like so many belt buckles. A brass channeling was used and form fitted around these panels to provide strength, brass being a material that is also solderable. The glass used in these shades was invariably opalescent and almost invariably caramel in color. One wonders why this rather bland tone was so popular; the supposition can only be that such a hue fitted in with just about any other color combination the purchaser may have had in his home. Two general shapes of panels were produced: the C curve, a single bend, and the S curve, a double bend, though not of necessity making an even division of the panel into thirds. With their rimming of brass channeling, such panels were placed into a holding template, soldered together and formed into a basic shape. Individual stylizations were then added. In many instances, a flat strip of brass was passed over the seams dividing the panels; ornate stampings might be used here. Where such stampings were made of white metal eventual strain set in diminishing the life of the shade and leading to the eventual repair or replacement of the frame. We have had a great many such fixtures in for treatment. While many bent panel lamps needed no skirt, the design of the bend carrying the eye gracefully downward, most of them did re-

Fig. 1.2 Old frames reglassed and up-classed. These will hang in a cluster at various levels.

quire the addition of a crown. In the main, these small pieces also were curved and put together in the same manner as the body of the lamp, the flare of the curve facing in the same direction. A wide band of brass or brass filigree might then be used to mark the separation of crown and body; the manner of application of such a demarcation was again up to individual stylization.

Certain of the bent panel lamps required a skirt as well as a crown. These included the so-called "fruit" lamps. In these instances, the bent panel was foreshortened in design so as to come up to a strong right angle line against which a skirt of small pieces of glass continued the slope. As before, the seam between skirt and body was usually hidden by a decorative flat strip of brass or white metal.

An alternate method of attaching the panels was sometimes employed. In cases where it was more convenient, for purposes of design or ease of fabrication, not to rim each panel with brass and solder them together, clips were used to secure the panels individually to the frame. Variations of this technique developed almost simultaneously with the cutting of channels into some frames, top and bottom, with either rigid or flexible metal sidings. We will consider these instances later in this book in the chapter on repairs. Skirt pieces were also treated this way in certain frames.

Following the surge of interest in stained glass lampshades in the 1920s and 1930s, a violent repudiation became manifest. In later years, interest in these products not only waned but became what one can only characterize as an active disdain. The cause of this was the nature of the material with which the shades were made—the glass itself. As the shades went out of fashion (and the fact that they never entirely did so is demonstrated by the considerable number of them that still survive in pristine condition), people began relegating them to attics and basements, where careless storage resulted in a panel or two becoming cracked or broken. These being difficult and costly to replace, the lampshade was considered useless and sent to the garbage heap. Where more considerate heads prevailed, rescues were accomplished which have paid off handsomely in dollars and cents, such lamps going at auction for between four and nine hundred dollars. The lucky inheritors of "grandmother's old lampshades" may well forgive the old lady for the storehouse of trash they had to plow through to find them.

Today a number of businesses are busily engaged in the reproduction of many of these old shades—both bent panel and Tiffany-type—for a burgeoning market. In fact, the market has become so large as to cause a critical shortage of stained glass, and the existing factories cannot keep up with the demand. Prices of these new goods vary from extremely cheap for some of the less ornate bent panel shades, to quite dear (in the hundreds of dollars) for the lacy Tiffany styles. Yet the critical eye can easily tell the difference between the old and the new. For all their exuberance of color and copycat originality, these recent arrivals have a raw look, a demeanor of inexperience that fades them to insignificant late arrivals when compared to the aged benevolence of the true antiques. If you can afford one of these antiques in good condition, you're probably in pretty good condition yourself. Certainly, rather than buying a new one (even if you are lucky enough to have an old one), you will find as much, if not more, joy in creating one with your own hands.

PLASTIC VERSUS STAINED GLASS

We have no argument with individuals who prefer one craft modality over another; we reserve our ire for those who cannot tell them apart. Despite the fact they may be exhibiting under a sign that plainly proclaims their medium, few workers in stained glass have escaped the question: "Is this really glass or is it plastic?" The fact is that people are more used to plastic than to glass, especially in lampshades, and they find it hard to believe, as we were recently informed by a prospective client, that "glass can so perfectly mimic plastic." The fact that the shoe is actually on the other foot, that plastic lampshades have been copying glass ones, doesn't shoo away the basic misunderstanding. The more exposure the general public gets to stained glass in general and to lampshades in particular, the more knowledgeable they will become and the more ready they will be to accept stained glass as a part of the decor of their home. It goes without saying that for the craftsman anxious to sell his wares, or the hobby shop involved in selling supplies, this is a consummation devoutly to be wished. The differences between plastic and stained glass should be explained to anyone curious enough to ask. A lampshade of plastic cannot compare to one of stained glass in beauty, selection of color tone, texture, character—or, in some instances, even price. Generally the glass one will be more expensive, but then, you pay for what you get. We've gotten a number of stained glass shades in for repair whose owners have decided that they would rather put the money into plastic. We were happy to take the stained glass off their hands; in this instance at least, we had no argument with their choice.

OPALESCENT OR TRANSPARENT GLASS?

In choosing to make a stained glass lamp, you must have a knowledge of stained glass itself. This is true even if you are depending on someone else to make the shade for you. Very rarely should a shade be made entirely of transparent glass. We have stated previously that a stained glass shade is really a lightbox; such a device must be constructed so that light from within can illuminate the entire surface. Actual lightboxes have a backing of reflective material—tinfoil, for example—which will throw the luminescence where it is wanted. The shade must achieve the same effect through the quality of the glass. Only opalescent glass will catch the light between its surfaces and run it round the shade to show an even dispersion of the bulb's output and a uniform exhibition of the beauties of the workmanship. This does not mean that transparent glass has no place in these creations. Quite the contrary, such glass employed in "touches" here and there will add a sparkle to and set off the opalescent colors like gems in a setting. We do not feel, however, that using transparent glass in amounts sufficient to allow the bulb to be seen adds anything to the lamp's beauty or effect. Long panel lamps, especially when made of antique or cathedral glass, will show no color—or practically none—with the light off, even in the sunniest room and only the "hot spot" of the bulb with the light on.

You can, if you insist on using transparent glass, treat it in one of several ways that will allow it to reflect more light and show less bulb. Placing one surface in hydrofluoric acid will "fog" the treated side and make it less apt to allow the passage of light. You must be careful not to allow the acid to work on it too long, however, or it will eat into the glass, making the surface pitted and uneven. Sandblasting one surface will also do the trick—though you have to be pretty determined to avoid using opalescent glass to go ahead with this. Probably the simplest way to treat transparent glass is to spray one side of your lamp with Glass Frosting® after it is all put together. This quick-drying, nontoxic material is available at many hardware or glazier's stores. Its use requires clean glass surface; all flux residues must be assiduously wiped off, and the underlying surface should be dry. The material comes in a spray can which must be kept at room temperature (70°F) for at least one hour before use. The can is shaken vigorously prior to use (there are agitators within it to stir up the material), and the nozzle is held from twelve to eighteen inches away from the surface to be treated. The spray is applied with a side-to-side hand motion for even application. If too much spray is applied at once, it will condense and form rivulets down the glass. If you want a heavily frosted effect, you must apply many coats of this material, waiting a good thirty minutes between applications.

TYPES OF STAINED GLASS

We have been using the terms "opalescent" and "transparent" glass pretty freely. Perhaps it is best, at this point, to define exactly what we mean. When we speak of opalescent glass, we are talking of glass sheets of multiple colors of a consistency impenetrable to vision, though not entirely to light. Thus, while one cannot see through this glass, enough light will come through it to give the glass an effect of "lighting up" from within. Such glass reflects light well and will present its color scheme whether backlighted or not; a lamp made of this material need not be turned on to look beautiful, though when lighted its beauty is even more to be appreciated. Opalescent glass (with the exception of pure white) rarely comes in a solid color. Occasionally as many as three or four colors may be mixed in a sheet in great whorls and shades. Needless to say, this alone can make it a very exciting glass to work with—and a dangerous one as far as combining different colors is concerned. It is a physically harder glass than the transparent, and a special cutter (opalescent, Fletcher® # 06 or 07) should be used when working with it. Opalescent glass is somewhat more difficult to cut than other types, and the use of an improper cutter will make it an unhappy experience; break lines tend to run off the score lines if they do not have clean cut score lines to follow. Use of the proper cutter will allow you to enjoy your acquaintance with this material.

Transparent glass is a general term combining the handblown, generally imported, "antique" and the home-grown "cathedral" glasses. While the hues and tones of antique glass represent the height of perfection of stained glass, not much of it is usually incorporated into lampshades. There are two reasons for this: its cost (it is the most expensive of the stained glasses) and its utter transparency. While this latter characteristic is a prized item in a window, in a lamp it can only be employed in moderation, as we have explained. The same is true of the transparent cathedral or "double rolled" domestic glasses. However, certain types of these, though they reflect light poorly, transmit it equally poorly, allowing their use in shades to a greater extent than the totally clear. Such glasses may have a roughened back (moss-backed, granite-backed, shell-backed) or a demented front (Flemish, rondelite) with impressed lines or channels running in all directions. Flemish and rondelite are hard to cut because of this channeling, but light passing through them, or through the roughened back glasses, is so fragmented that objects seen through their surfaces appear blurry. Incidentally, it doesn't matter which surface you use as the "front" of your lamp, though of course, any roughened back glass would have to be cut on its smooth side. To allow for the roughened side to be "up," you would just reverse your pattern.

Mirror, though not a stained glass, has been used in lampshades quite dramatically. To all intents and purposes, it would be considered an opalescent glass.

ADVANTAGES OF DOING IT YOURSELF

While the cost factor of a completed lamp done by someone else has brought individuals to the idea of doing it themselves and thereby saving money, this should not, important as it is, be the sole reason for going into a craft field. One does not, after all, make one's own refrigerator, furniture or silverware strictly with the idea of saving money. We have known individuals who have done such things because they were also interested in having a unique item or set of items coming out exactly as they had planned them.

This, then, is the main advantage of doing something yourself. There is no question that in any field of endeavor, you will save money by not hiring out the work; but if you do not enjoy doing the work, you are wasting time—an item more expensive than any salvage of funds. This is especially true in the hobby field, where the advantages of doing it yourself mean relaxation, involvement, creativity—and even destruction.

It is a good feeling to be able to destroy a piece of your work knowing that it is not worthy of your better efforts. You can always salvage the glass and the lead from your failures and start over, and you can't do that with painting or ceramics. You can't develop self-criticism with someone else's work—only your own will do. And a sharpness of judgment and self-evaluation comes out of this learned ability for self-criticism.

Stained glass is a very flexible craft. Just because an item is assembled, this doesn't mean it is done. Some of the finest shades turned out by our students were redone several times before they approached anything like the original intent. When you buy someone else's work you are not involved with it personally no matter how lovely it may be. When someone buys a piece of work from you which you know to be good (even if that someone is yourself) the feeling is quite unique. Give yourself a chance to experience it.

ARTISTRY IS A MATTER OF DEGREE

Artistry is not a matter of any earned degree. A Masters in Art intimates knowledge of the subject; it does not necessarily imply inspiration. One individual's accomplishment is another's primary faltering, but don't be frightened by the word Art. It should not discourage anyone from creating according to his lights—especially in the field of stained glass. A good part of the trouble with this medium, and one reason why we have so much difficulty with students criticizing their own work, is due to the work being so colorful and unique that even poor work is made to look good. So don't shy away from initial attempts thinking you are not artistic; chances are you'll go to the other extreme on seeing the completed project. In lampmaking, especially, artistic ability is not a prerequisite. Lamps are basically geometric shapes. Artistic touches, if any, can be added as they are learned. In this book, we will concentrate on the technique and the shapes so that, as your artistic ability develops, you will have a firm grounding that will allow you to express it. We have included enough basic patterns to give you a start. We think that those we gave you dimensions for look best at the dimensions given. Those without dimensions can be adapted to any size once you get a feel for the effects various sizes and designs have on their surroundings.

Chapter 2

Getting Down To Basics

THE WORKSPACE

THE WORKSPACE

An area with plenty of natural daylight is the best workspace. Unfortunately, individuals working in this most light-dependent of crafts usually find themselves in a basement or cellar. If that's where the room is, then you'll have to sacrifice the north light and sunshine because space is an absolute necessity both for ease of operation and to avoid accidents. You will be working with sharp pieces of glass, chemicals and hot irons; they will all work on you if you don't give them room to breathe. You can always walk up the stairs to hold a color up to natural light, and once you have it set in your mind, you can use your lightbox to make comparisons with other colors.

Your workspace should be as large as you can make it. You *can* work in a closet, if that's all you have; after a while, however, you'll acquire all sorts of hang-ups. Don't spread yourself thin, but do spread yourself out. Leave space to walk about, and use the space you have as efficiently as possible. The more room you find, the more you'll find to fill it; at least fill it with items of convenience—like aisles.

The largest objects in your workspace will be your worktable and your glass storage bins. The worktable, ideally, should have a top composed of a four- by eight-foot sheet of plywood 3/4 inch thick. This may rest on sawhorses or, better yet, on a frame built for it out of two by fours with corner legs. The room beneath may be used for the storage of lead, work in progress, drawings and other large and bulky objects. It is imperative that your worktable be firm. If it is going to wiggle about while you work because one leg is shorter than another or because the top is not balanced properly, your end products are going to look seasick. If you haven't the room for this much table, compromise it to the space available. It still must be firm.

The glass storage bins will conform to the size of glass you buy. (Fig. 2.1.) If you are not using full sheets—and most hobbyists do not, since a full sheet of cathedral glass is four feet by eight feet—you may be using half sheets. Half sheets have their own size wooden case, and you may be able to get hold of a few of these from your supplier. If this is still too much glass for you, try wooden

Fig. 2.1 Scrap glass pieces can be filed in boxes according to color and used as necessary.

crates from your local supermarket. These will stack nicely and, with some additions to the wooden slats already present, will make good holding bins. You may want to add some cigar boxes or old file drawers to the glass bin section to hold smaller pieces arranged by color. As you keep working with your material, you will accumulate more and more scrap glass which can be used for future projects—providing you can store them and readily find them again.

The third major item of furniture for your workspace is the lightbox. Lamps do not require the large lightboxes that windows need. You might try your local surgical supply house for a used X-ray view box. (Fig. 2.2.) You can get these either

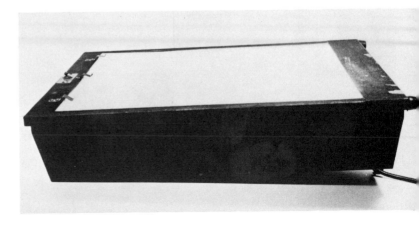

Fig. 2.2 An X-ray view box can serve nicely as a lightbox.

eight by ten inches or eleven by seventeen inches, and they make dandy lightboxes. If you want to you can, of course, make one yourself. Be sure to use fluorescent bulbs to get as even a spread of light as possible. Remember that daylight is the only true light for deciding upon the color of a piece of stained glass.

If you are working on a tiled floor, be sure to protect it in some way—either newspapers (dangerous, they slide) or a piece of old carpet will save you the trouble of taking up the flooring material (a hobby you might not like nearly as much as making lamps). Even with the best of care, small slivers of glass will be ground into the floor by your feet. We have found that a piece of 1/4-inch plywood placed around the worktable floor offers the best protection.

The best place to keep your tools is either on your table in a rotating toolholder or arranged on a pegboard within easy reach. (Fig. 2.3.) Whatever you do, avoid cluttering up your worktable with storage. Put things away as you use them. Nothing is more discouraging than going to your work area anxious to get started after a hard day and finding the worktable piled high from your last session. By the time you finish putting everything away so you can start, you may well be ready to quit.

NECESSARY TOOLS AND SUPPLIES

The glass cutter. A good Fletcher cutter sells for under a dollar. (Fig. 2.4.) You should have several of them—some with plain ends and some with balls, some for opalescent and some for transparent glass. If you treat the cutter well and use it correctly, it will last you a long time, but don't limit yourself to only one cutter. If you misplace it (and you will), you'll spend a lot of your craft time looking for it. If you want to really treat yourself, you might equip your worktable with a carbide cutter. This looks just like your regular cutter, but the wheel is quite different, presenting a longer lasting, sharper cutting edge than any other type of wheel. This cutter is expensive, between four and five dollars, and one will probably do you. Keep it in a safe place and away from your other cutters so you don't get it mixed with them. It is color coded if you do happen to get it confused with the others.

Fig. 2.3 Two very handy types of rotating tool caddies—for large tools and small parts.

Fig. 2.4 A Fletcher glass cutter. Lying down on the job? No, just waiting for a pickup.

Pencils with sharp points. Everyone knows these are necessary, but rare is the work area that has enough of them. Keep a box on hand. If you are working in your basement, especially, it will save you a lot of trips up and down the stairs.

A ruler or straight edge. This should be not less than twelve inches in length. An additional yardstick or two will help.

Paper for sketching. This can be a brown kraft paper or any type of drawing paper that will show lines clearly. Do *not* use paper bags that have been torn apart. Economy is one thing, but you are supposed to be doing this for fun, not as an exercise in frugality. Add to this, graph paper.

Pattern paper. This is a medium weight oaktag which must be to exact thickness or the cutter will not ride on it. Shirt cardboard will not do. Keep your shirt on.

Carbon paper. You may use pencil carbon or you may buy professional carbon paper from a studio. Pencil carbon is cheaper, though more fragile, and will do for a start. Several sheets may be taped together.

Plywood board. You may use this or the top of your worktable. The board is used to hold the pieces together while you are working on them. Its size is dependent on the size of lamp you are making. It should be the same thickness as your tabletop. If you are working on several projects at once, you may need several boards.

Lathe strips, or some type of thin wood strips. The dimensions of a yardstick would be a good guide. Furring strips from your local lumberyard will do.

Magic marker. This should have a medium inkflow with a tip approximately 1/16 inch wide. A tip thicker than this will give you trouble later on when you go to cut the pattern. The marker is used by beginners instead of pattern scissors or pattern knives.

Pattern scissors and pattern knives. If you think stained glass is going to be your hobby for a long while, you cannot do better than to invest in one of these. The scissors are more expensive but easier to use. Neither of these items is as essential in lampmaking as in other phases of stained glass fabrications.

Glass pliers and grozing pliers. These are both essential tools for any sort of accurate work. Glass pliers possess a wide (1 or ¾ inch) jaw and are used to break glass away from the score which cannot be broken by hand or with the glass cutter. Grozing pliers have a small jaw which is curved to allow maximum use against the edges of cut surfaces of the glass. The process of "grozing" involves the grinding away of small splinters and pinpoints of glass that remain along this surface making it uneven and impossible to seat correctly in the holding material—lead or copper foil.

Lead knife. A cheap way of getting round this tool is to purchase a linoleum knife and sharpen it on the outside curve. It will already be sharpened on the inner curve but this is of no use to you. Be assured that such a substitute is by no means a lead knife, but it will at least give you some idea of what a real lead knife does. When you become totally dissatisfied with it, then you are ready to involve yourself in the expense of a real lead knife. If you are completely satisfied with what the lino knife does for you after six months or so, we suggest that you take up another hobby. Do *not* use a razor blade to cut lead came; it is a very dangerous procedure.

Glass. If you are just starting this hobby, buy only enough glass to complete your initial project. It is a good idea not to stock up with glass you have no immediate intention of using, but on the other hand, do not scrimp and save to the extent that you measure each piece so that you have nothing left over. Invariably this will mean a number of trips to your supplier to replace colors you've run short of because of breakage or poor planning. It will be your luck then to find such colors out of stock.

Lead. Came is purchased in strands six feet long. You cannot buy five feet, four inches of it. Some suppliers roll it, others do not. It is better unrolled if you can get it that way. Buy as many strands as you need for your current project. If you have to buy a lot of it for whatever reason, wrap what you are not going to use immediately in some sort of protective covering—plastic will do—to prevent the lead from oxidizing. The tough oxide coating thus formed will not take solder and will make a lot of scrubbing of the joints necessary that might easily have been avoided.

Solder. Only one type of solder is used in stained glass work—sixty percent tin, forty percent lead. Ask for 60/40 solder. As for "core" solder, stay away from it. Such solder contains a flux and its use in stained glass work will only lead to grief. What you want is 60/40 solid core wire solder. A diameter of ⅛ inch is most workable; less than that and the solder melts out of your hand at an alarming rate, thicker and it becomes too bulky to work well. Bar solder is never used.

Flux. A liquid flux is our preference. This is an organic acid, though it resembles an oil in viscosity. It is harmless to fingers and causes no noxious fumes. The chief constituent is oleic acid. We prefer the white to the yellow. This is an inexpensive item provided you do not keep spilling it.

Flux brush. As simple an item as this is, the lack of it will keep you from doing any extensive soldering. This is a stiff-bristled "acid" brush, the purpose of which is not merely application of the flux to the area to be soldered, but an actual scrubbing of the flux into the pores of the metal.

Wire brush. A small wire brush is a great convenience, but be careful the wires are not so stiff they injure the lead. Such a brush is used to remove the oxide coat on lead came, thereby exposing a shiny surface that will take the solder.

Soldering iron. An iron of from 80 to 120 watts can do the job, depending on the size joints you have in mind. Whatever kind of iron you have at home should be tried out first. We even allow beginning students to bring soldering guns to class, if that is what they happen to already own. If they do any extensive work making lamps, they will soon become dissatisfied with them; if not, they have saved themselves a purchase. If you have no iron at home, do *not* buy one of the cheap two or three dollar soldering irons you may find around in stores. They burn out, burn lead, burn your fingers and generally burn you up. Spend a few dollars more on a good iron and travel first class.

Nails. Do not use finishing nails or carpet tacks. If you do not have professional leading nails use ¾-inch common nails or, better yet, the same size horseshoe nails. Leading nails must be slim with some sort of head for grasping them and pulling them out of the board into which they are going to be tacked— not nailed, tacked. Do not use railroad spikes, masonry nails, roofing nails, electric staples or tiny molding brads; your fingers are at stake.

Thumbtacks. The use of these or pushpins will allow you to keep your hands free during the drawing and pattern-making stage of the work. The long pushpins can occasionally be used as leading nails.

Eraser. A large artist's eraser is best. You cannot depend on the ones on your pencils, because they get dirty fast and you'll be forever cleaning them. You will be changing a lot of lines during the sketching phase of your design (and possibly thereafter), and nothing is more confusing than a partially erased guideline (does it belong there or doesn't it?). When you remove such a line, be sure you remove it completely. If you try to do this using a poor eraser, you may end up removing your paper as well.

Charcoal. Sticks are best. Artists sketch with charcoal; it is a very flexible entity, and lines can be changed or modified easily. Prototype sketches may be made in pencil; enlargements call for charcoal.

Hammer. If you do not have a professional leading knife with a weighted handle for tapping, keep a diminutive hammer on your worktable. Do not use a ball peen hammer or an old shoe to tap your nails into place.

CUTTING GLASS

To attempt a project as sophisticated as a lampshade without having had any prior experience of stained glass techniques argues not only an adventurous spirit, but a bottomless pocketbook and an unbounded frustration index as well. It is not our purpose to delve deeply into standard stained glass procedures here (they have been covered in our book *How to Work in Stained Glass*, published by the Chilton Book Company), but we feel that a review of some of them might be in order. Glass cutting falls naturally into six steps.

1. Holding the cutter. The experienced user places the glass cutter between the first and second fingers, as illustrated in Fig. 2.5, with the thumb supporting the cutter on the underside. Use a free wrist motion, and keep your

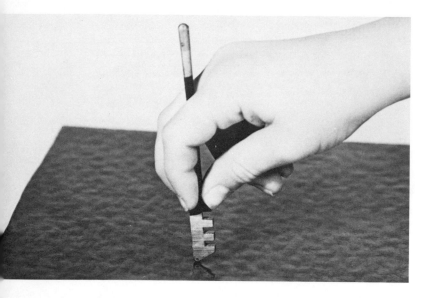

Fig. 2.5 Proper way to hold a glass cutter.

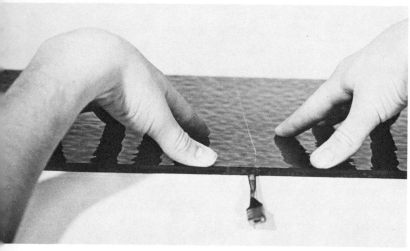

Fig. 2.6 One way to break the score.

Fig. 2.7 What happens when the score isn't deep enough.

arm limber all the way up to the shoulder. Do not grasp the cutter as though it were an instrument of destruction or it will become one. Do not allow your fingers to slide down upon the grozing teeth—you will never be able to cut accurately that way. The flattened area on the shaft is where your three-finger grip should be. Your cutting force comes from the shoulder, not the wrist. Your wrist guides it. Learn to apply your weight correctly. Always cut standing.

2. *Cleaning the glass.* Use a good liquid cleaner, one that will not make the surface slippery.

3. *Scoring the glass.* When you make your score be sure your glass is on a flat surface. To make a straight cut, draw the cutter along a straight edge only once. Do not repeat the cut. Rescoring the line at any point will ruin your cutter wheel. Begin your score close to the top edge of the glass and allow the cutter to run off the bottom edge. Use enough pressure to make a light score— you will hear the sound of the wheel plowing through the glass—but don't make it so light that you are unable to fracture the surface. If you can't get a fingernail into the resulting score line, it is not deep enough. Don't make your score so heavy that glass flakes jump out at you as your cutter moves along. A little practice will help immeasurably.

4. *Break the cut immediately.* Making another score before the previous one has been broken out may result in injury. There are several methods of breaking out a score line. You may do it by placing the glass cutter handle directly beneath the score line and pressing to either side. The glass will break cleanly. You may break the score by hand by grasping the glass on either side of the score line with thumbs lined up parallel to the score. The pull is out and down; the glass will break easily. (See Figs. 2.6 and 2.7.) For pieces too small to be broken by either of the above methods, glass pliers or grozing pliers may be brought into play. For long, thin strips, you may call upon running pliers. We do not use the grozing teeth—the notched edges along the bottom surface—of the glass cutter in stained glass work. Always break the glass from the bottom; never turn it over to whack it from the top.

5. *Always cut to a pattern.* The tolerances required between the pieces being leaded is critical. Only by making certain that your glass pieces conform to a premeasured template (pattern) do you stand any chance of making seams meet. This is most especially true in lampshades, the fabrication of which requires the exact enclosure of a geometric space. If you have difficulty following a straight edge or cutting to a pattern, practice by drawing a pencil line on paper and placing it under the glass. Use clear glass, and follow the line with a glass cutter. This technique is for practice only and should never be substituted for a pattern/template maneuver when doing any serious cutting. (See Figs. 2.8 through 2.11.)

6. *Care for your cutter.* Keeping your cutter in a baby jar with a mixture of light oil and kerosene will maintain it well. Unless the wheel turns freely, a glass cutter is quickly ruined. Do not allow your cutter wheel to rest in direct contact with the bottom of the glass jar. It is a good idea to pad the jar bottom with a piece of steel wool. The wheel will thus be lubricated and cleaned while it is being stored. Never use turpentine as a lubricant for glass cutters.

Fig. 2.8 Pattern on the glass. Note that we could save a cut by lining up the straight edges.

Fig. 2.9 Cutting to a pattern.

WORKING WITH LEAD

The lead came employed in making lamps is pure lead which is extruded by machine into strands six feet in length. Lead came is divided into two main styles—H and U, depending on the number of channels present. H lead has two channels with a central wall, or "heart," and resembles the letter H in cross section. It is an "inside" lead, that is, it is used within the body of the work, not along an outside edge; a piece of glass fits on either side within its channels. U lead resembles the letter U in cross section and is used along the outer border of a lamp. Within these two basic categories are any number of sizes and styles, most of which are not used in making lampshades.

Came is measured across its nonchanneled side. Two sizes of H are employed in shades, ¼ inch and ⅜ inch. Less frequently, a 3/16 inch lead may be used, but this is more likely to see service as an interior decoration within the body of a panel rather than strut a bend of the lamp proper. Such a small caliber of came is too likely to show glass edges as the panels are angled to complete the lamp's circle. We will have more to say of this later when we describe specific lampshades.

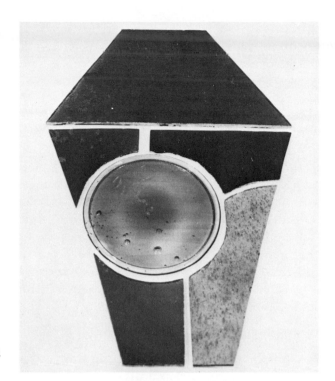

Fig. 2.10 Glass cut to pattern accurately.

Fig. 2.11 Planned dimensions. The line in the diamond is not an accident. It is a planned break called a "flint."

Two sizes of U leads are generally employed: 3/16 inch and ¼ inch. These are finishing leads which leave no loose channels along the surfaces of the glass. Occasionally a ⅜-inch U is used, but this is a pretty rare occurrence. 3/16 inch U is a square lead, that is, it has square corners; ¼ inch U is a rounded corner lead.

All sizes of lead came so far mentioned should be stretched slightly before using. This takes the kinks out of the came and makes the lead easier to work with. It is well to have a lathkin handy when working with came. This is an instrument whose sole purpose is opening the channels of came enough to allow the glass to seat properly within them. A piece of wood whittled to proper dimension and oiled may do the job or you may prefer to use a professional lathkin. One of our students modified a wooden spoon to do the job. Professional lathkins are made of metal and are quite sufficient, but so long as you get the cames open easily, it little matters what you use. Especially after stretching, the channels may be tight.

Lead is used in stained glass work because it is malleable, inexpensive and solderable. Other materials, such as brass caming (previously mentioned) and copper foil (to be discussed elsewhere), can be used in lamps.

Soldering Procedure

The process of soldering involves joining together metals by use of a solder and a flux. Once the flux has prepared the metals, by cleaning their surfaces of oxides and opening their pores to allow the solder to penetrate by capillary action, the solder is applied at a specific temperature just high enough to melt the solder without a consequent melting of the materials to be joined. Beginners may end up melting away the lead and leaving the solder untouched, so be assured that the lead will melt from the heat of the soldering iron. Care must therefore be taken to apply the iron to the solder at the juncture point of leads, solder and iron and to remove it when only the solder has responded to the heat. The soldered joint should be smooth and small—just large enough to hold the joint together, and not splashed all over the came for inches around. If a soldered joint has sharp edges, the iron was not hot enough and was "dragging" the solder. Such a cratered joint must be flattened smooth.

Steps to be taken in soldering are as follows:

1. Clean the lead surfaces to be treated with solder. Use your wire brush first to remove any oxide coating. When a shiny surface of metal appears, wipe again with a clean cloth.

2. Heat an iron and, while this is coming to temperature, flux the joints you are going to solder. It doesn't matter if you flux one at a time or all at once. Don't worry if the flux gets on the glass; it won't hurt it.

3. Make certain that your iron is not too hot for the lead. At first you might want to test it on a piece of scrap lead just to make sure. As your soldering experience grows, you will get to know exactly, by how the solder flows, if the iron is too hot or not. A rheostat-controlled iron will remain at a constant temperature. Incidentally don't worry about the glass. We have yet to see a piece of glass crack from a hot iron, and if any hot solder drops on the glass, it will fall away as soon as it has cooled with no marring of the glass surface.

Fig. 2.12 Soldering procedure. The solder runs off the hot tip of the iron for a continuous beading of the came where such is desired.

4. The actual soldering action may be done in one of two ways: you may dip your iron against the solder on the table and carry a small amount on the tip to the joint, or you may place an end of solder on the joint and touch it with the hot iron. (Fig. 2.12.) The iron itself need not be moved much for quick, effective soldering. The tip of the iron and the solder should do all the work. If you have to keep going back and forth with your iron to even out the joint, something is wrong. In fact, the more you try to even it out this way, the worse it will become until you finally end up by burning the lead.

The soldering tip is a critical portion of the iron. Various tips are sold to do different types of joints, but a good pyramidal or medium chisel ironclad tip is probably your best bet for lamp work.

A few hours of practice should be all you need to get the "feel" of proper soldering. If the proper temperature is present, the solder will flow out over the joint and solidify immediately leaving a neat, silvery, slightly raised area covering the seam.

THE SKETCH—INITIAL IDEA TO FINAL DESIGN

Neither masterpieces nor disasters spring full-fledged from the mind of their creator. It takes as much time and effort (and sometimes more) to make a mess as it takes to make a thing of beauty. While there are certain skills in the fingers of the advanced not available to the neophyte, everyone starts even with the original conception, and if this is faulty, nothing else, no matter how exquisite the glass cutting or how clever the leading, will make for an artistic final product. And, if you are honest with yourself and allow the piece to stand, you will probably find it chiding you always as a presentation gone awry; a ragamuffin in a Balenciaga. (Fig. 2.13.)

It has been our experience that end results are seeded in the initial sketch. From this, of course, the concept is developed and organized. Too many individuals are either in such a hurry to cut the glass that they do not fully develop their initial sketch to the cartoon stage, using it instead merely as a note in a progression of increasingly wavering ideas that blunder to a standstill, or they use the sketch itself as the cartoon.

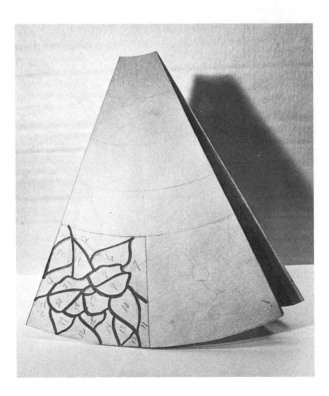

Fig. 2.13 A sketch transferred to the pattern for evaluation.

The initial sketch is neither less nor more than an embryonic idea trying to grow into a lamp. (Fig. 2.14.) It is a strictly transitory stage between what the worker has in mind and his expression of that idea in his chosen modality, in this instance, glass. In every case the sketch, a form of shorthand, must when completed be reevaluated in terms of the characteristics of one's chosen material. Otherwise one is liable to end up with a mute testimony to big ideas, small technique. To attempt to proceed with the work on the basis of an uncompleted sketch with no cartoon (specific blueprint) but with the thought in mind that you will figure out the difficulties as you go along is to waste time and materials. You will have when done, at the very best, a compromised piece of work.

Similarly, it is wrong to overembellish a sketch, to make it top-heavy, as it were, with projections not suited to the medium, and then proceed to bend the medium to fit the sketch. A lot of grandiose ideas have thus come to grief. Beginners, especially, tend to overcomplexity of design. This is not to suggest that lack of imagination be the order of the day, but it is best to refrain from using the sketch as a flying carpet of ideas. A lot of them will degenerate into throw rugs. Just because you can draw it with a pencil doesn't mean that you can cut it out of glass, that it will lead properly, that it will solder well or that the whole thing wouldn't do better as a watercolor.

MAKING THE PATTERN

Patterns are cut from the cartoon—the initial sketch devoid of all extraneous lines, put into final form and purified for glass. Pattern pieces are cut from an oaktag thick enough to allow the shoulder of the glass cutter to ride the pattern's

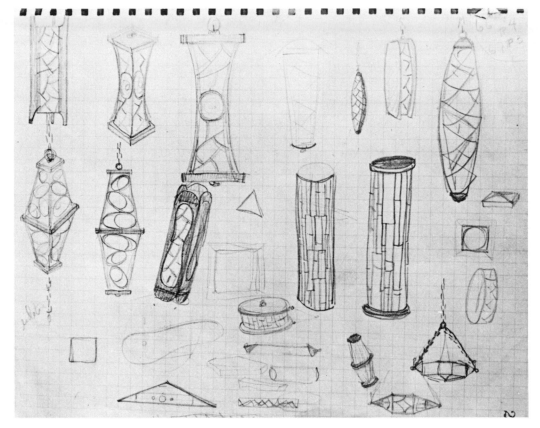

Fig. 2.14   Initial sketches of lamps from the authors' notebook.

rim while its wheel cuts the glass surface. If the pattern is too thick, the cutter's wheel will not cut efficiently; if the pattern is too thin, it will fray from the pressure. The pattern is used on top of, never under, the glass. (Fig. 2.15.)

If you are making a pyramidal lamp, or any lamp which by its nature involves the exact duplication of a great number of panels, it is best to make a master pattern for a single panel and from that a working pattern. Each time you use the working pattern, it should be rechecked against the master pattern for shrinkage from fraying. It is difficult to say how many cuts one can make from a particular pattern before it will begin to develop misshapen edges from the pressure of the glass cutter. It is also difficult to tell once this has happened without a comparison with an unused pattern.

When your working pattern begins to show wear, it is quite simple to make another from the master pattern. It goes without saying that you should never use the master itself to cut from. (Fig. 2.16.) Some workers like to make the master pattern from sheet metal and only the working patterns from pattern paper. Sheet metal, no matter how thin, does not cut quite like paper and a tinsnips is more awkward to use than a scissors. It is imperative, therefore, that any sheet metal master pattern be checked and double-checked for accuracy before working patterns are cut from it. Measure it against a T or L square. Once you are satisfied that you have cut it accurately, smooth down all sharp edges

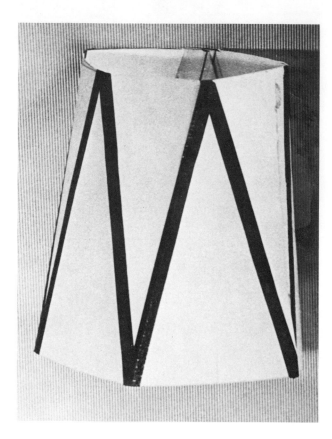

Fig. 2.15 A paper pattern folded to shape. This will be a small lampshade. It will be leaded.

with Carborundum® paper or a fine file. When making working patterns from the master be certain to use a sharp-pointed pencil to track around it. Otherwise you will add an extra dimension to the new pattern from the pencil which can throw your whole lamp off. We like to recheck each new pattern against the master after we have cut it. It is easier to trim the pattern down at this point than to trim the glass down later.

THINK IN 3-D

Words such as circumference, radius, diameter and pi are directly related to the planning of your lampshades. It is not necessary to be a theoretical physicist to produce a lampshade, but in order to produce what you have in mind in glass you have to be able to visualize two-dimensional drawings within the framework of a three-dimensional reference. How large do you *feel* a lamp must be to accommodate a diameter of twelve, sixteen or twenty-four inches? Cultivating this kind of instinct will help you to automatically rough out the type of lamp in your mind that will best fill such and such a space. You should be able to tell a customer fairly rapidly what size lamp he will need for a particular spot in his home. Acquiring this subtle flair for dimensional perspicacity will also help you decide the necessity for a crown or not, what type of skirt will serve and if the panels should be bent or straight. If you can take all these things into account before you even begin sketching, you will save a lot of time and come up with a far better product.

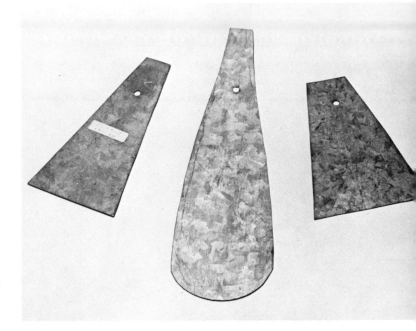

Fig. 2.16 Some metal master patterns. Paper patterns are then made from these.

There is no way to acquire this ability other than by making and looking at a lot of lamps. Look at lamps in stores, in different rooms in homes, over tables, over pianos. Eventually you will start to get a feeling for the quantity of space they carve out of any given area. Then begin to vary ideas you have seen with your own designs. Don't be afraid to make mistakes. Make them. Don't be afraid to break glass. Follow a poor design to its logical termination and discover what makes it poor.

The procedures and patterns in this book will produce beautiful lamps, but we hope they will do more. We hope they will stimulate you to design your own patterns and develop your own procedures. Each of these designs has pleased somebody since each was made on a specific commission. They are yours to copy or improve upon.

The Final Design—Function and Decor

Diogenes with his lamp was not too clear on where he was going, and many lamp enthusiasts since have followed his example. His search for an honest man might well have concluded promptly and successfully if he had had enough light to see by. While no stained glass lampshade need be conceived solely for a utilitarian purpose, each should be able to transmit light. It is a little silly to construct a lamp for reading and need a floodlight on top of it to see the book. Similarly, a hallway light emanating a clinging luminescence, no matter how gorgeous, will not prevent you from breaking your neck over shadowy objects on the floor.

So decide how much light you want your lamp to produce and use a glass and design calculated to transmit the proper radiance. Know which way the majority of the light should be guided—whether through the sides of the lamp, from the bottom or from the top. In some cases, all three directions are equally necessary, as certain individuals want to see both through and by their lamp and also be able to locate a reflection from it on the ceiling. Such projects should not be fitted with vase caps or any other such cover-all top which will block the egress of the light. Classically, lanterns transmit little light through the sides but quite a bit through top and bottom. The light transmission characteristics of most lamps depend on their design. Learn to take advantage of and modify designs to suit your needs.

Chapter 3
Fabricating Your Lamp

CROWNS AND SKIRTS

The crown is considered to be the top portion of the lampshade. Generally, but by no means invariably, it is a separate piece of glass. Its function is mostly decorative—to carry the eye along a graceful line and thus give the composition a finished effect. Certain lamps, without a crown, appear foreshortened and ineffectual; they leave the eye dangling in space. (Fig. 3.1.)

Crowns may be bent or straight regardless of the linear quality of the panels composing the body of the lamp. The addition of a bent crown to a straight panel lamp is a flourish which can add character to the lamp by surprising the eye. A straight panel lamp may also narrow its lines in an upward progression straight through the crown. Less choice is available if you are making a bent panel lamp and decide to make your crown out of straight pieces of glass. Now you are allowing the eye to travel nicely along a convex surface which abruptly shoots upward like a volcano. The effect can be disconcerting.

Fig. 3.1 A crown of straight pieces flared from the center. Note the round, ornate "story" skirt despite this being a pyramidal lamp.

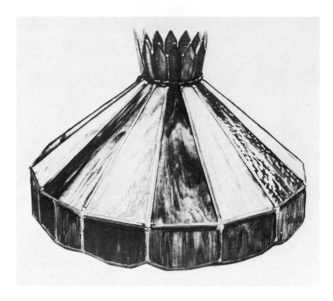

Fig. 3.2 A crown going straight up. The lamp appears unfinished and might look better with no crown at all.

Two things can be done to modify this visual leap into nowhere. (Fig. 3.2.) Straight crowns added to bent panel lamps can be flared anywhere from thirty to ninety degrees from the vertical plane. Also, the crown pieces must be made larger than would be the case if they were curved. Both of these techniques delay the eye long enough so that the sudden change in direction does not come as an inaesthetic shock. (Fig. 3.3.) Most bent panel lamps in which the panel is curved as a single piece of glass, rather than as multiple pieces, have curved crowns as well; the crown curve complements the panel curve. (Fig. 3.4.) Either each belly flows outward in a parallel bulge or the curve of the crown sinks inward, continuing the panel curve as a brief S-shaped motif. Straight panel crowns are not usually found on bent panels (molded by heating the glass in a kiln on a special form; see Chapter 11). If you have a lamp with such curved panels and a straight crown, the chances are that it has been repaired by someone who did not know how to remake the missing curved crown pieces and just redid the entire crown straight.

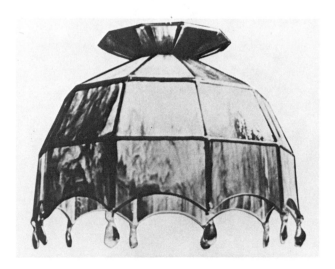

Fig. 3.3 A widely flared crown which *does* give a finished appearance to this lamp. Note the well placed navettes hanging from the scallops. They provide just the right touch; the addition of an ornate skirt as well would be too much.

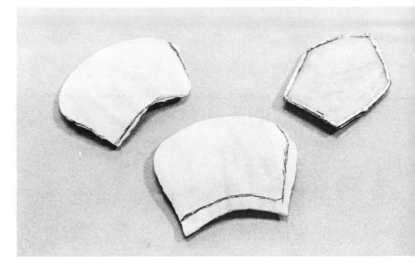

Fig. 3.4 Curved crown pieces in various stages. Many of these pieces require trimming down when they come from the kiln. The piece in the foreground has been marked; the one above it has been grozed almost to size. In the upper right another piece, at the proper size, has been foiled and tinned.

The separation of the crown pieces from the body varies in distance according to the disposition of the designer. In cases where the heat-molded panel is shaped so as to be both crown and body in one fell swoop, obviously no separation at all between the two elements is possible. A false sense of separation may be imparted to the lamp by fitting a piece of filigree around the bend of body and crown. In the fabrication of such a lamp, fewer pieces need be made. Commercial lamps can be knocked out this way fairly rapidly, but the skilled workman usually desires to work with more pieces as this gives him more mobility in design.

The opposite effect occurs in lamps that have over an inch of separation between crown and body with some sort of metallic decorative design worked in between. Brass filigree is most often used, but glass rods, seashells, gemstones and other multimedia can be employed as decor and spacemakers here. (Fig. 3.5.) Care must be taken that such material, meant to represent a boundary be-

Fig. 3.5 Filigree neckpiece made of brass. This will separate crown and body.

Fig. 3.6 The structure beneath the crown, seen from the top; the supporting strap that lets it all hang down.

Fig. 3.7 All the pieces are properly spaced—we hope. The last one will tell.

Fig. 3.8 The crown flare continues the S curve of the individual panels. Note the ornate skirt done in white metal and backed up by the glass.

Fig. 3.9 The ornate skirt in a closer view. When the lamp is lit these figures stand out dramatically against the luminescent glass.

tween the anatomical features of the shade, does not become so ornate that it overpowers the basic work. If this happens, you may as well throw the lamp away and use your demarcation decor as a necklace.

Crowns are also used quite functionally to hide the skeleton holding the lamp aloft. Often it is necessary to use a steel or copper plate to suspend a shade; a metal strapping of some sort must almost always be employed (see Chapter 4). (Fig. 3.6.) In many instances such a brace or plate is the main support of all the individual struts and thus may of necessity be bulky enough to depress a delicate design. A well-placed, well-designed crown will not only serve its own purpose for existing but will also serve to glorify the stevedore labor going on below it. (Figs. 3.7 and 3.8.)

Design-wise, the skirt does pretty much for the bottom of the lamp what the crown does for the top. It is a more dangerous feature, however, as the tendency to overdo it is far from rare. Workers seem to be more apt to hang things than to raise them. While they usually keep their crowns straightforward, the tendency to let the skirts fly wild is universal. Aside from overornamenting the internal design, the urge to bedeck the glass with beads, navettes, glass jewels and whatnots hinging down between the scallops of the skirt can make the whole thing into some nightmarish mobile. Simplicity is the key. (Figs. 3.9 and 3.10.) Unlike the crown, it is common to find lamps of molded, bent panels with

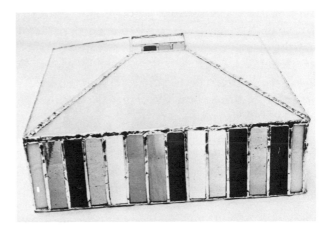

Fig. 3.10 A lovely, very effective skirt of long, straight pieces.

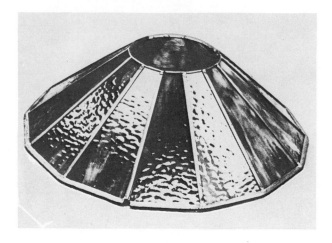

Fig. 3.11 A simple panel line without skirt or crown.

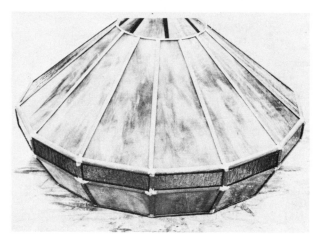

Fig. 3.12 The same panel idea with a broken, straight line and a tucked under skirt.

skirts that are straight. The line of the skirt is used to carry the eye downward from the bend of the panel. Whether the panel is literally curved or straight but at an angle (as in pyramidal lamps), a straight skirt will add the proper finishing touch. A properly sized skirt will also serve to hide the bulb or allow a globe to peek under to just the right amount. (Figs. 3.11 and 3.12.)

Skirts may be either scalloped, straight or uneven. (Fig. 3.13.) The scallop is the usual design as it is easy to accomplish and breaks up the severe straight-line aspect of most beginners' lamps. The straight-line skirt may be used as part of a scalloped edge where the leading border is scalloped only as an afterthought against an internal straight lead line. Uneven borders can be most pleasing and stylized, but they must be planned. A border that is uneven by accident does not give quite the same effect.

Most straight-line skirts are wide and fairly ornate within their extra dimension. Examples are found in the bent panel "fruited" skirts (Fig. 3.14) or in almost any other paneled lamp. The width and detail are dependent on the designer and the size of the lamp. You can easily overwhelm a small bathroom lamp, with an overindulgent skirt. The bordering straight-line edge of such a skirt may have the usual lead channeling or brass came for extra support.

Fig. 3.13 Broken panels with a straight skirt and a small flared crown. It could be argued that this lamp has no skirt at all, but the eye treats the bottom break as a finishing touch, much as it would a skirt.

Brass came or a heavily tinned lead border is quite common as the border of the uneven skirt. Such lampshades are difficult to place on a table since they have to rest on a number of uneven projections (these had better be able to take the weight). Uneven border lamps can be in reality even border lamps with bunches of grapes hanging down at equal intervals. This will still give an off the shoulder air of improvisation if the areas between form a perfect geometric pattern. The true uneven border lamp is most difficult to design and almost of necessity must have an internal structure of "Tiffany-type" small-pieced glass (see Chapter 10 and Figs. 3.14 through 3.18.)

CALCULATING YOUR SPACE

Lamps are calculated "in the flat." That is, they are first drawn on paper. You should have in mind the size diameter lamp you want to make before doing any designing. Remember that the diameter need not be the measurement within

Fig. 3.14 An organized, complicated, multipieced "fruit" skirt on a tiered lamp. Note that the paneling of the skirt fits the body of the lamp.

Fig. 3.15 A complex skirt with a paneled lamp which is *not* paneled with the body of the lamp but rather forms a true circle.

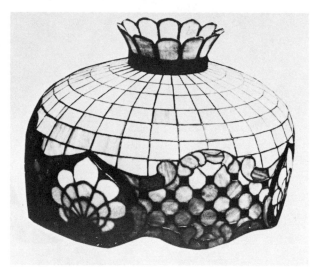

Fig. 3.16 A complicated skirt and a bent, flared crown of a so-called "Tiffany-type" small-pieced lamp. Note the straight lines going up the sides as well as horizontally.

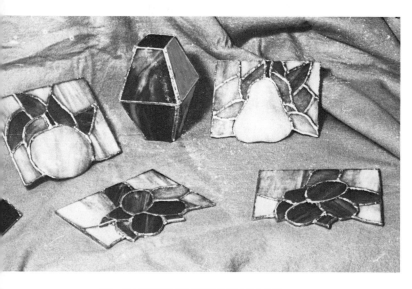

Fig. 3.17 Some skirt pieces, some with bent fruit in them. These are, in fact, small panels. They are all foiled, and the edge foiling is narrow enough to slip into the lead caming that will form the struts of the lamp.

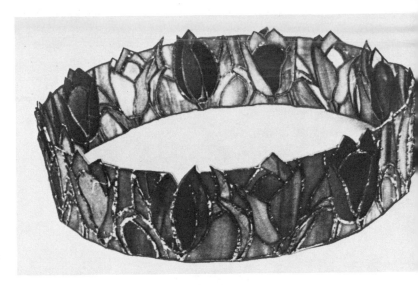

Fig. 3.18 Lamp skirt demonstrating uneven border.

the skirt—your lamp may curve downward into the skirt so that the widest part will be above it. The diameter is the straight-line distance across the lamp from the outside of one piece of glass to the outside of another directly across from it. There is no relationship between the diameter of the lamp's widest space and that of the top hole through which the bulb and wiring will go. The diameter of this top opening is dependent solely on the design of the lamp and may change as you go along depending on how strictly you stick to your design. Don't plan the size of this top space to the extent of acquiring the hardware necessary to bridge or fill it; you may find you are off the mark when the lamp is completed. We advise all beginning lampmakers to first make their lamp and then fit the vase caps and hardware to the top hole they come out with. This saves a lot of returns of materials.

The basic diameter of the lamp proper, however, can easily be worked out on paper. From the diameter you can project the circumference on the formula: the circumference equals pi times the diameter (C = πD; π equals 3.1416). Thus, if you want a lamp twenty-two inches at its widest point and you want to draw the circumference as a circle on paper, you would multiply 22 inches by 3.14 and come out with a circumference of 69 inches. This will give you an idea of the widest circle of space the lamp will take up. To visualize your lamp's diameter, measure off sixty-nine inches on a string, tie the ends and lay it out. Of course this tells you nothing of the height, and in those cases where the lamps are laid out flat and then folded to a circle, this stringed space cannot be used as a guide. It can be so used when lamps employing a mold are to be made, since the mold can be produced to exactly the diameter enclosed by your string and sloped to whatever height you desire.

THE CARDBOARD MOCK-UP

Many students make several paper prototypes before they attempt even the cardboard one. This is wise especially where a difficult or original shape is being put together. We are firmly of the opinion that no lampshade should be at-

Fig. 3.19 The cardboard mock-up of a lamp in the flat.

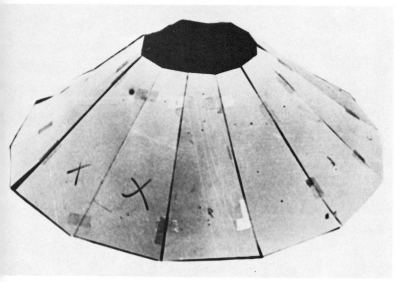

Fig. 3.20 The same mock-up shown dimensionally.

tempted unless a prototype is first made in cardboard. It is easier to cut paper and cardboard than glass—and it's a lot cheaper. No matter how precisely you may have designed the shade of your dreams, reality can give it a different light. Projects that are too complicated for cardboard are assuredly too complicated for glass—better to find this out right away and discard the project than struggle through to final exhaustion.

Once you have your sketch laid out on kraft paper, transfer it to pattern paper and cut out the panels. (Figs. 3.19 and 3.20.) Use Scotch® tape to hold and hinge them. Your final result may be a bit floppy, but if it goes wrong any-where—if it is too high or too broad or just too awkward—you have the advantage of being able to modify it with the snip of a scissors. If you are satisfied with the basic shape and want the prototype absolutely rigid, get hold of some cardboard boxes—thick, corrugated cardboard boxes—and cut sheets from them. (Figs. 3.21 through 3.24.) You can make this material hinge readily by cutting through one side of it. It will then fold nicely against the uncut side. Make cer-

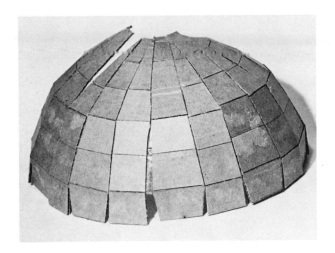

Fig. 3.21 Cardboard form for a tiered shade.

tain that you cut your pieces of cardboard from the pattern as accurately as if you were cutting the actual glass pieces. Sloppiness here will provide a form that won't go together and that will tell you nothing about the glass form to come.

If you intend using the cardboard form as a mold as well, each piece should be cut a trifle smaller (1/16 of an inch will do) than the same piece cut in glass. You may have to use two patterns—one for the mold and one for the glass. If you make the cardboard mold the same size as the glass pieces, you will have trouble matching up the glass seams as the underlying cardboard will take up too much room. A lot of solder can go down the drain trying to close opened seams if you disregard this factor.

An understanding of how a mold is used is basic to certain types of lamps. The cardboard mold is first made to as perfect a size as possible, and all the seams are closed securely with Scotch tape. Any other type of tape is too thick and will give a bumpy surface. Do not allow the Scotch tape to fold in any way—this will also provide bumps you do not need. Once the mold is completed cut your glass to pattern. When the first two pieces are cut, place them on the mold rimmed either with lead or copper (your pattern must compensate for whichever metal you use) and tack them together with solder. Each additional piece is added this way until you have covered half the mold. The glass pieces are then

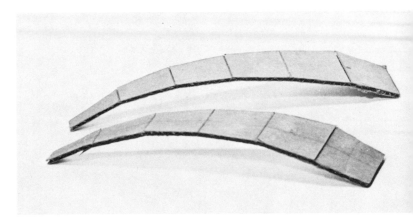

Fig. 3.22 Individual tiers from the above model.

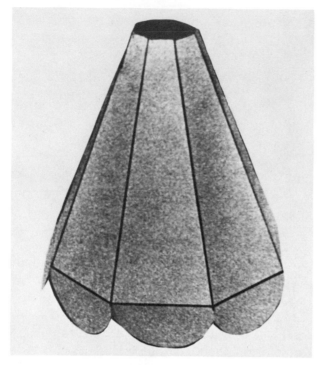

Fig. 3.23 A base lamp form.

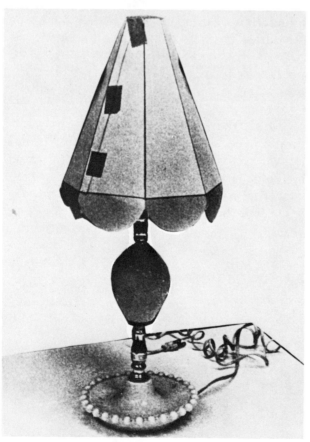

Fig. 3.24 Try the shade out on a base before proceeding further.

reinforced with additional tackings of solder and may or may not be removed from the mold. The second half of the mold is employed in the same manner. The two glass halves (now exact duplicates of, though slightly larger than, the mold) are then soldered together. The lamp should now be exactly the shape you wish. One or a dozen of these same lamps can be created from the same mold. The only additional work involved is to provide a final soldering of the seams and whatever additional ornamentation is required.

KITCHEN, HALLWAY, BEDROOM OR BATH?

It's a good idea to keep in mind where your lamp is going to hang out. A hallway light may be totally out of place over a dining table; a bathroom fixture can be all wet in your boudoir. Certain characteristics may be impressed into your design depending on the individuality of the room involved; these are generally more subtle than overt, but they can make or break an overall effect. For example, bathroom lamps tend to be as small as hallway lamps, but much brighter. Illumination is a more important factor when combing your hair than when finding your coat or climbing stairs. The type of glass used will thus vary depending on the room. The design should also be modified to mirror the precincts it enhances. Apples and bananas grow better in kitchens and pantries than in bedrooms, and the requisite incandescence is again more practical than provocative. Bedroom lamps are wanted more on bases than as swingers but may hang quite low to the floor with a soft, upward streaming luminescence. The design then, would have to cope with this. A lamp for a pool table would provide a long, downward reflected light, either in pairs or as a threesome exactly duplicated; such a trio would hardly serve as nightlights in a nursery. Providing only one style for all occasions disregards the basic premise of lighting (lighting allows the vision to be exercised) and ignores the fact that vision is a state of mind which can be modified, experimented with, teased, distorted, emotionalized, dulled, enhanced and colored—all with stained glass lamps.

FOIL OR CAME?

From its inception centuries ago, stained glass has been used in conjunction with lead. The comparatively cheap, easily soldered metal was, until the time of Tiffany, the most widely used material for holding and designing colored glasses. In the 1920s Tiffany found lead too bulky for the multiple-cornered, many-tiered lamps he had in mind; the came could not turn the corners of his patterns gracefully. He (or one of his workers) devised a method of holding the glass together using a thin copper foil approximately .002 inch in thickness. Tough even in these dimensions, the copper was as flexible and solderable as lead and served the purpose perfectly. Strips of copper were cut from sheets to the required tolerances. Since most machine-made glass was (and is) approximately ⅛ inch in thickness, a foil of ¼ inch wrapped around the glass left 1/16 inch on either side for purchase, and this was enough to cover the center portion of the border and meet the corresponding border of the glass to which it was to be joined. The thin foil fitted well into every nook and cranny of the piece of glass around which it was wrapped. No came, no matter how thin, com-

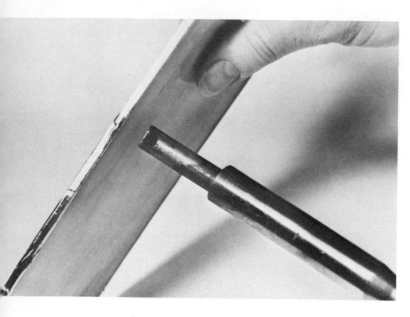

Fig. 3.25   Tinning a foiled piece of glass.

pared with it for flexibility, but the lead, being more rigid, held the glass better. This problem was solved by "tinning" the seams of foil after the glass was wrapped in them and placed in proper sequence. "Tinning" was simply running solder over the seams of copper showing to either side of the glass—approximately 1/16 of an inch from each piece, or a total of ¼ inch. Eventually this was deemed to be too wide a joint, and the pieces of glass were wrapped in foil so that most of the copper overlay was against the back of the glass (which became the inside of the lamp). About 1/16 of an inch total was thereby presented to the front of the lamp for tinning. The juncture was so delicate as to almost show the edges of the glass it was supposed to be protecting, and this gave a lacy appearance to the finished product that has never been surpassed.

Today we use an adhesive-backed copper foil that sticks closely to the multiple surfaces of these small-pieced lamps. (Fig. 3.25.) It takes a very skilled and patient workman indeed to wrap small pieces of glass with this material so that the overlay is even from front to back. The less overlay you leave in front, the more delicate the join will be with the neighboring pieces. There is a 1/16-inch adhesive foil that gives an even more delicate juncture; this should be used only with the thinnest antique glasses, however, as it does not allow enough purchase on ⅛-inch, machine-made glass. We suggest that only the ¼-inch foil be used on the small-pieced, Tiffany lamps and that the worker disregard the extra foil that will appear within the lamp as he diminishes the amount on the front. You will need this support from behind to hold the pieces in place.

Once the pieces are in place and soldered, all foiled elements should be "beaded." (Fig. 3.26.) This provides a raised soldered surface over each seam and gives the effect of one continuous flow of metal over all the joints. Beading must be done with a soldering iron at medium heat so that the solder does not flow through the seam and flatten out or melt through to the other side. The raised surface of solder should be smooth and thin and should effectively hold the pieces of the lamp together.

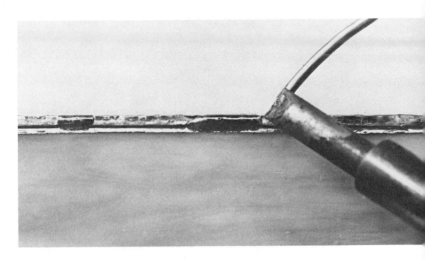

Fig. 3.26 Beading a seam. Note how the solder bulges over the gap.

Generally speaking, foil should not be used where large panels are to be employed. For one thing, such panels aesthetically require a more forceful linear quality than the foil can achieve, and for another, the long span of glass calls for a more supportive material than copper. The amount of beading that would have to be done would be a waste of time and solder. Lead came is far more at home with paneled lamps than copper foil could ever be, and the individual who uses the latter to produce the former is providing himself with a lot of extra labor for no real gain. The oft repeated reason for foiling large-paneled lamps, that foil provides for a lighter lamp, makes very little sense inasmuch as a foiled lamp and a leaded lamp are both hung in exactly the same fashion. The creation of an occasional foiled large-paneled lamp has its place, but the general rule of came and foil stands: large panels—came; small pieces—foil. In most instances, the individual who has never worked with came, who has been started on foil by an instructor "because it is easier," attempts to fit the one method of which he is aware to all occasions. This particular pretense is an art in itself.

BEGINNING AND ADVANCED PRODUCTIONS

Certain lampshades are easier than others; certain workers are more apt than others. Nonetheless, all beginners in this field should start their lampshade experience with a pyramidal lamp. The pyramidal lamp is neither the simplest nor most difficult of shades, but it is probably the one offering the most experience and, as such, the logical place to begin. As far as cutting and breaking out the glass, an angled panel is by no means as simple as it looks, and whereas a small, multiple-surfaced piece of glass for a Tiffany shade may look difficult to cut, it is only tedious. The straight lines of the pyramidal lamp offer an exercise in discipline. Try sometime to put such a lamp together when the lines are off slightly. Finally, the pyramidal lamp offers the beginner a product for his pains that will not shame his endeavors unduly and the advanced glass worker a rapid review of what he already knows along with ideas for future modifications. From this point, beginner and advanced worker can start even. Such advanced productions as molded panel story lamps utilize many of the techniques and ideas of the pyramidal lampshade.

Fig. 3.27 A panel made of rondelite.

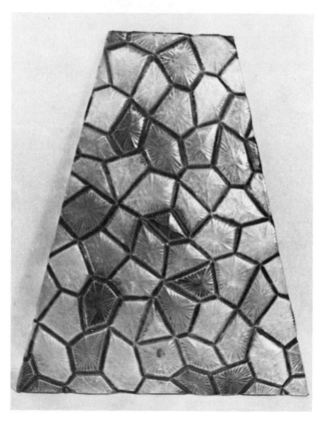

Fig. 3.28 A panel made of "mosaic glass." (This is true glass, not plastic.)

It is possible to provide yourself with a lamp every panel of which is a different type glass. Unfortunately it is liable to look less than radiant, more than redundant. To mix opalescent, streaky cathedral, Flemish and rondelite (Fig. 3.27) into one great potpourri just because you happen to have pieces of them on hand may serve the cause of efficiency but will do nothing for your aesthetic sense.

On the other hand, different glasses may certainly be mixed together just as colors may be mixed if the mixture is productive of any sort of meaning. (Fig. 3.28.) It is not necessary, for instance, to use granite-backed glass throughout a lamp. This glass can be mixed with clear or Flemish, depending on the design, the size of the pieces and the desired effect. Mixtures of glasses should be balanced so that the eye picks up and carries over a flow of design emphasized sporadically here and there by such variations.

This technique is enhanced by turning different sides of the glasses toward or away from the viewer. All textured glasses—rondelite, Flemish, moss-backed, granite-backed—may be so treated as they are more softened facing one way than another and yet leave no doubt as to their character. There is no right or wrong way to face any glass; it is strictly up to the worker to employ them in the manner he decides will best give his lamp a basic theme. Most of the differences and subtleties of these glasses become apparent only when the lamp is turned on, but that's part of the fun of making lamps of stained glass.

Chapter 4

Wiring and Hanging

A Lamp Must Be Sturdy

A good percentage of all lamps are of the hanging variety and as such are to be suspended over people and other items of greater or lesser value. It would not do to have your lamp plummet from its moorings at an inconvenient moment, nor is its effect to be enhanced by a gravitational slouch at the end of its chain. Provided that you have properly balanced your lamp when putting it together, it should hang accurately. You cannot make up the discrepancies in positioning after the fabrication of your lamp; eventually the pull of its weight will tip it, roll it, yaw it or slide it in the direction dictated by any inherent flaws. Once this happens, beware; it will not take long for leads or vase caps to pull away and down it comes.

There are a number of reasons why this happens. Carelessness in what too many workers feel is the "noncreative" electrical part is the main one. Some individuals have their lamps professionally wired and hung, but this does not teach them much about complementing their creative efforts with the functional final result. Stained glass lamps, unlike anything else made of this material, have to be structured for a very specific function; a knowledge of how this function is to be carried out should always be in the forefront of the creator's mind. A maker of stained glass windows need not bother about their installation, provided that he keeps within the boundaries provided him; someone else can put the windows in, and the artist misses nothing. But if someone other than yourself hangs and wires your lamps, you will never get the "feeling" of a misplaced strut or an unbalanced plate or a sloppily placed center hole. The instinctive grasp of knowing what can go wrong is acquired only by doing it wrong; if someone else does it for you, right or wrong, the experience is never acquired by the designer in you, and you may well continue to design yourself into any of the following traps.

Unbalanced sections. Certain glasses are heavier than others of the same thickness due to the different densities of the oxides providing their color. An exception to this is antique glass which may not only be heavier but also thicker by far than machine-made glass. Glasses unequal in weight which are used in only one or two portions of the lamp, as panels or as an aggregate of small pieces, may disturb the balance of the lamp and cause it to tip. Be sure to use glass of the same weight, especially in paneled lamps, to avoid this.

Unbalanced design. A repetitive design in a "story" lamp simplifies its construction and makes the lamp easier to stabilize when it is hung. If you are going to do, let us say, four quite different designs in the four quadrants of a story lamp, you should not overburden any particular quadrant with excess leading, foiling, soldering, jewels, rocks and seashells or you will make the lamp too heavy on that side. Some workers get so carried away by their design, that they really go off balance. (Fig. 4.1.) Gemstones cut into thin slabs so the light shows through can be a lovely addition to a lamp—provided that they are either put in more than one section or that care is taken to balance them out with something of equal weight elsewhere. Otherwise you are liable to have those rocks on your head.

Poorly mixing foil and came. Believe it or not there are individuals who will start with a specific foil or lead, run out of it, and finish up with whatever they have on hand. If half a lamp is leaded and the other half foiled, you may defend it as vehemently as you desire on aesthetic grounds (someone will always believe you and consider you an innovator), but you will have a tough time getting it off the ground.

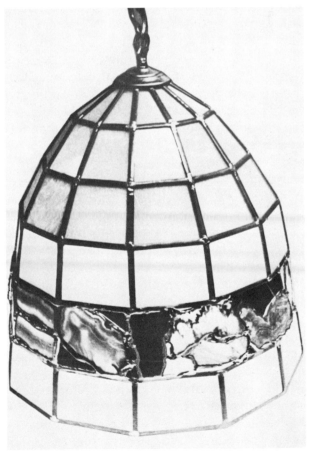

Fig. 4.1 Tiered lampshade employing thin mineral rock slabs in the lower tier. These transmit light well, but because of their irregular shape, they must be foiled into place.

Incomplete soldering of the joints. All joints, inside and out, must be soldered completely and not merely tacked together. Any joint that is not thoroughly fluxed may appear to be soldered (or have a lump of solder sitting on it), but such joints must eventually give way under stress. Review your soldering technique if your joints are breaking down; a well-soldered joint should have a smooth, even flow of solder bridging the seam.

Burned leads. Any such struts with holes through them from the use of too hot an iron should be replaced. Attempting to fill these gaps with solder makes the strut look horrible and further weakens it so that eventually the panel will start to jiggle. If it jiggles enough, it may fall out.

Poorly tinned foil. Whether your foiled piece is heavy or light, it should be beaded firmly to all adjoining pieces. If you can see the seam through the solder, the beading has not been sufficient. It is imperative that foiled pieces be soldered firmly together on the inside of the lamp, though beading, if carried out thoroughly on the front, is not necessary within. If you are making a foiled lamp and you do not tin properly, you probably will not have to worry about its falling apart in the air; very likely you will not get it off the table.

Use of improper material for the plate. By the plate we mean that circular piece of metal used to support the lamp from the top. Though certain sizes of these are available commercially, not all of them solder. Brass solders, but brass plating does not; steel does not, but galvanized steel does. The problem with many metals is that if you work on them long enough with strong hydrochloric acid and keep scarifying the surface to take the solder, the solder will appear to flow smoothly enough onto them, only to have the joint break down eventually in midair. We have seen such lamps, even after weeks of hanging, begin to yaw dangerously to one side and dangle as the struts peeled away from the top plate because of "forced" soldering. Choose a metal for your plate that you know will solder well, and then use plenty of solder. In most instances you are going to hide the plate with a crown anyway; but even if you are not, it is better to completely solder all around the struts and top plate than to tack them neatly and risk their pulling away. Galvanized sheet metal works very well for such top plates—better even than brass—but even this material must be completely soldered, inside and out, to the top of the lamp in order to acquire and maintain a purchase. Never use any brass-plated material for this purpose.

The center hole not centered. When preparing your top plate, take the time to find the exact center and drill your center hole exactly there. Since the drill bit is liable to slip on the metal, once you have established where your center hole should be, make a dot with a felt-tipped pen and put a nail hole through it. This will give enough purchase to your drill bit to lock it into place. Be sure you clamp the plate to the table so that the bit does not twirl it around, mashing the metal and lacerating your fingers. Drill the hole (standard size is $\frac{3}{8}$ inch) with a graduated bit until you get up to dimension. Then file the inside surface with a round bastard file, first snipping off any points with a fine tinsnip. Remeasure to the *center* of the hole as a final check for accuracy.

The top plate miscut. It is not easy to cut sheet metal (even the thin metal) accurately with a tinsnip the first time, or even the second or third time, you try. A technique is required to follow the line you have placed while getting the cut, waste metal out of your way—it insists on curling up into your hand. Small wonder that a number of workers get the top plate cut as best they can and then find it does not exactly fit the top of the lamp. While a certain amount of latitude is allowed here, care must be taken that the top plate is not so mis-shaped that it does not touch the top circle of lead all around. If there is one area that is flattened where it should be round and so misses contact with the top lead, and you try to bridge with solder here, you can be certain that eventually this is the section that will pull away. It would be much better to recut and rehole your top plate, wasted motion though you may feel it to be, rather than patch one that really doesn't fit. To come out with a top plate that does fit:

1. With a piece of kraft paper take the exact boundaries of the top of your lamp. Place the kraft paper atop the lamp and with your fingers press down all around so that the top circle is exactly indented into the paper.

2. With a sharp scissors cut the kraft paper to the exact size of the indented surface.

3. Place the kraft paper template back on the lamp. The chances are good that the top of your lamp is not exactly even; whether it is or not, mark one strut and mark the paper in the corresponding place to give yourself a key to fit the metal plate to the same place. Your kraft paper template should sit on top of and almost completely cover the leaded surface. It must not extend over the sides anywhere. It is best if a small rim of lead is seen surrounding the template; you will use this surface to solder the plate to the lamp.

4. Hold the paper firmly over pattern paper and trace around the edges with a sharp pencil.

5. Recut the pattern from the pattern paper and transfer this onto the sheet metal with a felt-tipped, fine pointed pen. Don't go too fast or the ink will not take. Some workers transfer directly from kraft paper to sheet metal on the theory that the more often you transfer a pattern, the more margin you leave for error. We feel that the percentage of error is greater in using the thin, less rigid kraft paper as a guide than it is with the pattern paper.

6. Once the pattern is transferred to the sheet metal, mark the key line from the kraft paper, get a sharp tinsnips and start cutting. (Fig. 4.2.) Cut a little at a

Fig. 4.2 Top sheet metal plate with center hole. The plate is soldered all around to the top flanges of lead came inside and out.

Fig. 4.3 A commercial "strapping" with a predrilled center hole supports this lantern.

time being careful not to blur the ink line with your fingers. Keep cutting away the waste; don't try to fold it out of the way. Cut as accurately as possible. When you have the plate all cut out, try it atop the lamp. If it fits, add your center hole and you are done.

The top strap misplaced. Instead of having their top surfaces completely covered with a plate, many lamps are designed to be supported by a bar or strap of metal which can be either straight or bent to provide maximum bracing. (Fig. 4.3.) The majority of old, molded bent panel lamps use bent straps which are screwed into the sides of the frame below the crown, where extra metal was often added to give the screws effective purchase. This technique can be done easily enough, provided that the screw holes are even on both sides of your lamp and that you have a strong enough framework to allow for this type of bracing. It is not advisable to place screw holes into either the lead struts or crown framework as this metal is not rigid enough to hold them.

If you want to use a bent strap and have made one of a material that will not solder, wrap some copper foil around the ends, tin it, and then solder it to the top of your lamp. Again, make sure both sides are even. Straight metal rods will work nicely and simply as top braces. Wrap their ends with copper foil and solder two of them into place with just room enough between them for a standard size nipple. The check ring and socket at the bottom of the nipple and the lamp hook above, with a few lock nuts in between to take up any excess space, will stabilize the nipple and allow the lamp to hang evenly. If it is uneven, you can easily move the nipple to the right or left by releasing the pressure on it through the bars. In this instance, even if you haven't gotten your bar exactly even, you can compensate for it.

The above is a fairly general rundown on what you can do to suspend your lamp accurately. As for the wiring and the actual hanging, these activities will neither unbalance nor rebalance a lamp. The exception to this is if the vase caps are misplaced.

Vase caps are the brass cones that many workers use to hold their lamps in the air. They come in many different sizes—from one inch to twelve—and are usually used in a pyramidal or cylindrical lamp, a smaller one on the bottom of the top circle of lead and a larger one on the top. The top edge of the lamp is thus caught between them; when pressure is applied by means of the socket below and the lamp hook above, the shade is firmly held. Problems arise with vase caps if they are the wrong size or if they are not positioned properly. In such instances, the lamp will slide or tip to one side, and if the bottom cap is too small, it will begin to break out of the ceiling as the ineffective cap pulls through the top hole.

TYPES OF CHAINS AND FIXTURES

There are almost enough types of chain available to satisfy a host of Marley's ghosts, and they vary in price from very cheap to very expensive. Following are a few of the most popular and their description:

1. *Oval* is the commonest and cheapest of the decorative chains. It comes in brass, black and nickel, as well as pewter and white.

2. *Medium Spanish* has an extremely lengthened oval loop with decorative impressions stamped into the thin, flat links.

3. *Gothic* has an octagonal link with flattened, unengraved surfaces.

4. *Sunburst* has engraved oval, rounded links alternating with flattened, wider surfaced links more ornately engraved. The differences in links are striking.

5. *Mediterranean* has twisted links in long ovals, the metal turned on itself like licorice.

There are also a number of handmade decorative chains composed of one or two regular oval links with exquisitely shaped and engraved, stylized links between. (Fig. 4.4.) Almost any type of lamp should look good with these; unfortunately, if the lamp's workmanship is poor, it will be made to look even worse in comparison.

Fig. 4.4 Types of brass fittings and decorative pieces. On the left, vase caps of different design. Above left, a globe holder. Top center, a decorative finial. On the upper right, a brass base. Lower right, a decorative canopy. Lower center, decorative brass plate. Many of these items cannot be found any longer.

Canopies. These are caps used to hide the ceiling electrical box into which a lamp is wired. They can be purchased either plain or quite fancy.

Sockets. Either porcelain, Bakelite® or brass-plated sockets can be used in stained glass lamps. Different lengths are available. If you can, get the socket without an on-off switch or chain. You will be controlling the current either from the cord or from a wall switch, and the socket should be as free from extraneous detail as possible to give a neat appearance to the inside of the lamp.

Nipples. We advise the use of brass running thread nipples, ⅛ IP. Occasionally we use steel, zinc-plated nipples (galvanized) for special work. It is difficult to select any specific length of nipple as a standard since lamp styles vary so widely. We try to have on hand sizes from three quarters of an inch to at least an inch and a half, and we also keep several two and a half-inch ones available just in case. Keep a hacksaw with a sharp blade in your studio; it comes in handy not only for cutting reinforced lead came but also for trimming nipples to the proper size. Somehow, no matter what variety of sizes you maintain, invariably a lamp will come along that requires a nipple just a trifle shorter than any you have in stock. A good bench vise is a necessity here—one that will hold the nipple tight enough to be sawed but not so tight that the threads will be crushed. When trimming nipples with a hacksaw, try to keep it to one cut. Don't let the saw bounce off and start three or four different cuts. You won't be able to screw the nipple into anything with the threads all hacked up.

Die Cast Loops. These are the lamp "rings" or "hooks" which join the lamp to the chain. The bottom link of the chain is opened with a chain pliers and hooked into the loop, which screws onto the protruding nipple, which is in turn fixed into the socket below through the vase caps. Such loops come in brass, copper and black to match the chain, but such matching is far from essential. They are also available in a number of ornate shapes. (Fig. 4.5.)

Lamp Wire. Regular electrical wire is used in producing stained glass lamps. From the socket it goes through the hole in the nipple, through the corresponding hole in the die cast loop and up the chain, through the hole in the canopy to the electrical box. Thread it through the chain every other link so

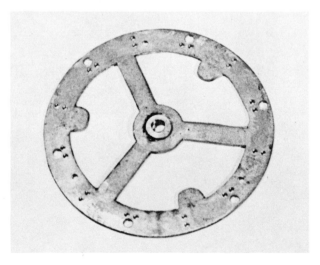

Fig. 4.5 An old hanging plate. This is placed within the top hole of the lamp and suspends it securely.

A standing Tiffany-type shade (maker unknown, an old lamp).

Standing "ball" lamp. *(Courtesy of Clemence Stanley)*

that it does not become an eyesore. Be careful if you are swagging your lamp and threading an excess amount of chain that the weight of the chain does not pull your lamp off the table while you are threading the wire through it.

Chain Pliers. If you once attempt to open the links of decorative chain without this handy gadget, you will quickly come to the conclusion that it is well worth any price. In fact it does not cost too much. Without a pair of chain pliers, two pairs of ordinary pliers and some vigorous tugging at the offending link will just about get it open, and almost as much trouble is required to close it again. With this instrument, opening and closing links of chain—a process you may have to go through several times with one lamp—becomes a matter of routine.

Vase Caps. We have mentioned these items previously and include them now for the sake of completeness. They come only in brass color, and if you wish to change their color to match the chain, you must paint them. If you intend to paint them, wipe them down first with acetone or a similar solvent to remove any grime or any spray coating placed on them in the factory which will prevent the paint from taking. Vase caps come brass brush finished (very shiny and new looking with a high polish) or unfinished (rather dull, but more interesting in appearance for certain types of lamps). There are certain solutions available to darken the brass almost to an antique finish—ammonium hydroxide, for one—and the more times you apply and wipe off such a solution, the darker and more antique-looking your vase cap becomes. We have found that this is not really a permanent change, however, the cap reverting after a while pretty much to its natural color. We have tried spraying a treated vase cap with lacquer in an attempt to maintain it, but the difference has never seemed worth the work involved. Nor is painting these caps the answer, as the paint tends to chip in time and the natural color then shows through in bits and pieces making the thing look worse than ever. Probably the best thing to do is to use the caps as they are and not worry about their matching or not matching the chain. After a few days, you won't even notice.

SWAGGING OR CAPPING?

Swagging a lamp involves placing it wherever you want it, regardless of where the socket may be, and walking the electrical wire and chain back to the socket in artistic loops along the ceiling and down the wall. At its best, this technique provides an aesthetic method of placing an important piece of room furniture, at its worst it can look forced. One swagged lamp in a room is generally enough; wire and chain criss-crossing the ceiling makes for confusion. The choice is yours how deep the swag and how many loops of chain to make. Swags can be all of a depth or can get deeper as they go. Three loops of chain should be enough for anybody.

Capping, on the other hand, is placing your lamp into an existing fixture. An electrical box placed in the ceiling is usually covered by a canopy, but you can make a false swag from such a box if it is not placed to your liking; generally it is over a table or where a table is meant to go. There is certainly no difference in designing a lamp for a swag arrangement or for capping into an existing box, but there is a difference in how such lamps are hung. The amount of weight a lamp carries matters little if it is to go into an existing electrical box which was made for a lamp and is probably reinforced to take the additional load that plaster alone is not prepared for. The swagged lamp is going to go, in all likelihood, into either plaster or drywall, which is even worse. Very little, if any, support is offered by this material, and if you do not make adequate preparations, your lamp may end up in your lap. It's a good idea to reconnoiter the area to be used for swagging and to reinforce it not only to take the weight of your lamp, but to take more than that weight. After all, you may want to hang a bigger lamp as you continue work in this field. So get above the ceiling if you can and put an additional beam across the existing beams to take the load. If you can't get into this space, you had better find what beams are available as close as possible to where you want to hang the lamp and use one of them. It is not a good idea to use "mollies" or any retaining devices with a very heavy lamp. The risk of the lamp pulling them through the ceiling is too great. Medium weight lamps may well be held with such plaster retaining devices if you want to take the chance, but if you are in any doubt whatsoever, cannot find a beam and yet want the lamp in a specific area, call an electrician.

PLACING YOUR LAMP—HOW HIGH OR HOW LOW?

A question constantly asked by individuals making or buying a stained glass lamp for the first time is: how large a bulb can I safely put in it without cracking the glass? The answer, of course, is that it doesn't matter as the heat from the most powerful bulb will not affect the glass. With this in mind, one must realize that the placement of any stained glass lamp does not, therefore, depend on how much radiance the bulb is allowed to put forth. Neither glass, solder nor lead is susceptible to the heat; rather it is the other way around, and the bulb must give way before the amounts of the former materials, a surplus of which will make the brightest bulb glow but dimly. Such lamps may well be closer to the floor, as their function is more decorative than visual and the light they do put out is more effective at that level. These lamps to either side of a sofa even at ankle level enhance their surroundings and provide a unique decor. On the other hand, lamps for reading, gaming or dining should be hung high enough to light what is going on below but low enough to be easily seen.

Stained glass shades hung too high will show only the bulb and its glare on their inner surfaces. They must swing just above eye level for their beauty to be apparent. If you have to go much higher than eye level, the bare bulbs will show too much, and you should use a globe. A globe will not make up for the higher positioning, but it will give a better effect. Globes are sold by size according to their "collar." (Fig. 4.6.) They require a special holding device which becomes part of your lamp's electrical system. Thumb screws across this holder secure the globe to the lamp. Make sure that the thumb screws fit the holes before you buy the holder, especially if you don't have too much room inside your lamp to maneuver. A thumb screw frozen in a hole too small for it can be disastrous when you are trying to get the globe off with one hand to change the bulb so that your lamp will come alive again.

Fig. 4.6 A globe with globe holder. Note the set screw. The collar of the globe is within the holder.

If you are able to hang your lamp just above eye level and you want as much light as possible, there are two things you can do. Since you will be able to see just under the skirt but not much further (unless you do not have your lamp over a table and so can sit directly beneath it), you can get a Dura Lite® bulb in either 100 or 150 watts which will give a globe effect and yet provide the convenience of a bulb. It gives more of a "hot spot" than a globe, but from the side you probably won't notice that. The other thing you can do is provide your lamp with a "cluster" socket which gives room for three bulbs at angles from each other. A lot of the old lamps were wired this way, and the three bare bulbs of the cluster socket may still be seen in a great many of them to this day, but most of the customers for whom we make lamps prefer to have globes.

HANGING VERSUS TABLE LAMPS

Almost any lamp designed for hanging can be used as well for a table lamp if a complementary base can be provided. The reverse is not always true; most table lamps are pretty specific. If you decide to convert a hanging shade to a table lamp, you must keep certain considerations in mind.

Size. Obviously you don't want your base overpowered by your lamp. Extremes are simple enough to decide, but is there a rule of dimension here? We feel that if the bottom edge of a shade—whether skirt edge or lamp edge—comes down over more than thirty percent of the base, it is probably too long for that particular base. There are, of course, exceptions to this and the eye may decide that a certain combination is aesthetically correct even if fifty percent of the base is covered, but such instances are rare. At the other extreme, decision is far more difficult. Certain shades may be quite small and yet fit a large base well if they are employed as a part of the decor of the base and not as a covering for it. It is most important that the proper base be found for such a marriage and that things are not thrown together just because they are on hand. Attempting to force a small lamp to "top up" a large base gives a ludicrous effect.

Design. Another good rule of thumb is not to use an ornate lamp upon an ornate base. Ideally lamp and base should set each other off so that each contributes an individual glow that blends to produce one good result. This does not mean that ornate bases must of necessity squelch their shades, but that shades should be designed to complement the bases; they cannot fight each other. It is much easier to design or fit a lamp to a simple base than to one which pretty much has made up its mind to be the whole show.

Physical modifications. Probably the easiest way to fit any shade to any base—and we are talking now of shades and bases that were not made for each other—is to use our old friend, the sheet metal plate. The problem here is that many old lamp frames are difficult to solder; if you run into this, you will have to juggle nuts and finials to hold your plate to the shade with pressure. If you are making your own lamp for a base, you can fit whatever modifications of the basic shape you need into your design. Most bases have some type of holding device built into their shape, and it is easy enough to match this up with your shade if you are starting from scratch. (Figs. 4.7 through 4.9.)

Fig. 4.7   Wiring for bulbs to either side of this shade is run across the top plate and taped down to avoid being seen.

Fig. 4.8   With the shade hanging, the top plate and wiring will not be noticed. This is an example of a long-paneled lamp with scalloped skirt. A dieter's nightmare, it was made by an individual who had recently lost a lot of weight. Look for the message. *(Courtesy of Larry Gargulio)*

52   WIRING AND HANGING

Fig. 4.9 The top plate soldered to the supporting sides converts a hanging lamp to a base lamp. The lines on the top are guidelines for locating the center hole.

BASES

Almost everything from cut glass to steel shrapnel, from ceramic turns to driftwood, has at one time or other been used as a base on which to place a lamp. If your pleasure is to employ such "found" bases, you must allow your ingenuity full play in electrifying the piece and in choosing the style of lampshade to cap it with. There is potentially a lot of fun, and a lot of disaster, at your fingertips. If you prefer to play it a little safer and save a lot of work, you should be content to employ standard bases for your lamps. There is still plenty of variety.

Bulbholders. These bases are bare above the socket and made for lampshades which clip onto the bulb with a pair of metal prongs. To transform these to carry stained glass, you have to modify the existing shape by soldering an arm to reach above the socket to whatever height you desire. You may want to have the base fitted with a harp instead; a lot depends on the style of the shade you intend to use. (Figs. 4.10 and 4.11.)

Harp bases. The harp is an oval piece of metal framing the socket and extending above it for half a foot or more. On top of the harp is a small screw plate which will take a finial. Stained glass shades may be fitted to such harps by use of the metal plate described in the preceding pages. Harps are sold separately in lamp supply stores, and if you feel the harp you have is not sturdy enough for the lamp you have in mind, you may be able to replace it. (Figs. 4.12 and 4.13.)

Flat bases. A flattened metal surface is provided here on which the shade can rest. This is usually threaded to take a finial. A vase cap will fit nicely on such a space; this type of fixture provides maximum support for the shade. (Figs. 4.14 and 4.15.)

The pipe base. This is, in effect, half a harp. Such a pipe, threaded at the end, can come out of a base in any direction, and a lamp (generally a small one) will continue in the direction indicated. A great deal of variety is afforded

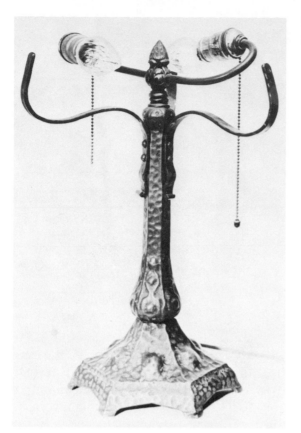

Fig. 4.10 A rather unusual base found in an antique store.

Fig. 4.12 Lamp base found in an antique store.

Fig. 4.13 A shade, found in another store and repaired by the authors, went well with the above base. With only slight modification, the harp-stand was just right for the center hole in the shade.

Fig. 4.11 Luckily the shade for the above base was found there as well. One missing glass panel was replaced by the authors.

Fig. 4.14   Another antique store base.

Fig. 4.15   Above base matched with this shade, which we had hanging around.

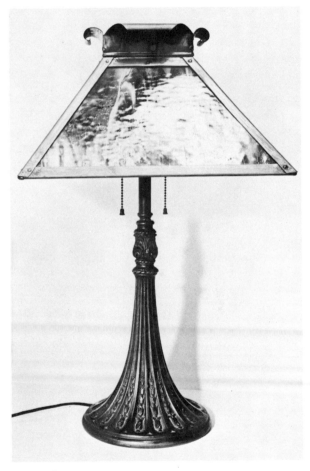

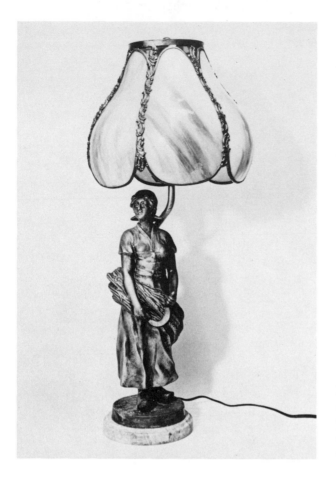

Fig. 4.16   A lovely combination of base and shade. The pipe support of this base allows the shade to be turned upwards as well, but we prefer it this way.

here, and the lamp may be placed so the light falls either toward or away from the base. A sheet metal plate is probably the best holding device. (Fig. 4.16.)

THE ANTIQUE SHOP

A great source for fixtures of all types is the antique shop. Bases especially may be found that, cleaned up and established with a stained glass shade, will make a stunning addition to your home. We have picked up many superb bases in this fashion. (Figs. 4.17 and 4.18.) Many of them we have not as yet used, some of them we may never use, but we have them on hand for when the urge strikes or a commission arrives. Don't worry if you have to clean up such finds; soap and water and a little polish will generally do the trick. Of course if more extensive repair work is involved, whether the base was worth it would have to depend upon how much you wanted the base. It's a good idea to rewire all bases so purchased. Most of the time the wiring that comes with them is broken anyway, but even where it is not, the wires are pretty well dried out and the insulation split. If the wiring looks pretty good outside the base, best check it within. More heat transfer and drying of the wires takes place inside. If you do decide to re- wire your base, don't just pull the old wires out haphazardly after cutting them. They may follow a certain pathway of tricky bends which you will have a time

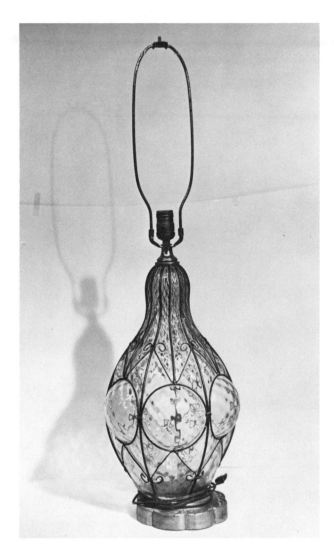

Fig. 4.17 An Italian base, lovely in itself, to which no shade has yet been fitted. One will come along or will be made in time. This base was purchased at a garage sale for $4.00.

reworking. Study how they are folded into the lamp base before you yank them; a lot of time can be saved in this manner.

If you can salvage the socket on your old base, you are in pretty good shape. Most of the time sockets are pitted and corroded with age and disuse and can furnish a problem as far as removal is concerned. Sometimes such a socket is special to the base, and you may not be able to rematch it. Note this before sinking your money into this particular find. (Fig. 4.19.)

Remember that not only bases but also stained glass shades may be located in antique shops. If these are in good condition, they will probably sell for a good deal of money; however, you may be fortunate enough to find one or two that are in desperate need of repair—either they have four out of eight bent panels missing from their frame or half the glass may be smashed. You may just be able to pick these up for a song and remake the panels or repair the glass yourself, either of which will leave you with an expensive, hard-to-find shade that may well go hand in hand with a base from that selfsame shop. (Figs. 4.20 and 4.21.)

Fig. 4.18 A ceramic base lovely in design from that same sale. We'll find the shade for it someday.

Fig. 4.19 Small bases need not be overwhelmed by chunky shades. Here is a bedroom lamp with a brightly lit, decorative shade in square, broken panels. Note the scalloped bottom. *(Courtesy of Elliott Wiener)*

Fig. 4.20 An unusual base which is a small lamp in itself. The bottom glass portion lights up.

Fig. 4.22 The base of this "mini-lamp" is sand cast lead. A pipe stand carries the shade. The pipe curves round the bulb and affixes near the socket.

A FIXTURE NEED NOT BE FIXED

The usual run of practical lights for rooms are pretty well immobile. They serve only one function—providing illumination. (Fig. 4.22.) Stained glass shades, however, can within reason be transferred from room to room, provided that their specificity is not such that they demand one room alone. Furthermore, as you keep making them your critical appraisal will begin to change, and you may want to substitute a more original for a more prosaic shade. A more original shade may call for a different type of hanging or even for a base instead of a swag. Since you are in control, since these are your creations, you can keep changing them around, selling off or giving as gifts the ones you no longer care for and continually expanding both your collection and your art. Few things can be this rewarding.

Fig. 4.21 The base (left) forms an interesting ensemble with its shade. This lamp, originally brought in for repair, was purchased by us.

PART II
Procedures

Chapter 5
The Lantern

A lantern is defined as a transparent case, portable in nature, for enclosing and protecting a light. (Fig. 5.1.) A lamp is not thought of as portable. We have stylized the definition of a lantern somewhat and are more prone to think of it as an elongated light case, ornate with colored glass in a patterned design, rather small in diameter as compared to a lamp, and much thinner than a lamp. Be that as it may, the crossover point between lantern and lamp is still pretty individualistic. The patterns in this chapter will give an idea of what the typical, and a few nontypical, lanterns can look like.

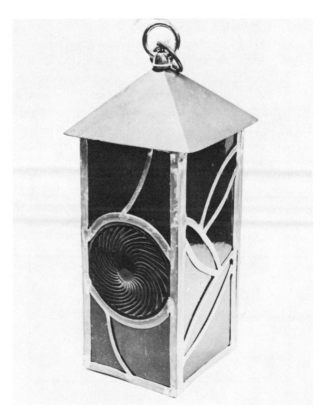

Fig. 5.1 A typical lantern (one side containing an old rondel) with a copper top.

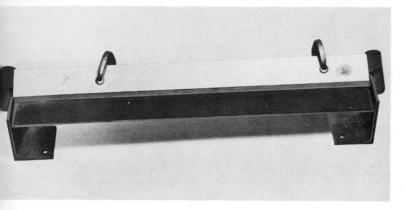

Fig. 5.2 A bending brake. The clamps are removed, the material to be bent is placed under the removable aluminum brace, the clamps are replaced, and the side is bent up with the help of the two steel rods that fit in the holes at left and right corners. The bending brake should be screwed into a firm base.

This does not mean that we have given up on portability. All our lanterns can be carried about using a candle to provide luminescence. They are quite lovely that way and provide effects not possible with lamps per se. The history of the lantern goes back rather a long way. Recall, if you will, Wee Willie Winkie of nursery rhyme fame. Wee Willie (the nickname given to William, Prince of Orange, and later William III of England) runs through the town with a lantern which we like to think was made of lead and sparkling stained glass. If you doubt this was really something to shout about, try the patterns herein.

DESIGNS AND CONSTRUCTIONS

Figure 5.3 is a Japanese style lantern with a lot of character in the copper topping. A bending brake (Fig. 5.2) was used to provide the sharp folds that give it an almost pleated effect. This instrument holds the metal firmly in position while giving the user a chance to make clean, neat folds. The main glass section is rectangular in design with internal lines breaking up alternating panels. A rather squat skirt complements the shape and adds to the diminutive but rather jolly proportion. We advise the use of a wide lead here, even a ⅜ inch, to help bring out the sturdy appearance of this lantern.

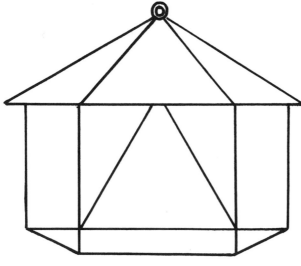

Fig. 5.3.

Fig. 5.4.

Figure 5.4 shows two panels in a typical rectangular pattern. Two rondels are placed against a central diamond around the corner. Rondels can either be purchased as such—they are either spun or pressed glass circles showing whorls of color and texture—or they can be falsely produced by the simple expedient of cutting circles out of glass. (Fig. 5.5.) True rondels have a beauty and individuality that cannot be simulated; glass circles will still give your lantern an interesting design. This lantern has a well-balanced linear quality. Note the small break, or flint, in the left hand corner of the diamond panel. This adds a touch of asymmetry to the scheme. There is such a thing as being too well-balanced.

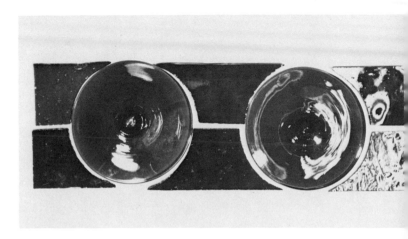

Fig. 5.5   Lantern glass cut to size.

A workmanlike lantern also including rondels is here shown in Figure 5.6, but this lantern lacks the frilled skirt of copper of Figure 5.4, giving a more spare appearance. This design has a rather no-nonsense cut to it, but it is ruggedly attractive nonetheless. The top is the same style as in the previous figure. Figure 5.7 is another basic pattern for a rondel lantern with a rounded top.

Two large rondels give this rather narrow lantern (Fig. 5.8) a wider look than it would otherwise have. Note that the panels are similar. Little other designing is necessary. It is exactly here in this "little else" that many beginners go overboard with pettifogging details. The skirt, scalloped deeply, livens up this classically plain design. When scalloping such a piece of metal, whether with copper or sheet metal, never do it freehand. Make specific inked lines and follow them. The scallops must all look the same.

Here is a soft look in an octagonal style (Fig. 5.9). A sharper peak to the cap complements the lengthy panels and the long lines within do the same. The four-corner "lead in" panels give the lantern its octagonal shape. The width of these will determine the diameter of the lantern, but if you make them too wide, you will lose the design. They should be no more than one-third the width of the main panels. A simple skirt is all that is needed. Such a design can also apply to a four-panel lantern using the lead-in panels as borders on the main panels with just four pieces of skirt necessary.

We present Figure 5.10, a bowed design imparted to all panels. You may use pieces of rondel for the broken central circle or may just cut glass to fit. The central lead line is the pivot for the bend or bow. You need not repeat the broken central circle in all aspects; two opposing ones are enough. The slightly scalloped skirt complements the top capping.

Fig. 5.6.

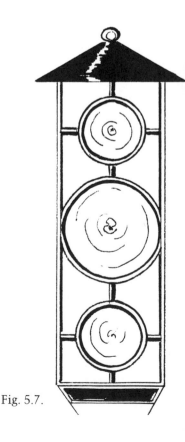

Fig. 5.7.

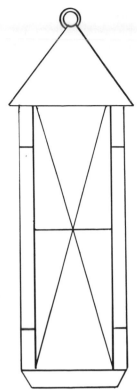

Fig. 5.9.

Fig. 5.8.

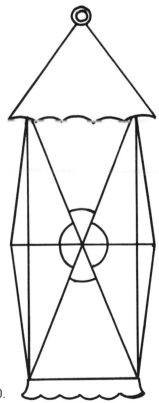

Fig. 5.10.

65

Figure 5.11 shows four free-swinging uncapped panels. The opening top and bottom adds to the spur of the moment effect, though care in planning and time in executing these panels is necessary. This lantern is a real beauty and will give you a great feeling of satisfaction if you do it right. Make sure that the panels match in dimension and that you put them together evenly at right angles. The internal design may be modified, but not too much or the panels will look too plain. Use rondels here, not glass circles. This lantern is suspended internally by a holed four-corner plate of sheet metal soldered to the struts of the design and the four dips of the upper portion of the panels. Solder should be applied to the top and bottom of the plate. Catch as many of those internal lead lines as you can with solder and adhere them to the plate. You cannot err on the side of strength.

Figure 5.12 is a veritable rustle of rondels climbing over all the surfaces, some appearing from the bottom, others vanishing over the top. Two half-rondels form the center of the panel, giving a follow through from one panel to the next. There is quite a bit of small piece cutting in this one—all that background—but you will find it worth it. A square cut rectangular sheet metal or copper skirt makes a handsome border. No frills on the top plate here, please.

Figure 5.13 is a lovely flowing design in feminine style with panels intermixed of rondels, circles and ranging curves. A lot of work has to go into the top cap, which shows a beautiful, pagodalike quality, to lead in the design of the glass. The peak is extremely sharp and quite tall; it should be reinforced within to take the weight of the lantern. One strut within will secure the outside loop. This of course must be done from below before the top cap is seated and soldered to the upper lead of the lantern. Note the small scalloping of the edges of the cap and the similar areas in the tiny skirt, which is just wide enough to allow the passage of a long, thin bulb.

Figure 5.14 is a change from all those curves, a straight-line design that is still intriguing and not at all "boxlike." You can use up a lot of your scrap pieces of glass in this one. So far in describing these designs, we have said nothing about color, a subject difficult enough to discuss with examples in front of one. We will inject a cautionary note here regarding color: don't mix all your colors together in a piece such as this just because it offers you the opportunity to do so. Your design will be stronger with a mixture of delicate hues and tones than with a rainbow effect. Stick to a primary tone and modify it from there, always remembering to come back to it somewhere along the line. Remember also that lanterns can be made from clear glass if you wish—either antique or cathedral—since, due to their pieced panels, they do not show the bulb as readily as the unbroken long, straight-paneled lamps do. The choice of glass is quite important; there is less a chance of mixing different pieces of opalescent colors than antique or cathedral colors, as the opalescents (in a lantern such as this, for example), will tend to clash more.

A small, softly flowing design with a rondel as the center of one panel and crossed lead lines the other is shown in Figure 5.15. This is a good design for beginners to start with.

Figure 5.16 is a complementary design to Figure 5.15 though slightly more intricate. No rondels here, just lead lines in fairly straight order. No skirt is needed.

Fig. 5.11.

Fig. 5.12.

Fig. 5.13.

Fig. 5.14.

Fig. 5.15.

Fig. 5.16.

Fig. 5.17.

Figure 5.17 shows a few modified lantern TV night lights that are simple but effective. The two background styles have copper tops curved to a greater or lesser degree over glass edges. The small skirt should also be glass. The bulb and socket should be almost miniature and can lie free within. The foreground light has sloping sides of opalescent glass and a three-corner rondel design front and back. A wooden border or a glass one will serve. Again, the light and socket within can lie free. If the bulb gets too hot, let it lie on a piece of sheet metal. This design has enough height so that if you want a fixed bulb, you can wire one into a sheet metal floor.

Here is a trio of lanterns in Figure 5.18 showing different design "faces." The design is not overly impressive in a line drawing, but used with the proper colors of stained glass, it quickly takes on a life of its own.

Figure 5.19 shows alternating diamond panels in a bowed design only two panels of which are bowed. The two diamond panels are of necessity straight panels, while their opposing panels bow out slightly. You can get the bowing even in these panels by placing a pea or a bean under the center section of the panel to be bowed and sloping up to that point. Do not leed this panel first and then try to bow it; allow the glass to rest, centrally, on the object used to take it off the table, then lead it when it is already in the bowed state thus presented by the glass. It is a little tricky the first time, but you will soon get the hang of it. Remember that the opposing panels are larger than the diamond panels. Instead of the diamond, however, all lines meet at a central point which becomes the center focus of the slight bow. If you take out the diamond panel, continue all lines to the center, and then erase the diamond, you will have the design of the bowed panels.

Figure 5.20 is another bowed design whose panels are all the same. Bowing takes place away from the center line. It might be wise to first make a cardboard mock-up of this one and then fit your glass over it. If you don't want to take the time for this, it is possible to bow this freehand; use something underneath that will provide the height you need, and use the same thing for all the panels. Use glass strips for the skirt.

Figure 5.21 is an alternate design to Figure 5.20 offering a plumper and more stolid look. For the holed, thin skirt you might try the tin or sheet metal strap-

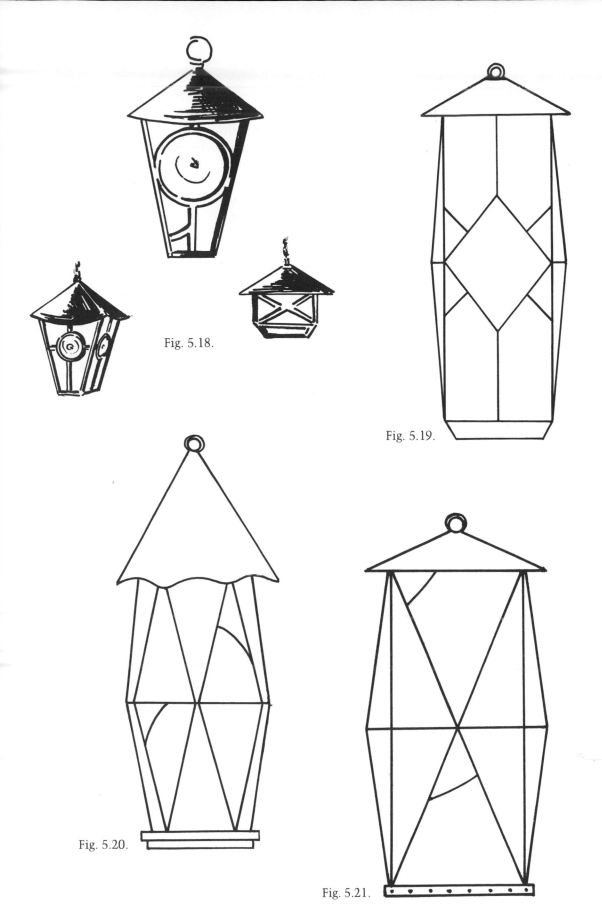

Fig. 5.18.

Fig. 5.19.

Fig. 5.20.

Fig. 5.21.

ping used in chairs and also by plasterers (it solders well). The shallow cap goes with the overall presentation.

Figure 5.22 is a twinned pyramidal lantern presenting an enigma as well as a lovely finished product to the viewer: how to do a bulb change? The two halves are joined together by small clips on the bottom which fit into small wire loops on the top. One at each corner will do. A flange of lead runs over the seam and is soldered only to the lead of the bottom panel so that it will hide all these mysterious goings-on.

Figure 5.23 is another pyramidal lamp design showing more detail. Each half is married to the other via the central lead line. You could also make this lamp by leaving out the lower point. Then the panel shown would be a complete side and, bent inward against the center lead, could meet three opposing sides to form a truncated pyramidal shade whose skirt would be this lower portion.

We have been dealing mostly with metal tops for our lamps; here are two views of a glass one in Figure 5.24. The top view shows the design with the central hole; the bottom shows the extension from the table. Glass tops can be used to support lanterns provided that the hole is small enough and the amount of weight is not excessive. Otherwise, metal bracings must be used from within. Small vase caps will usually do the trick.

Figure 5.25 is a double pyramid lantern with a very ornate interior design. Compare this with Figure 5.26.

This is the same basic shape as Figure 5.25, but a completely different appearance is given by a more muted pattern within the panels. The center break line makes this lantern appear (it is not) longer than the previous one.

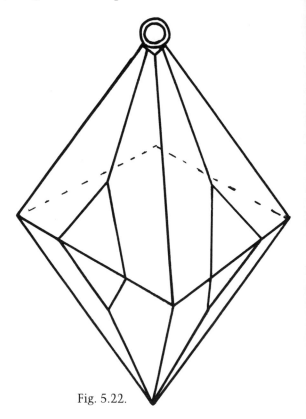

Fig. 5.22.

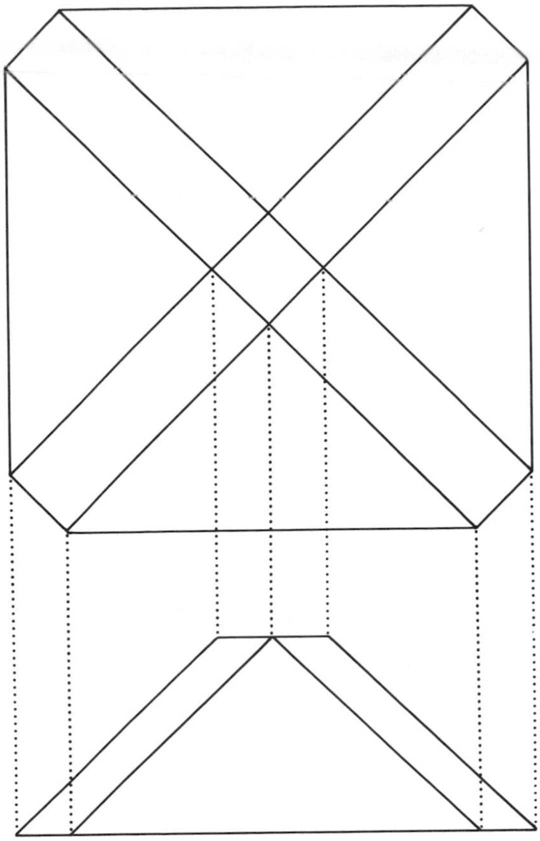

Fig. 5.24.

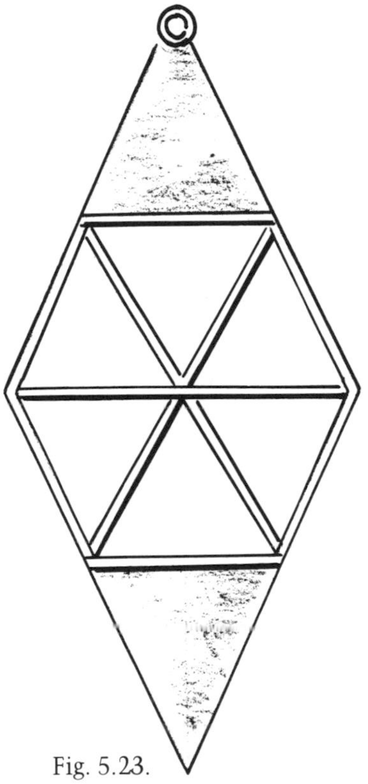

Fig. 5.23.

Fig. 5.25.

Fig. 5.26.

ODD AND EVEN PANELS

We have seen some pretty odd panels made by beginners, but the oddity we are discussing at the moment is geometric, not aesthetic. Most lanterns are composed of an even number of panels, generally four, though six and eight can be produced easily enough. Occasionally one runs across the odd numbered lantern. Such a form is not difficult to make providing you follow a mold; without a mold, you will have difficulty. The odd numbered panel lantern, unless the panels angle at pleasing degrees, will tend to appear absent-minded. The odd numbered lantern must be so constructed as to present a recognizably purposeful look. Therefore, while such a lantern can be done and can provide interest, don't try to get away with breaking a panel of an even numbered lamp and forcing together what remains. (See Figs. 5.27 and 5.28.)

GETTING THE RIGHT ANGLE EVEN

Since most lanterns are composed of four sides (as in Fig. 5.29), they are basically right angled shapes, either squares or rectangles. It is imperative when putting the sides together that you make sure the angle between them is ninety degrees. Somehow individuals have gotten the idea that there is really nothing to producing right angled, even sides, that it is, in fact, less difficult than putting

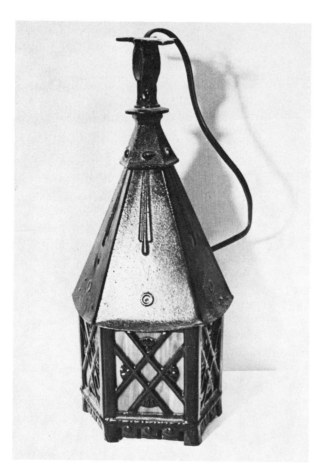

Fig. 5.27 Old five-sided lantern. The frame was found in an antique store, and the glass was added by the authors.

Fig. 5.28 Old lantern, four sided. The peaked roof is almost characteristic of these lamps. Alternating glass panels are present.

together a pyramidal lamp containing a number of thirty or forty-five degree angles. The fact of the matter is that a pyramidal lamp, the multiple panels of which can really only go together in one way, seeks its own angles between panels, and so long as each panel touches the table, the angle between is automatically formed. Not so with a four panel lantern. These angles can go pretty much any way and will unless you check them carefully. Unfortunately the fact that an angle is off is not always immediately apparent. Usually you discover it when the lantern is all together and you are busy soldering up the sides. It is a good idea, therefore, to double-check for right angles directly after tacking the sides together. Once you are satisfied the right angle is in good shape, solder the two sides completely along the seam. Then do the same with the other half of the lantern. Put the two sides together and check the angles with a rule. Then make the final tacking and soldering and you have your lantern together.

Another mistake to watch for is not getting the sides even. Carelessness is working here. Again the individual may feel that since he has only four panels to take care of, instead of fourteen—as he may have had in his last lamp—he couldn't possibly go wrong. The other problem is the individual who knows that his sides are off but who feels it won't show up in such a simple shape. He may end up by

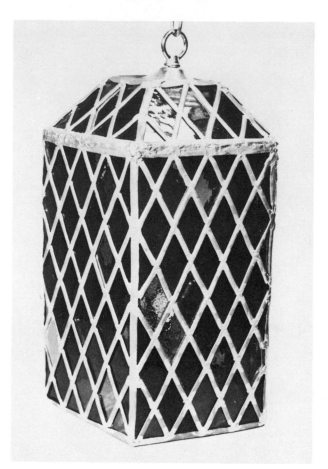

Fig. 5.29 Large lantern of small, leaded glass pieces. *(Courtesy of Clemence Stanley)*

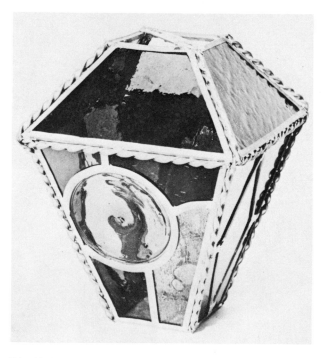

Fig. 5.30 Rondel-diamond lantern employing glass for a top roof. Note the twisted lead over the side seams and horizontal joinings.

hacking glass and spewing solder to salvage his project. Eventually, if he has any sort of pride in his work, he will have to take it all apart and start over.

There is always the question of how to solder right angle shapes, whether corner to corner or overlapping one corner. This is a matter of individual taste and does not bear on the sturdiness of the lamp, but be sure that you solder all four corners the same way. As for the seam at these edges, there should be no reason to even consider covering it; it should be so tight that covering it just to hide poor technique doesn't even come into the picture. If you want to cover it because it bothers you, or because covering it will make the lantern look better, then you have several choices. You can run a bead of solder evenly over it, you can use U came to form a corner or you can twist the came into a decorative corner stripping that will add luster to the edges. (Fig. 5.30.) Tack this firmly but neatly with solder every few inches so that the stripping will not come away from the edge.

If you want to cover right angle corners with brass came, this choice, as well, is open to you. Try to tack the brass to the underlying lead at places where it will not show. Don't try to chase hot solder with your soldering iron when you make a mistake and some solder gets on the brass. Attempting to roll solder back to a joint, especially where brass is involved, is hopeless. You will just end up with even more solder melting onto the brass, and there you'll be with silver puddles splashed on your yellow struts. There is no good way to get this off, either. Some solutions will make solder brassy, but somehow it is never the same color brassy that you need. If a little solder splashes on any lamp strut, leave it alone. Whether the underlying metal is sheet metal, lead, brass or copper, the solder is on it for good. If you avoid sloppy technique in the first place, you won't have to worry about solder getting out of control.

DESIGNING THE METAL TOP

Heavy sheet copper is the best metal you can use for lantern tops. (Fig. 5.31.) It is malleable, has a pleasing color, is easily solderable and cuts and bends better than any other metal. Galvanized sheet metal is next. As stated previously, you can make lantern tops out of glass, but we feel that the contrast between copper and glass, while not essential for every lantern, forms a striking combination that the producer of any stained glass lamp should be familiar with. (Figs. 5.32 through 5.34.)

Sheet copper is not easy to locate in most hobby stores, but many plumbers' supply houses will be able to sell you what you need. Copper usually comes in a roll about a foot wide, so the first thing you have to do is flatten it and get the bumps out of it. We place our copper on a smooth piece of steel plating and then gently pound out any discrepancies in the surface with a rubber hammer. Make sure you use one with a wide surface—more like a mallet—or you will leave indentations in the copper which will not come out. If there are occasions when you might want to leave decorative indentations in the copper, tools are available especially for this purpose. This is another advantage that copper alone has.

We first work out our top plate in the flat—as we do most lamps—and make a pattern of it (Figs. 5.35 through 5.37). The original design is done freehand,

Fig. 5.31 Custom-made lantern skeleton. Just cut your glass and clip it into place.

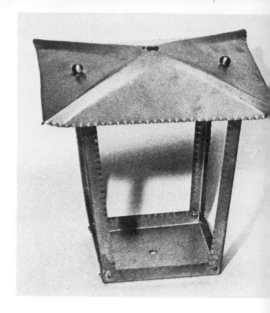

Fig. 5.32 Two lantern tops, with the paper template for the one on the right lying in front of it. A slot is cut in the metal to match that in the paper, and the metal is pushed out until the cut ends overlap. Solder is then applied to this seam. The wider the slot, the higher will be the peak of the top.

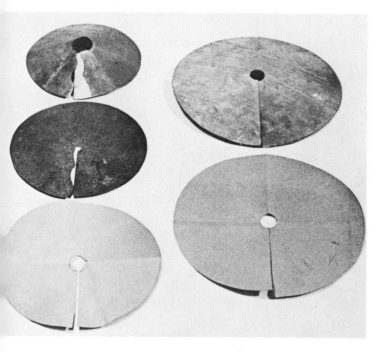

Fig. 5.34 Top: A master metal pattern for decorative pieces. Inside or outside lines can be used. A number of such pieces put together will form a dome (see Globe Shade, Chapter 9). Center: a decorative copper circle. Bottom left: a standing base; bottom right: a "soft" lantern top—not peaked—also made of copper, in this instance hammered, not bent, into shape.

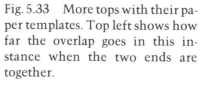

Fig. 5.33 More tops with their paper templates. Top left shows how far the overlap goes in this instance when the two ends are together.

Fig. 5.35 Stages in making a lantern peaked top. The shape is first cut out of cardboard. For purposes of illustration we have darkened the "working portion." The cardboard is bent firmly along previously measured lines radiating from a central point at the top. These spaces, including the non-working space (not colored), are all even. To acquire the original pattern for this: draw a circle with a compass and, selecting two points slightly above the points where the horizontal diameter intersects the periphery of the circle, draw two lines from them to the center of the circle. These will be the top edges of your pattern. Dividing the space between these lines will give you a pattern which you can then transfer to cardboard.

Fig. 5.36 The cardboard is then bent around ...

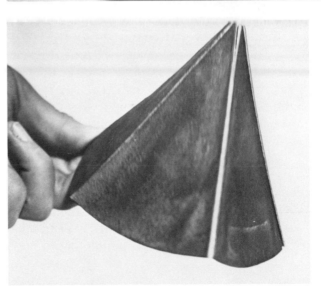

Fig. 5.37 ...until the nonworking space is tucked under one of the working flaps. This will be the shape of your lantern top.

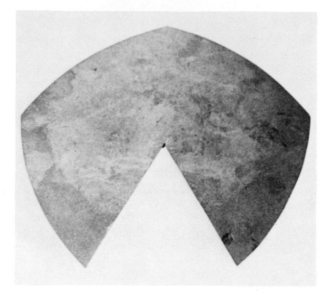

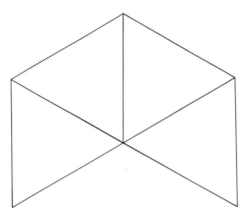

Fig. 5.38 The same thing done in metal. The pie-shaped area removed in front will determine the height of the top since the greater the arc of circumference removed, the smaller the circumference along the bottom when the two ends are brought together. The rest has been shaped and all that now remains is the placing of the lines along which the piece will be bent to shape in the bending brake. Lines will go from the central peak to the three points on the perimeter, so three bends will be required to bring the ends together. When the ends are soldered, the top is done. Angles of the bends are worked out first in cardboard as shown. The top will resemble that on the left in Figure 5.32.

and modifications are then added using French curves and rulers. We always have in mind the type of lantern we are going to fit. We almost never make just one top—when we make one, we make a dozen. Doing them en masse saves a lot of time, and they may be stored up against the time we will need them.

Once the design has been decided upon and worked out in pattern paper and heavy cardboard to make certain that it will follow the lines we want emphasized, we draw it in ink on the copper and cut it out with a tinsnips (Fig. 5.38). The edges are smoothed with Carborundum® paper. The blank is then placed on the bending brake, and the proper angles are set. The bend is made in one motion; four motions or so later we have our top. When the two free ends are soldered together firmly from the inside, the piece is ready. There can be some slight difficulty in the soldering. You cannot comfortably hold this top in your hands and apply a lot of heat to it because copper conducts heat well. To avoid slippage of the ends—which must be absolutely even—and burnt fingers, we manipulate the top in a vice. This can take a lot of doing, but it is either that or make a jig for the metal which would have to be changed for each different shape. Another way this might be done is to clamp one end of the cap with a screw C clamp, solder the remainder of the seam, and then remove the clamp and finish the job. As long as the soldering can be done without the joint moving, it does not matter which method you use.

CHOICE OF BULBS

Since we prefer not to make lanterns from opalescent glass, and because of the long, narrow shape of most lanterns, we use many decorative style bulbs. There are numerous types of these on the market which will show quite nicely through the lead interstices. We also use long bulbs similar to those in aquarium fish tanks. We use both incandescent and fluorescent. The long bulbs will light even the longest lantern well. Never allow the end of such a bulb to protrude through the end of the lantern; ideally the bulb should stop a good two inches away from the bottom opening of the lamp. Long bulbs have another advantage in that they are easier to get in and out of those lanterns that have long bodies and short bottom openings.

SCONCES

The sconce is a wall lamp, and almost any lantern can be made into a sconce by removing one panel and placing it flush against the wall or by moving the socket from above to below and supporting the lantern from a wall brace (Fig. 5.39).

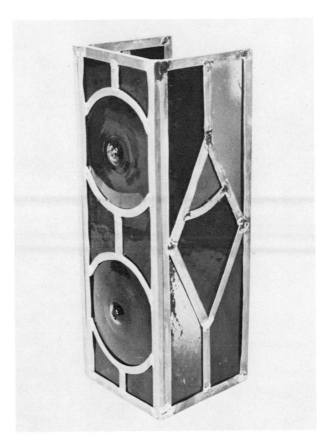

Fig. 5.39 A lantern sconce. The back will be a metal plate fastened to the wall.

This is not to say that sconces are not designed as such; not all sconces come to life as modified stained glass lanterns. A great deal of their designing, nonetheless, follows that of lanterns with the exception of the way they are lighted and placed. We prefer to use opalescent glass in our own sconces, but we have made small-pieced ones with transparent glass. Attaching sconces to the wall can prove a bother, and while we are quite willing to design them, we generally leave their wiring and installation to an electrician. You might well do the same. (See Figs. 5.40 and 5.41.)

CANDLEHOLDERS

The flickering of a flame behind an artistically woven barrier of stained glass is a charming sight easy to produce. Such panels can be cut in miniature candle form, arranged in a circle, leaded and soldered together with very little effort. When we make them, we produce a dozen or so at a time using copper foil or "back-to-back" 1/16 U lead. This particular lead can be wrapped around the individual pieces of glass and its ends soldered closed. Then one piece of glass is soldered to another at point areas to make the circle. A piece of our friendly sheet metal beneath, cut to fit and soldered to the bottom of the glass pieces, provides a base. The candle need only be set on top of it and lighted (the flame will not crack the glass).

If you want to improvise on this arrangement, try bending your glass pieces on a mold in a kiln (see Chapter 11). This graceful flare will enhance your candle-

Fig. 5.40   Sconce patterns.

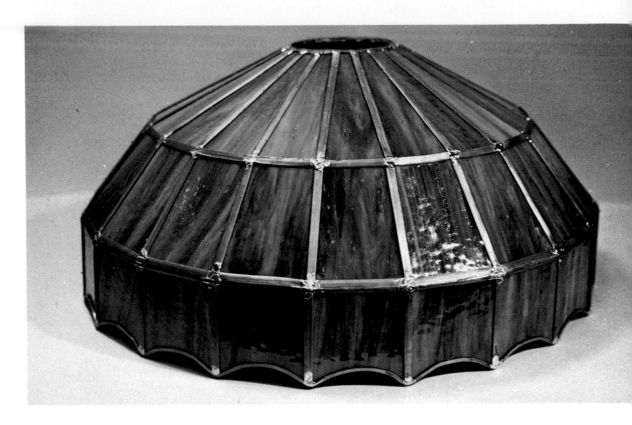

Basic tiered pyramidal shade, no crown.

Tiered, crowned pyramidal shade with offset design.

Tiered pyramidal shade with ornate skirt.

Tubular lamp. *(Courtesy of Clemence Stanley)*

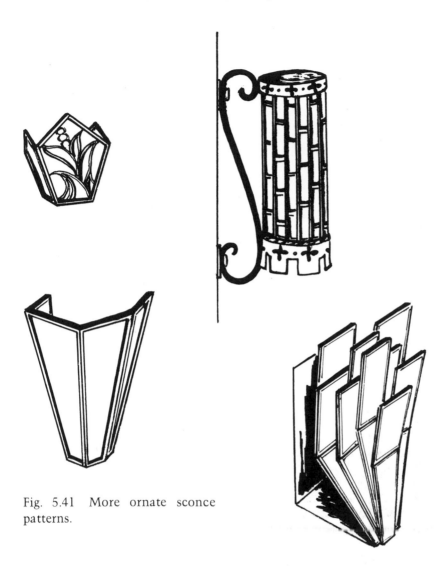

Fig. 5.41 More ornate sconce patterns.

holder, provided that you remember your pieces of glass must be longer to make up for the bend. It is best to use copper foil on such bent pieces of glass; lead came here is too bulky. The foil must wrap around the entire piece of glass and must be tinned even if the bent pieces you design touch briefly only in one area.

We have made very simplified but effective candleholders out of glass "globs." These preformed, rounded chunks of glass (not "chunk" glass) can be laid on a table on their flat bottom surface and leaded together with just enough room in the center to provide for a candle. They become colorful candle supporters. The candle is held by pressure in the middle of the ring. These holders don't look like much until a candle is actually provided; the candle itself adds to the design and grace of the total form. (See Figs. 5.42 through 5.49.)

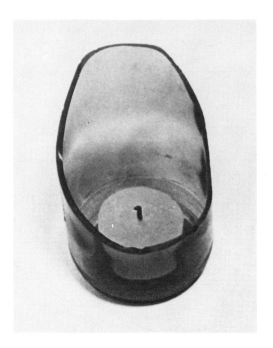

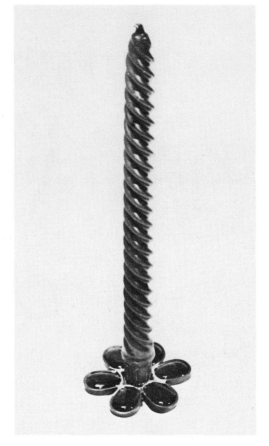

Fig. 5.42 Candleholder cut from a bottle. A score line was run around a bottle (beer bottles work best, champagne bottles least well), and the bottle was placed first in hot, then in cold, water. This method generally works well for shapes which cannot be cut by commercial bottle cutters that stick to straight circular lines.

Fig. 5.43 A candleholder made of glass globs. If you'd rather light a candle, here's one you might try.

Fig. 5.44 Chandelier containing stained glass panels and candleholders. We present them curved, but they can be produced like miniature lanterns. You could also cut sections of bottles for this design.

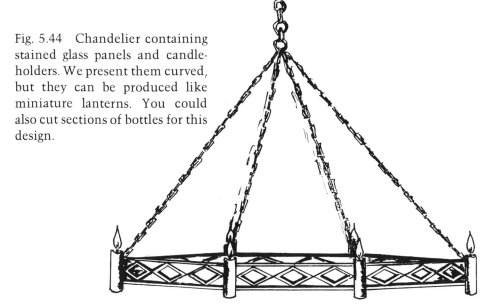

82

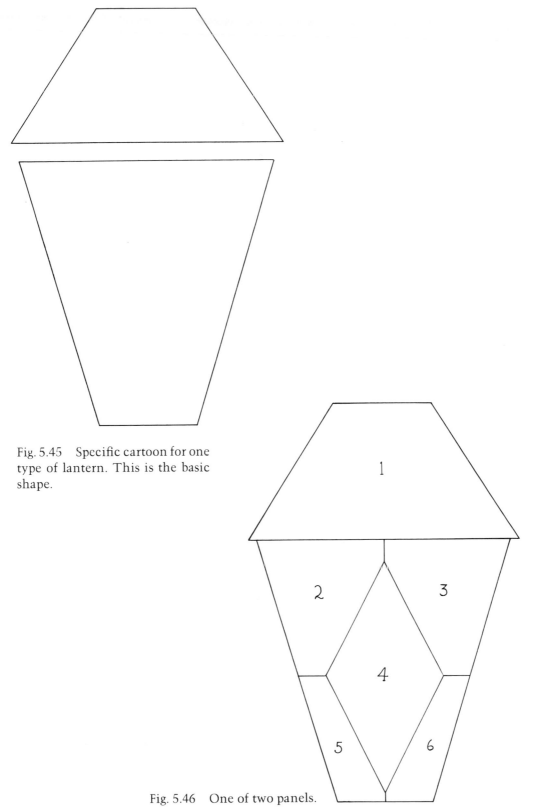

Fig. 5.45   Specific cartoon for one type of lantern. This is the basic shape.

Fig. 5.46   One of two panels.

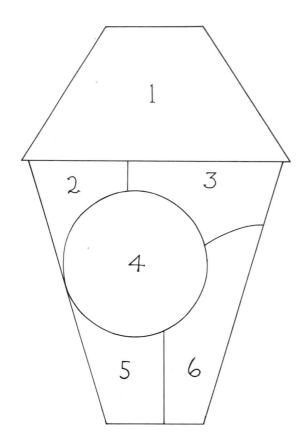

Fig. 5.47   One of the other two panels.

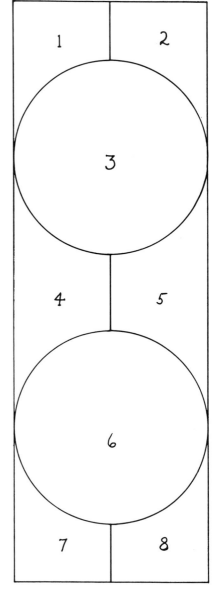

Fig. 5.48   A cartoon for a specific lantern. One of two panels.

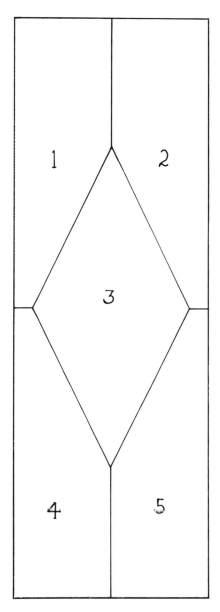

Fig. 5.49   The same lantern. One
of the other two panels.

Chapter 6

The Straight Panel Lamp

PYRAMID STYLE WITH ADDED SKIRT

This is the one most beginning students start with (Fig. 6.1). It provides a beautiful effect and can be made with quite basic instruction. But it can also be done quite badly if the instructions are not followed point by point, and inasmuch as such instructions are also employed, though modified to suit the case, in other lamps, we shall establish such a guide in its most basic form.

1. Decide on the dimension of your lamp (see Chapter 2).

2. Decide on the number of panels it will take to fill this dimension. As an example, let us say you want a diameter of twenty-four inches. Calculate the circumference of your lamp by the formula pi times the diameter, in this case, approximately seventy-five inches. A ten-panel lamp, therefore, will have individual panels measuring at the bottom 7.5 inches. For a fourteen-panel lamp, the measurement would be considerably less per panel, for a sixteen-panel lamp still less. Use graph paper to see what the panels will look like in the varying widths; it is hard to keep in your mind. Once you have decided, add the widths of two more panels to your circumference and draw your circumference as a circle on

Fig. 6.1 Standard "Carrousel" pyramidal type lamp with scalloped skirt.

a piece of graph paper. Extra panels should not appear, only the actual ones that you intend to produce should be drawn in. When you have drawn your circle and measured off the bottom dimensions of the panels on it, you should have an area of circle left over corresponding to the area of two extra panels. This space is very important; without it you will have a leaded dinner plate, not a lamp. The space so left over is proportional to the height of your lamp since the greater the arc that is removed, the closer the height approaches the length of each panel. This can be larger or smaller depending on how large or small you make your center hole. As we have said previously, don't worry about the dimensions of this center hole having to correspond to the sizes of commercial vase caps. These items come in practically every size varying about one-eighth of an inch, and there will surely be one to fit your lamp.

3. With this much done, trace your design onto pattern paper using a good carbon paper. Use a ruler and compass to make your lines; never do this free-hand. Then cut the pattern using a regular scissors. Pattern scissors are not necessary here because of the angle the glass will take within the lead.

4. When your panels are all cut, lay them out on the worktable. They will, of course, fall into the same circle as before. Since you have cut away the space for the two extra panels, you will now have an uncompleted circle of paper panels each measuring the same as the next. Scotch tape them together only on the side facing you. We suggest you do this top, bottom and middle.

5. Now, with your hand in the center hole area, raise the panels from the table until the leading edge of the free panel to one side of the empty space meets the leading edge of its neighbor across from it. Scotch tape them together here.

6. Measure your diameter. It should agree pretty accurately with what you had planned as a figure. If it does not, you must fill in or widen the empty area by extending or subtracting from the bottom measurements of your individual panels. It is a lot easier to do this in paper than in glass. Producing the lamp in this way as a mock-up will also give you an idea of the height of the panels. Remember that, for purposes of construction, the height of the panels has nothing to do with the height of the lamp which is only a point in space where the final pyramid comes together. You can truncate this pyramid to make the panels as long or as short as you want. In designing, however, we must think first of theoretical height.

7. Once you have decided upon the panels for your mock-up, your dimensions are set except for how low you want the skirt to fall. The skirt, unless you somehow flare it away from the midline, will not change any of your dimensions. The only dimension you are bound to, in the skirt, is the bottom edge of each panel. The skirt edges, no matter what kind of interior design you use, must match them. Cut your skirt shape out of pattern paper and attach it to your panel mock-up all around the lamp so you can see what it will look like. If you are going to break up your skirt pieces with some internal design, you might want to draw this on the pattern pieces (on one or two of them, anyway), but it is not necessary to cut them out. In fact, you will have problems if you do.

8. With the shape and dimensions of your lamp decided upon, retrace new patterns from pattern paper. Do not take your mock-up apart to use the pieces as

patterns. You will want to consult your prototype as you go along, and if you try to get the pieces apart, most of them will tear from the Scotch tape anyway.

9. Using the master pattern to make working patterns (remember you only need two—one for the panel and one for the skirt), cut your glass to fit. The pattern always goes on top of the glass.

10. Put your glass pieces together just as you did your prototype. Lead as you go in the following manner:

a. With your first panel cut to size, tap two leading nails into the worktable or workboard and brace an edge of your panel against them. Brace it first with another nail on top and two more on the bottom.

b. Cut a piece of ¼ inch H lead (we prefer it rounded rather than flat for design's sake) and fit it to the leading edge of the glass panel making sure you leave room on top and bottom for the parallel rim leads to run by. In other words, the rib leads that you will now be placing should be smaller than the panels by about ¼ inch. Do not force these rib leads into place. The usual hang-up is at either cut end where a point of the channel, pushed inward by the knife, may form an obstruction which will not allow the glass to be seated properly. Make it a habit, after cutting such leads, to take the blade of your lead knife and smooth open the channels at either end. If you don't do this and attempt to force the glass into the channels by forcefully tapping it with the weighted end of your lead knife or with a hammer (which is even worse), you will either crimp the lead beyond repair or break the glass. The trouble with crimping the lead in this manner is that usually it is the bottom channel that is so treated—a fact that is not discovered until the entire shade is put together. Even though this does not usually show from the outside, it is sloppy and shows extremely well from the inside. It also tends to weaken the support of the particular panel it is supposed to maintain, and if the crimping is bad enough, it will throw off the placement of all succeeding leads. (See Fig. 6.2.)

c. With all your panels placed in exactly the same manner as the first two and with leading nails supporting them as you go, you should end up with an

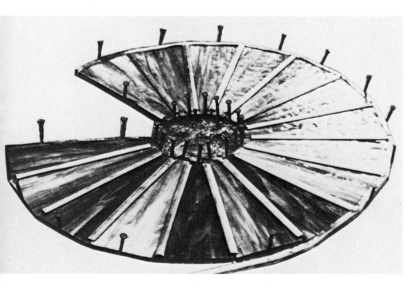

Fig. 6.2 The panels laid out in the flat. The outer rim of lead is being applied.

Fig. 6.3 The same technique for a tiered shade. Here one tier is being formed. Leading nails are used to hold small scrap pieces of lead against the caming so the nails themselves do not indent the channels and yet apply enough pressure to hold the required shape.

incomplete circle of panels interspersed with lead ribbing which has left a brief space top and bottom of the panels.

d. Take a long piece of 3/16 inch U lead and, starting at the bottom of your first panel, remove the leading nails and fit the bottom of the panels within the single channel of came (Fig. 6.3). The nails should then be replaced as each individual panel is so treated. You will have to angle the lead as you go from panel to panel; be careful not to allow slack here. One reason the leading nails are replaced is to snug the lead tightly against the glass. Use your fingers to mold the came to the corner angles of the panels. This long strand may get in your way, but don't let it dangle off the table or its weight will pull against you. Try to keep the portion that you are not using coiled on the table in the general curve you are trying to accomplish. At the last panel, cut the lead even with the glass.

e. The top curve is leaded following the same procedure in a manner mirroring what you have just done to lead the bottom. The fit will be tighter. (Fig. 6.4.) Once again, be careful not to crimp that bottom channel of came when

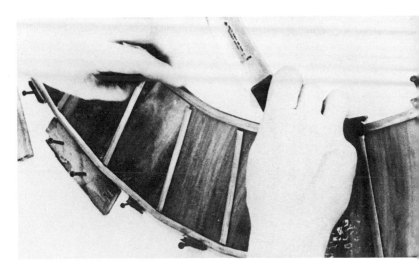

Fig. 6.4 A tier of glass pieces almost complete. The top lead rim is being applied.

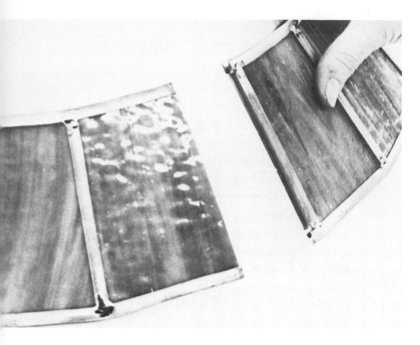

Fig. 6.5 The ring of leaded, soldered pieces, previously laid flat on the table, is being closed. The unleaded side must fit into the open channel of the leaded side. Note the overlap of lead on the right. The glass, on the left, has its lead cut short top and bottom to compensate for this.

working in these tight quarters. Using the tip of your leading knife, raise the edges of the panels slightly from the table to allow the lead channel to go easily beneath them. Cut the came even with the glass edges.

f. Solder all joints facing upwards. Flux and wire brush all joints prior to soldering. These joints should not be merely tacked; they should be strong, smooth and evenly covered with solder. It does not take an excessive but an even amount of solder well placed to cover a joint space well. Do not solder any joints that are not facing you.

11. Remove all leading nails and place one hand in the center of the top circle. Gently raise the panels from the table with one hand while bringing the ends around with the other. As you lift upwards, you must make sure that each panel's bottom edge comes in contact with the table. Then gently, a little at a time, close the circle. (Fig. 6.5.) You should have the edge of one free panel leaded and the edge of the opposing one free. The object of the game is to fit the free edge of the one panel into the empty channel of the other (Fig. 6.6). This will automatically close the circle accurately. As far as the top and bottom leads are concerned, flap up one to make sure the glass is meeting accurately, then flap it down so that it meets the other lead and solder this seam. An alternate method here is to cut one lead short and leave the other long so it laps over at this point. It still must be soldered. Once the top lead is soldered, turn the lamp over and solder the bottom leads. Then place the lamp right side up on the table to make sure that it maintains its proper shape.

12. There are a number of ways to place skirts on lamps. Skirts can be made all of a piece and then put on as a unit, or they can be added piece by piece (see next section, The Tiered Pyramidal Shade; see also Figs. 10.3–10.6). We will discuss the unit method first. Lay out the pieces of your skirt. Take a length of 3/16 inch U came, stretch it, open it with a lathkin and lay it flat against a long piece

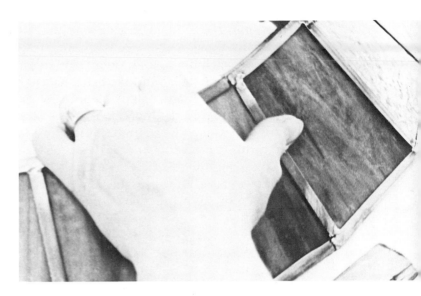

Fig. 6.6 A perfect joint; even the overlap of lead fits in neatly.

of wood which is firmly attached to the worktable with C clamps. Place the back part of the came (the flattened surface of the 3/16 U) against the wood so that the channel faces away from you. The top of the skirt is thus nearer you. Fit the flat part of the skirt within the channel and cut ribs from ¼ inch H came to fit between the glass pieces. As in the case of the panels, do not make these the size of the pieces but rather somewhat smaller to allow for the leads that are going to be running top to bottom. Since you already have a lead running along the edge nearest you, the top of the skirt, you have only to allow for the top lead, which (since you are doing this upside down for the sake of convenience) will be the bottom, scalloped portion of the lamp skirt. Place this lead in the same method as the straight, back lead you did first, and use leading nails as previously when placing the panels. Make sure that it dips into the scalloped portion between the glass pieces enough to catch the lead ribs there. If you leave too much of a gap here, you will have trouble filling it with solder and trouble bending the skirt to shape since solder does not bend as well as came. In fact, it does not really bend at all, and more pieces of glass are broken in trying to bend them against inflexibly soldered areas than for any other reason.

With your skirt all lined up—and unlike the panels, it forms not a circle but a straight line—solder all the joints facing you. Once this is done, remove all the leading nails. Tip the line of skirt pieces up onto the scalloped surfaces and, putting force against the unsoldered side, bend them gently, a little at a time, into a circle. Once again, the edge of one piece of glass will be leaded with an empty channel of H lead protruding and the leading edge of its opposite number will not have any lead rib. Once again, this unleaded edge must be made to fit into the empty channel approaching it. Solder top and bottom, and your circle of skirt pieces is completed.

With any sort of luck this circle will exactly match the paneled circle, but putting both these circles together is sometimes a hair-raising experience. You know you have cut the glass accurately, taken accurate measurements and leaded perfectly. Still, until the last minute, the two circles may not seem to be going together, and then, at the last minute you *know* they are not going to match. What went wrong? Well, there is a basic factor, the placement of the individual panels upon the individual skirt pieces, that we have not yet discussed. Because of this we only tack panel and skirt together at this point and do not solder them solidly. You cannot tell, just by placing the ring of panel pieces upon the ring of skirt pieces whether the individual panels should move a little inward or a little outward to best match the underlying skirt piece. There is just enough play here to make this a problem. In order to keep this unknown factor within bounds, these lamps should be tacked on opposite, not conjoining, sides. Tack one panel, then go to the one across from it and position and tack it. Hopefully you will be able to even up the correct positioning between them. Tack at the corners of the panels so that, if you have to, you can break the join with a quick melt that won't allow solder to run all over the place. Even after this criss-crossing maneuver, you may find the panels to be slightly off as you test the panels not yet soldered. If this happens, do not attempt to make up this discrepancy in succeeding panels. Untack the panels so far concluded and reposition them.

Your first lampshade may or may not give you a lot of trouble in this regard. You may have no trouble with the first and run into the problem on your fifth or sixth. If so, by that time you will have had enough experience with such shades not to panic. If it happens on your first shade you may well find the problem a scary one. Just remember that if you have cut and measured accurately, you can get panels and skirt to fit—they have to fit. Keep maneuvering them until they do.

13. Once you have your shade together, tip it on its side and only then solder all inner joints. Wipe off the excess solder and flux residues, clean your lamp, and it is ready to be hung.

THE TIERED PYRAMIDAL SHADE

This is a "bent" panel lamp (Fig. 6.7) consisting of a two-pieced, angled body, a scalloped skirt and perhaps a flared crown. If so desired, the body can be made three- or four-pieced, with the pieces becoming consequently smaller (Fig. 6.8). The technique follows that of the pyramid lamp with added skirt up to the point of making the initial ring of panels. In this instance, we use an H lead, either ¼

Fig. 6.7 A tiered pyramidal shade completed. We have just seen the closure of one of the rings (Fig. 6.6). Such rings are then fitted one into the other in one method of production.

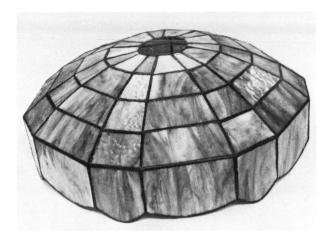

Fig. 6.8 A more complex tiered pyramidal shade made with copper foil.

Fig. 6.9 Pieces cut for a tiered pyramidal shade arranged to demonstrate their interrelationships and the "one to two" relationship of crown to neck pieces.

or 3/8 inch, on the top and bottom of the initial ring, rather than the 3/16 inch U leads we employed in the straight pyramidal lamp. Once the ring is formed, we use it as a base from which to make the other tiers. Only the crown, if there is to be one, is formed separately and then soldered to the top. (Fig. 6.9.)

With the first ring of the body formed, bent to shape and soldered closed, the pieces of the next ring, or tier, are placed within the empty channel of the H lead. Their corresponding ribs of lead are placed alongside them and tacked into position on the side facing the worker (Fig. 6.10). A slight slant forward may be given the first glass piece so placed to continue the basic bend the worker has in mind. These pieces, cut to a prior pattern following this bend, will conform naturally to it as they are placed in the lead. As more and more of the pieces are put into the lead, in order for their edges to meet, a uniform bend forward will become apparent. The lead ribs must also bend forward a little. Naturally, the moment of truth will arrive when you go to place the last piece. (Figs. 6.11 and 6.12.) However, you can easily tell as you go along if this last piece is going to fit

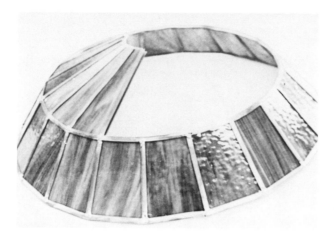

Fig. 6.10 Another way of making the tiered shade. The panels are fitted individually and support each other. The came is soldered as you go.

Fig. 6.11 The last piece of came being fitted to the shade in Fig. 6.10. There is no room for miscut panels here.

or not by how close your lead ribs are following the line of ribs below. If only one of them is a trifle off, that will knock the next one off line even more and so it will go until you can rest assured that your last piece will not fit. At the first sign of the line going crooked—fix it.

Once you have the two pieces of the body together, turn them over (Fig. 6.13) and add the skirt in the same way (the skirt may be leaded or foiled; see Figs. 10.3–10.6 for procedure with copper foil). Whereas the top body piece may have an H lead rimming it, the skirt bottom must close with a U lead. You may want a 3/16 U or a try with a slimmer ⅛ U lead. You must be careful with this one as it has a decided tendency to come away from the glass if the edges are not smooth.

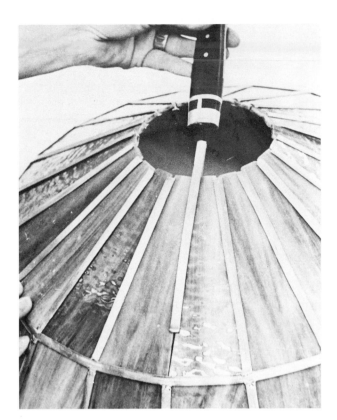

Fig. 6.12 Tapping the final piece of rib lead into place with the weighted back of the lead knife.

Fig. 6.13 Panels and skirt can be made separately and then joined or the pieces can be individually added. Here we see the skirt pieces being placed. Because of the sharp right angle bend here, a smaller lead is sometimes placed within the channel of the bordering lead which itself could not take the bend. This allows the skirt glass to fit straight in. Such a lead is here being added as the skirt pieces are placed. This "additive technique" is also used when two or more separate pieces form the skirt.

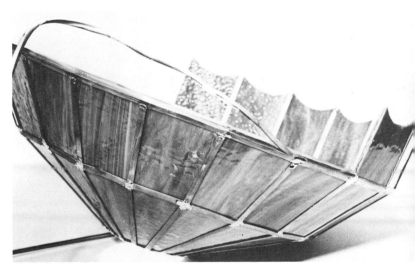

The crown for these style lamps is usually made separately, is usually wider than that for a typical straight panel pyramidal lamp and has more flare than the crown for such a lamp (Fig. 6.14). It is planned out the same as any other paneled ring; the less open space you leave between the first and last panels, the more flare you will get from the midline. Such a crown should also have 3/16 leads rimming it inside and out. It is then soldered on when the top of the lamp is completed. Crowns need not match the panels of the top layer of the lamp on

Fig. 6.14 Flared crown for a tiered pyramidal shade. If it is to be present at all, it must make its presence felt.

a one-to-one basis. Since this type of lamp generally ends up with a very slim neckline, you would have to cut a lot of thin panels to match it to the crown. You can alleviate this additional work—which adds nothing to the effect, unless you specifically want it to emphasize the area—by making the pieces of the crown complement the panel pieces on a one-to-two basis (see Fig. 6.9).

Another way of making this type of lamp is to make all the rings separately, rim each with a thin (3/16) H lead and force the flanges into one another to make it appear that only one lead was used. You can also use a thin H lead in the bottom of one ring and a wider one in the top of the ring below, a ⅜, for example, in which the thin lead can more easily be hidden. You can also make the rings rimmed with a 3/16 inch U lead all around and leave an open seam. To close this, either in this lamp or in the one previously described, you can use the twisted lead method (as described in the lantern section) and solder over the seam so that a smooth joint results or use a "belt" to cover it. Such a belt is made from 3/16 inch lead that has been flattened and stretched. It will just nicely cover the seam in these lamps and can be tacked to the lead ribs it passes by. Lead in this condition is fragile and easily burned by the iron, and holes will scarcely improve the area of the lamp you are trying to finish.

It is important to keep in mind when using the first method described, that the lead ribs, slanting forward as they do, can best be seated by cutting away a small portion of the bottom surface. This will compensate for the forward slant and provide for a smoother joint from the inside and an easier lie from the outside.

Once this type of lamp is completed, you can add overlays of decoration which will entirely change its character or leave it plain and classically simple. Modifications can be added to any of the tiers which will drastically change the design. In short, here is a good, solid workaday design from which you can proceed in any direction.

Stages in the construction of a tiered pyramidal lamp are as follows. (Figs. 6.15 to 6.23.)

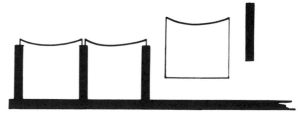

Fig. 6.15 The first tier (skirt) is being formed. (Dark lines are lead ribs and rim.)

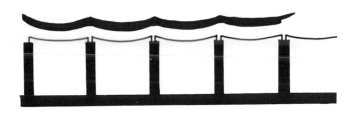

Fig. 6.16 The first tier completed, the bottom lead is being placed.

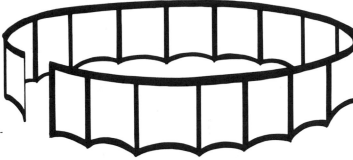

Fig. 6.17 The circle being completed; the tier closes.

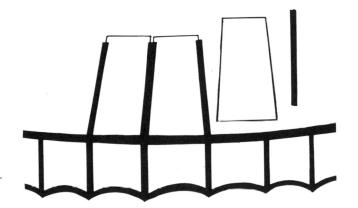

Fig. 6.18 The second tier (panels) being added.

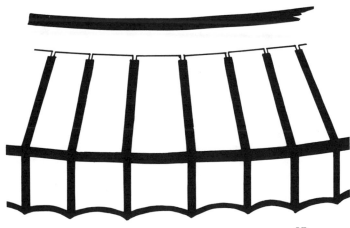

Fig. 6.19 The second tier completed, top H came lead is being added to the free glass edge.

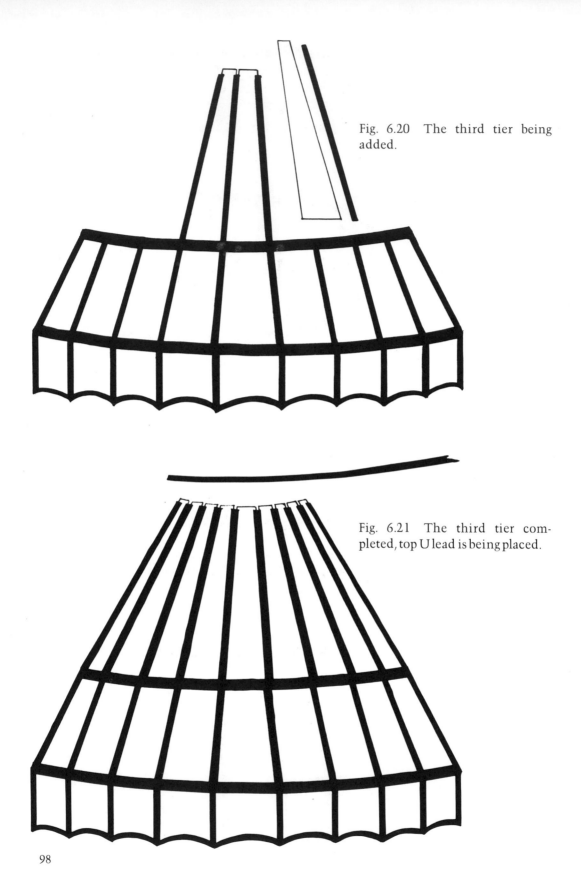

Fig. 6.20 The third tier being added.

Fig. 6.21 The third tier completed, top U lead is being placed.

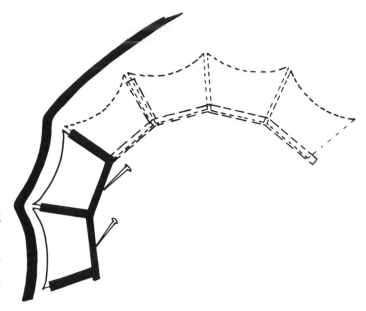

Fig. 6.22 The crown being formed. The first two pieces are placed; the dotted lines show the extrapolation of the circle. U came is used in both borders; H came is used for the ribs.

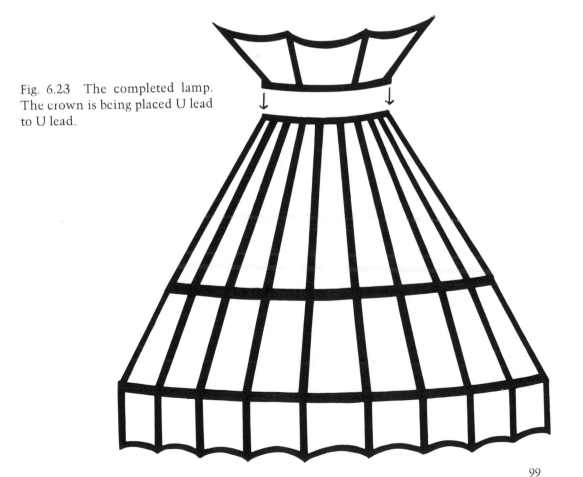

Fig. 6.23 The completed lamp. The crown is being placed U lead to U lead.

THE MULTI-PIECED PYRAMID

This is usually a straight pyramidal shade with its panels and possibly its skirt as well broken up into an internal design that can be as simple as a two- or three-piece break or so involved that it all but obscures the basic style of the shade. Nonetheless, each panel, no matter what its internal complexities, is treated as a unit, and these units are built into a shade along the same principles as those discussed for the straight pyramidal shade. (Figs. 6.24 through 6.26.) All internal lead lines must be securely soldered front and back before such panels can be manipulated into shade form. It is disconcerting when pieces of the design start dropping out of the panels during the excitement of putting the lamp together.

Fig. 6.24   A simple but effective multi-pieced pyramid lamp.

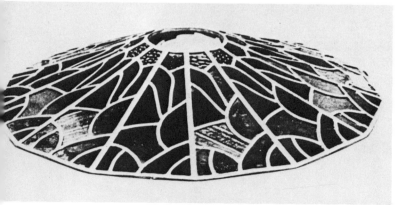

Fig. 6.25   A more complex multi-pieced pyramid shade. A skirt added to this should be simple so as not to clash with the upper panels.

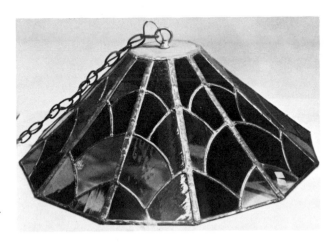

Fig. 6.26 Another style of multi-pieced pyramid shade.

The following are some cartoons for multi-pieced panels. (Figs. 6.27 to 6.29.)

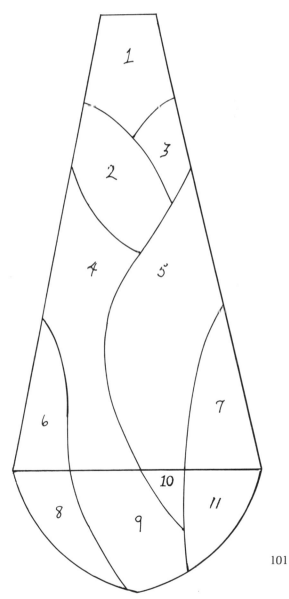

Fig. 6.27 A multi-pieced pyramidal panel.

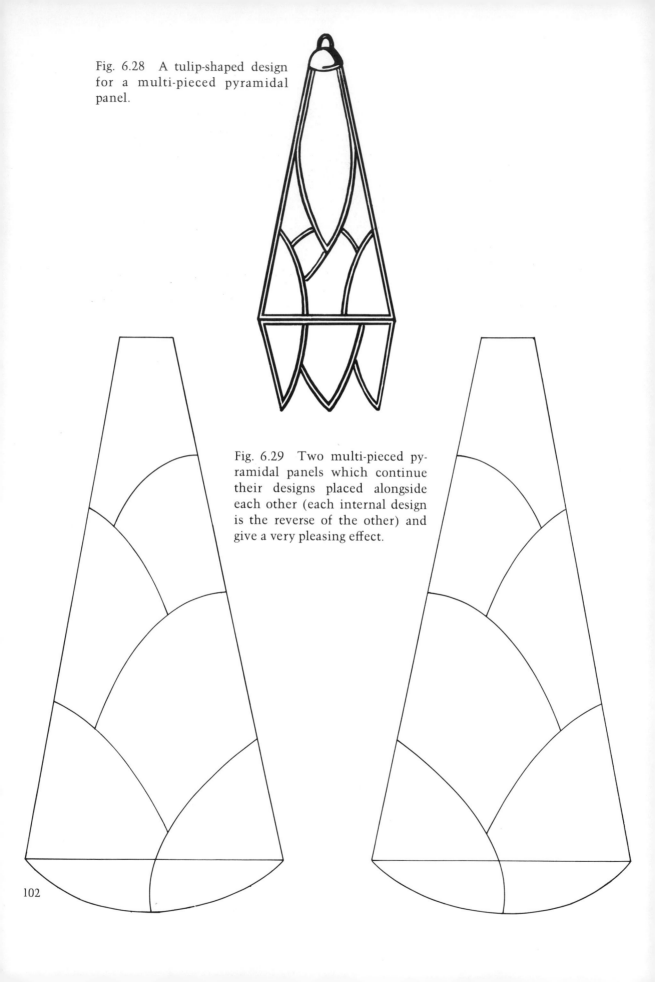

Fig. 6.28   A tulip-shaped design for a multi-pieced pyramidal panel.

Fig. 6.29   Two multi-pieced pyramidal panels which continue their designs placed alongside each other (each internal design is the reverse of the other) and give a very pleasing effect.

Tiered Pyramid Style with Ornate Skirt

The shape is that of a tiered pyramid, but the skirt is usually twice the width or more of the usual pyramid style and is broken into a patterned repetitive design that is almost "Tiffany-like" in nature. The amount of repetition within each panel usually depends upon how mosaic or how large the individual pieces are. Repetition comes more frequently in the smaller makeup and less, if at all, in skirt panels containing eight or nine pieces. Each skirt panel is treated as a unit and is made separately from the rest of the lamp even though the pattern may continue from one panel to the next (see Fig. 3.17). Old jewels, marbles, glass eyes, all can form part of the skirt pattern, and each pattern can form part of a unique shade. Effective also, in this style, is an uneven border skirt with fruit or some part of the design spilling down right out of the panel (see Fig. 6.30 and color section).

Fig. 6.30 Ornate skirts for a tiered pyramid shade. Panels shown are A, B and C, where C is then broken up into the designs presented. Crown E may or may not be added. If an ornate skirt is not desired, F may be used. Its concave surface provides a decorative effect. Panel E may be substituted for Panel B to give a different shape to the lamp.

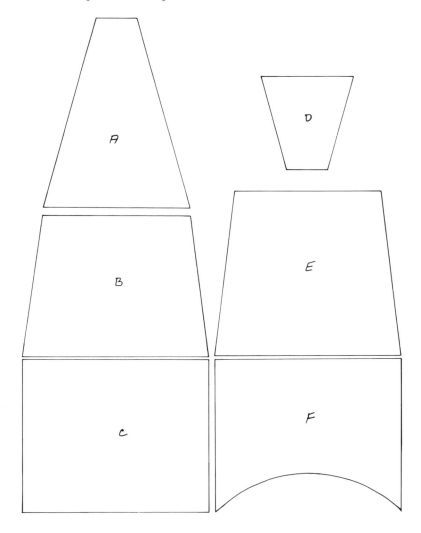

103

This was at one time a far more popular shade than it is at present; nevertheless, it would be a shame to leave it out of the collection. The style is almost that of a bowl light with straight sides. It can be modified from the single straight pyramid panel lamp to the "star lamp" which was so well known in the 1920s and 1930s. The star lamp was composed of small pyramids of glass going off in all directions and almost creating a sunburst effect from a central core. The true inverted pyramidal lamp has no skirt; it is just a cone of glass pressed flat against the ceiling with the bulb within. From this basic idea we have produced basket-type lamps hanging from three chains in a basic pyramidal shape and true dome lights with both molded and bent glass panels. The pyramidal shape can be modified to almost any occasion. (See Figs. 6.31 through 6.33.)

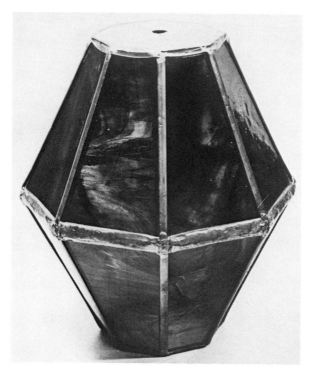

Fig. 6.31 Twinned inverted pyramid shade.

Fig. 6.32 Old style dome, inverted bowl type shade.

Fig. 6.33 Left: Standard pyramidal lamp pattern—panel and skirt. Right: A pyramidal tiered shade with a crown piece covering two vertical tiers. This can be made in either ten, twelve or fourteen panels (all cartoons should be first made in paper to judge their size).

Chapter 7
Tubular Shades

CALCULATING THE DESIGN

A popular design for tubular shades uses long, thin strips of glass, cut in varying lengths, running up and down the lamp (Fig. 7.1). Unfortunately, the sameness of all these thin strips scampering up and down the shade tires the eye rather quickly and the lamp becomes boring. The irregularity of the lead lines gives an improvisational effect to the piece. The thin piece strategy readily accom-

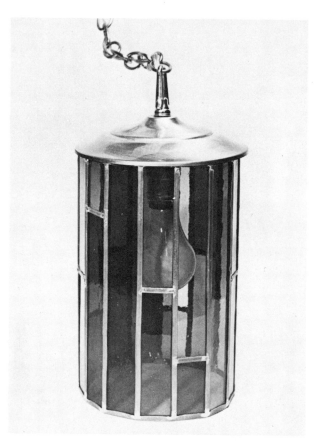

Fig. 7.1 A typical tubular lamp.

modates itself to this specific shape with very little work; the lamp is literally rolled up in thin pieces. Ease of construction does not necessarily mean that so interesting a shape as a tube should be limited by unambitious craftsmanship. While the strips of glass may well continue as background, the intrusion of a little foreground character would make the shade so much more interesting. We suggest that certain of the strips be cut in a design form so that lines undulate over the surface of the lamp instead of staggering quite so emphatically and mechanically. From there you can become involved in complexities that will serve to make what is basically a beginner's lamp into a force of its own. (Fig. 7.2.)

ROLLING THE TUBULAR SHADE

The design is, as usual, run out on kraft paper and then transferred to pattern paper. If you are just beginning to work in this shape, you had best stay with the routine approach to these lamps and cut glass strips with no impressed design. Strips are selected as to color and placed within the lamp so that no strips of the same color will coincide. Cutting these strips is not so easy a job as it may at first seem. Long, thin pieces are difficult to come by in glass. They tend to break

Fig. 7.2 Several designs for tubular shades.

short; either the break line curves away from the score line into the wanted piece or the line is chewed out from overgrozzing. The idea behind this lamp is to keep the vertical lead lines absolutely straight; they should not swerve to cover miscut edges of glass. The best method of cutting long thin glass strips is to use a running pliers.

The running pliers has no use other than to cut long, thin strips of glass. It is composed of a convex lower jaw and a concave upper one, the two fitting snugly together when the instrument is closed. A screw gauge is usually provided which allows a calculated pressure upon the glass to either side of the score line. Once the glass is scored, the edge of the piece is moved slightly off the table, and the running pliers grasps it. A scored line in the pliers' upper jaw matches up with the score line in the glass. The screw gauge is then turned so that the jaws of the pliers just lightly grasp the glass. A light pressure on the handles forces the convex lower jaw up against the bottom of the score line while the two pressure points of the upper jaw are forced down to either side of it. The score is thereby forced to "run," to extend a deep fissure along the length of the former scratch of the surface. This is possible because of the liquid nature of glass itself. Being a mechanical device, the running pliers manages to exert an exact pressure along the score line far more precise than your hands and miles above what you can expect from the hit or miss force exerted in tapping the glass. It is difficult to run any long score line by tapping the glass. The tapped piece cannot maintain that lengthy a punishment and will usually respond by breaking. If you attempt a tubular lampshade without a pair of running pliers in your armamentarium you will have a lot of scrap glass left over for candleholders.

Once you have enough pieces cut, spread them out over your cartoon and lead them up using H leads in the center portions and U leads on the outside. Solder all joints facing you. Then lift the piece from the table and curve it inward toward the unsoldered side. As it begins to curve together check that you don't have individual pieces of glass sneaking out of their lead framework. If you do, and you don't locate them here and now, you will have a very difficult time getting them back into position once the curve is completed. With the curve completed, and once again the two glass edges meet with one going into the lead caming on the other, solder the joints together and your lamp is completed.

MOLDING THE TUBULAR SHADE

Molding a tubular shade provides a lot more creative opportunities than rolling it. Find a mold that suits you—anything from a rolling pin to a Styrofoam® float—and stand it on end. Looking down on it from the top, get an exact dimension by taking a paper template. Transfer this to a piece of pattern paper. Now you know the circumference. Divide that into quadrants and decide on a repetitive design using pieces of glass which are not so large that they take the bend of your mold. The smaller the diameter of the mold, the smaller the glass pieces will have to be to follow it. On large molds you might be able to get away with small rondels; on small molds designing in miniature is called for. In either case, a good bit of ingenuity is necessary. The lead lines can be brought forth to emphasize and promulgate the pattern. Work directly on the mold, and if it is Styrofoam, use push pins to hold the glass pieces until you can tack their edges with solder. If your mold is wood or metal use clay or gum (chewing gum does nicely) or hot wax or even Scotch tape to hold the pieces temporarily in position. We like to use lead caming on these lamps rather than foil as we prefer the sturdy look and emphatic linear quality this material gives them. However, there is certainly no reason why you cannot work in foil using the same principles.

A vase cap will do nicely as a top for either molded or rolled tubular lamps. If you are fortunate enough to discover some old, high round lamp tops in an antique store, put them away until you have a chance to use one of them on a tubular lamp; chances are you will want to use them all that way.

Closed Tubular Shades

It is possible, and interesting, to design tubular shades which can be closed at either end, on top by the hanging plate, on the bottom by a decorative plate (Figs. 7.3 through 7.6). Remember you still have to have a way in to change the bulb, so don't get carried away. Obviously you can't solder the bottom closed. What you can do is prepare the bottom for a plate by building up a circle of lead with a closed

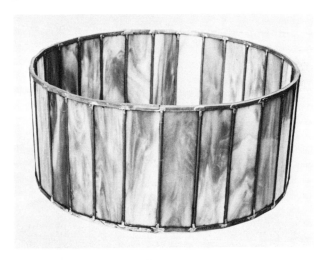

Fig. 7.3   A unique tubular shade starts as an ordinary design.

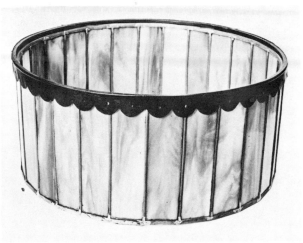

Fig. 7.4   To it is added a top border found in an antique store.

Fig. 7.5 The inside electrical material and bottom border are shown separately.

Fig. 7.6 The whole lamp combines all of the above in a striking arrangement.

ring of brass filigree soldered to it. You will then have a strong, fairly wide decorative surface. Drill holes into this surface and drill and tap a wide collar vase cap in the same places so you can then screw the vase cap into the bottom of the lamp. This gives an interesting finishing touch, and the cap is removable.

When drilling these holes, never lay your lamp on the table; without realizing it, you can build up pressure as you drill which is transmitted to the lamp. The glass is already in jeopardy from the vibration of the drill, and sooner or later it will break from the combination of pressure and vibration. When the time comes to drill holes, hang your lamp at a convenient height and, supporting the bottom of the lamp with fingertip pressure from within, drill the holes. It is almost impossible to break any glass this way. Drilling your finger is another matter.

Chapter 8

Square and Rectangular Shades

GETTING THE SIDES EVEN

Getting the sides even in the basic shapes involves the same difficulties as getting the sides even in lanterns (see Chapter 5). But square and rectangular shades have more surface area than lanterns, and the unevenness of the sides is magnified the longer the sides are. We cannot stress enough the fact that some workers—beginners especially—have the idea that right angles are easy to do and can be accomplished by eye alone. We have seen in the discussion of the pyramidal lamp (Chapter 6) how much play is possible in fitting the panel to the skirt; the same amount of play is possible fitting panel to panel in square and rectangular shades.

Such panels should all be joined in the same way, that is, if panel A is joined to panel B on the inside surface of the lead rim, then panel C should also be joined on the inside surface. Otherwise the panels will be uneven. We suggest you draw a template on graph paper and stand the sides of the lamp on top of it when you solder them. Do one-half at a time, tack it singly and then do the same with the other half (you can do this much by eye). The final joining of the two halves, however, should be done guided by your template. (Figs. 8.1 through 8.3.)

Be sure to use a heavy enough lead along the edges of rectangular shades so that you will not find the came coming away from the glass. This can be a long span for came to travel, especially if it is unaided by breaks in the panel. Indeed, such breaks may have to be designed to keep the top border of lead in place. We have sometimes had problems here when doing specific commissions for clients who did not want the panel broken with an interior design. A compromise was reached (it being impossible to design the lamp otherwise) when they allowed us to use an external overlay strapping of came in "belt" form to hold the lamp together. Adhesive-backed copper foil can also be the answer here if the weight is not so great that unsupported foil will also come away from the glass edge. Foil, however adherent it may be, is no help if the clients want a leaded shade (see section on Brass Came below).

Another difficulty with the sides may arise in the cutting. It is one thing to cheat a little when cutting out pyramidal panels that lie against each other to

114

form a multi-paneled top; you can nudge the leads a little to cover up flaws in the glass cutting provided they are not too outrageous. A square or rectangular paneled lamp has only four sides, and if they are not all cut absolutely accurately, the discrepancy will stand out like a sore thumb. It is hard to pretend that this is part of the design. Three out of the four edges can come out perfectly, and just as you are congratulating yourself on your technique, a piece chips off the fourth edge not large enough to unequivocally disbar the panel, but

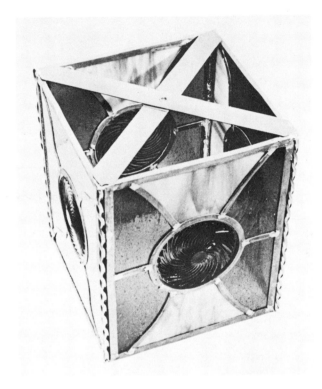

Fig. 8.1 A square lamp showing the supporting top straps, their corner arrangement and the center hole going through both straps.

Fig. 8.2 A right angle about to be formed using the underlying graph lines as a guide.

Fig. 8.3 Two sides being soldered together at right angles.

not small enough to give you a feeling of comfort, either. You are afraid that it will show, but you hope that you might get away with matching the rest of the edge to the fault by giving it a very gentle slope. While this may eventually come to look even to the eye, when you lead it you will find that somehow the other panels do not quite slope the same way. Now is the time when you will begin stealing from Peter to pay Paul. Attempting to move leads around so they cover the mistake or to disguise the deformed panel by adding solder, you will, in all probability, waste more time than you needed to correctly cut all the other panels. In the end, if you have any feeling for your craft, you will end up doing it over anyway. Why not save time and just do it over right away?

You can tell if a chip is going to show by trying a piece of lead on the edge right away. Never be afraid to cut another panel, even if it is only to teach yourself a lesson. You may not want to cut it right away, however. If you try two panels and the glass starts misbehaving one way or another, do not try a third. It will surely break wrong as well and you will feel so defeated that you won't be able to cut anything accurately thereafter. We have seen individuals go through an entire sheet of glass in this fashion. On the contrary, if the glass is not breaking well, leave it and take a walk, read a book or visit your spouse. Come back to it in half an hour or so, and you will be surprised at how much the glass has learned in the interim.

REINFORCING THE SIDES

A triangle is a very sturdy form, a square is more prone to a certain amount of "give." If your square or rectangular lamp gives, it will go askew at the corners and provide a wobbly base for the rest of the shade. In order to prevent this, you might reinforce the corners by beading solder along the inside edges, ironing the seam smooth and taking a length of ⅜ inch copper foil tape with an adhesive back and running it down the length of the seam so that the edges overlap onto the glass to either side. With a sharp knife cut a strip out of the central portion

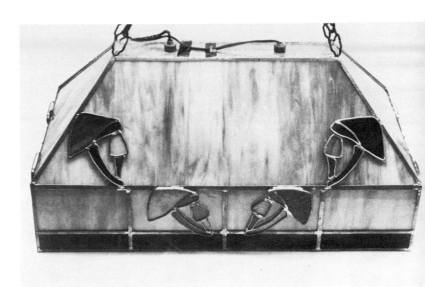

Fig. 8.4   The "mushroom" shade. The offset mushrooms not only add dimension to the sides but also brace the long panels by forming triangles at their ends.

of the tape allowing the underlying solder to show through. Now tin the tape strongly. Solder will flow through the central hole in the tape to the seam below, fixing the tape firmly. The two flared edges of the tape resting against the glass to either side will, when heavily tinned, act as a pyramidal brace in this area and prevent movement in the joint. Do not overuse this device, as too much tape spread against the corner glass will show through from the front as an unsightly bulge when the lamp is lit.

Along the sides proper, reinforcement might also be needed to maintain the integrity of the edge. If the lead came is not sufficiently braced, it will allow the glass edge to fall out from between its channels. Either an inlaid or offset design must be provided specifically to correct this. Even if this pulling away of the glass does not happen immediately when the lamp is hung, eventually the steady pull of gravity will cause the separation. Not only lamps but any object made of leaded glass subject to gravity will have the same problem. Ideally the designer will take this into account upon drawing his very first sketch (Fig. 8.4). What usually happens is that it is overlooked in the excitement of creation, and after the lamp has been hanging for three or four months (if not immediately), the parts start wandering. An inlaid design is possible then only if the entire lamp is redone; an offset design is more practical. Still, it is an annoying piece of knowledge to know that such a latter-day compromise is necessary because the initial design was poor. Essentially what you are doing is placing struts of lead as functional bridgework, a patchwork, journeyman task, on a completed project. It may always look like a tacked on feature.

INLAYS AND OFFSETS

An inlaid design is a design placed within the glass in which H cames are used to break the background glass into a pattern imposed upon it by the will of the designer. An offset design, on the other hand, is placed all of a piece *on* the underlying glass surface so that it stands away from the glass affording an emphasis and three-dimensional effect (Fig. 8.5). An offset design can, if used incorrectly, chop up an otherwise smooth flow of line. The production of both inlaid and offset designs follows certain rules which, while they are by no means inflexible, should not be compromised until the designer is fully conscious of their reasons for existing.

An inlaid design should not be crowded into a small space nor so busy that the eye gets confused by all the lead lines. An offset design can be crowded because the physical difference between background and foreground is so great that little chance for design confusion exists. An inlaid design need not be repetitive over the surface (unless the designer wants to have it so); an offset should be repetitive and balanced. Inlaid designs are produced by the use of H channel leads; offsets can be made of H and U leads or of 1/16 inch back to back lead (which allows them to stand away from the surface even more due to the extended flange of this channel). Offset designs can be added as an afterthought; inlays can't. An offset design must never be placed on a surface already containing a complicated inlay since a clash of the two is unavoidable. Generally speaking, if you intend to use an offset design, you will probably use no inlay at all other than the functional one to hold the lamp together. Even a functional inlay can get in the way of an offset if it involves close-knit lead lines. Both inlays and offsets may employ glass globs, jewels, decorative brass or other materials to enhance their meaning; however, both should not do this at once, even if this is the only inlay you are employing.

Finally, keep in mind the fact that the offset design is really a trick and as such can appear to be an easy way out of a situation that may really call for an inlay. Unless the offset ties in with the basic idea of the lamp, it will *look* like a trick, and if it does, the magic will go right out of your design.

SKIRTING THE EDGES

Large panel shades do not have to come equipped with square or rectangular skirts. Scallops or other cuts can break up the pattern; hanging beads, navettes or mobile skirts can add uniqueness and wit to a plain, geometric design (Figs. 8.6, 8.7 and 8.8). We recently made a "fish" lamp for clients to hang in a den. The

Fig. 8.5 The offset flower pattern makes this basically three-tiered shade interesting and unique. Glass globs were used in forming these offsets. (*Courtesy of Clemence Stanley*)

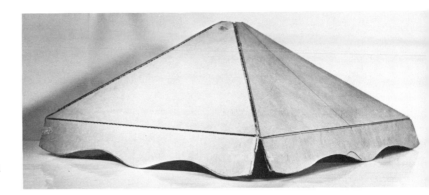

Fig. 8.6 Prototype panels with a small skirt. No design as yet.

Fig. 8.7 The design in the panels is complemented by a simple but tasteful moderate number of breaks in the skirt.

Fig. 8.8 A few hanging items for skirts. From the left: hearts without flowers, small jewels, navettes, large jewels.

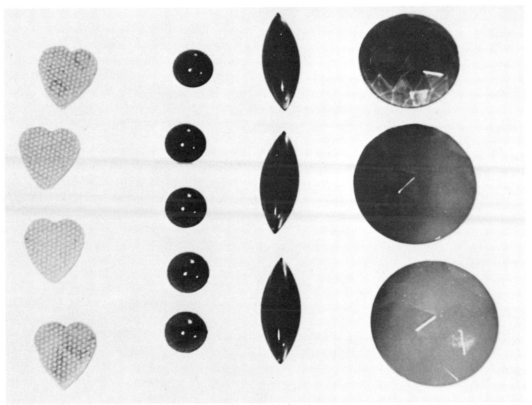

Fig. 8.9   A large panel lamp with no skirt.

Fig. 8.10   A large panel lamp with a rectangular skirt having a central design. Note the effectiveness of the fleur-de-lis with no extraneous lines in the entire remainder of the shade.

breaks in the panels were of a fish motif and for a skirt we hung free-swinging, stylized stained glass fish. All the fish, of course, were of the same design. It would have been a little much to start introducing a different species.

A number of square or rectangular shades have no skirt at all other than a strip of filigree running around the edges to set off a line of demarcation and provide a border. Others do not have even this. Whatever you use will depend on the function of the lamp. To employ lamps of this cut over a pool table and have beads or mobiles in the way would not be practical (Figs. 8.9, 8.10 and 8.11).

BRASS CAME—A SPECIFIC USE

The instance will arise when you must span a long edge of glass with no break allowable—neither inlaid nor offset. If the span is straight and subject to gravity, the lead came will surely pull away in time no matter how deep the channel. Even if you employ a ⅜ inch U lead and so do not see the perhaps ¼ inch space the glass is falling from the horizontal, you will know it is there by the way the rest of the lamp will look. In such cases brass channeling or caming should be used. This type of caming comes in different shapes and may be purchased at many hobby stores (Fig. 8.12). It will easily accommodate the usual cathedral

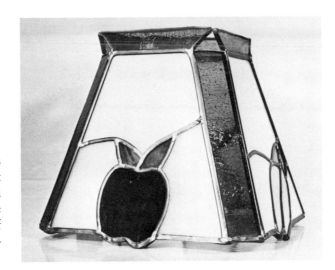

Fig. 8.11 There is no skirt on this basically rectangular shade, but with the story panels provided, a skirt is hardly necessary. Note the "lead in" panels at the corners of the main panels and the space between the crown pieces.

glass thickness of ⅛ inch within its channel. The brass strips are not long—about a foot seems to be standard in most stores—but you generally will not need more than that in individual lengths. If you do, solder what lengths you need together onto the glass and cut off the excess with a tinsnips. Such came is easy to work—again we are talking about a straight edge—and easily soldered. If you want to

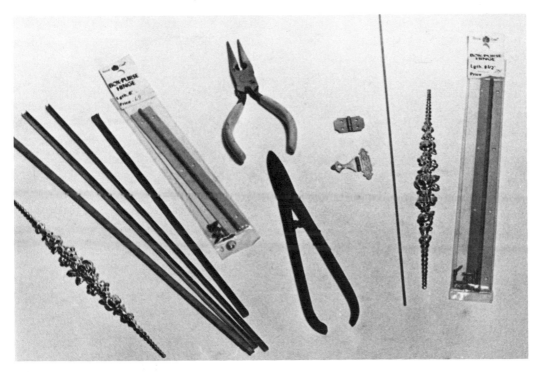

Fig. 8.12 Brass addenda for shades. From the left: filigree spear, brass channels, a brass hinge (piano type), a needlenose pliers and a tinsnips, two small brass hinges and a thin brass rod. Another filigree spear and hinge complete the armamentarium. All of these brass pieces were purchased in our local hobby shop.

wrap it around an edge that is not straight, its ability to respond is limited by the extent of the curve. Long, gradual curves offer few problems; anything more abrupt should be leaded or, if this is not feasible because of gravitational pull, at the least foiled. If even this will not hold pieces together because of the weight involved, then the entire lamp should be redesigned.

We do not suggest that you attempt to crimp sheet metal to make a came out of it.

ORNAMENTAL LEAD EFFECTS

The use of ornamental leads for offset designs in windows was greatly in vogue during the 1920s. Such mixtures of metal and glass, the one complementing the other, still produce a lovely dimensional facing which can be employed effectively on shades (Fig. 8.13). The use of such a device must be of necessity moderate. In the first place, you are liable to overpower the design and texture of your glass; in the second, lead offsets do not transmit light and may just get in the way. The technique of placing these ornaments so they add to rather than detract from the design, depends on delicacy of touch and the experience of the worker. Don't get carried away by the rarity or complexity of your leaded element; it is, after all, only a modifying factor. Be wary of a size imbalance: a leaded ornament that looks small and subtle in your hand may be too large or too ornate for a particular area of the shade. Too many shades are overdone with designed elements; the poor things appear to solicit bulb snatchers. It would be better to practice on simpler, unadorned shades for several projects before attempting to employ offset lead effects. Indeed, these effects should be worked on last of all.

CASTING YOUR OWN DESIGNS IN LEAD

Ornamental lead designs are not easily located. The ones you may find in the rummage box of a stained glass studio have probably come from old windows and may be oxidized beyond any use. In any event, if you are looking for a

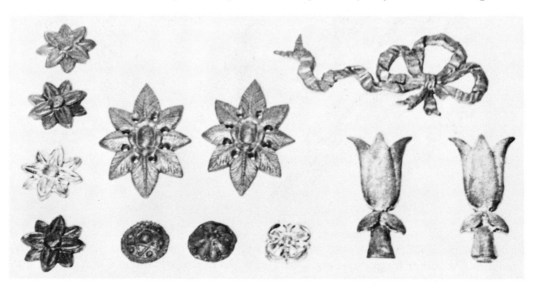

Fig. 8.13   Some decorative lead pieces. These are most effective for lamp ornamentation.

specific shape, you probably will not find it until you are well on your way in the employment of a substitute shape. It is possible, not without some inconvenience, to produce your own leaded shapes. All stained glass workers have scrap lead around; with this and a few elemental tools, you can turn out original leaded ornaments to your own specifications. Here's how:

1. Obtain the drawing of whatever shape you want to produce. We suggest you choose a simple one for your first attempt.

2. Get a block of wax about an inch thick. Candle wax will do; most hobby stores now carry this. Trace the outline of your drawing onto the wax.

3. Cut out the outline with a sharp knife. An X-acto® will do nicely.

4. Smooth and round the edges and add the interior design lines to the wax model. If you aren't able to borrow a wax-carving tool—dentists use them—purchase one from your local hobby store. You will need one on hand if you are going to do this often.

5. Once your carving is completed, find a piece of steel pipe into which your model will fit leaving about an inch of room top and bottom and along the sides.

6. Fit a wax stem to the model which is almost as thick as the model itself and which will protrude from the top of the pipe.

7. Mix some medium setting plaster. You may want to spend a little money to acquire a rubber bowl which will allow you to get a creamy consistency to the plaster through uniform mixing.

8. Set the pipe upright on a piece of wax paper and pour a little plaster into it. Put your wax mold into the pipe, holding it by the stem, and pour plaster all around it within the confines of the pipe. Hold off the pouring now and then tap the pipe smartly with your lead knife or some similar object around its circumference. This will send any air bubbles that are trapped in the plaster to the surface. Continue pouring until the pipe is filled. Allow the plaster to harden.

9. When the plaster has hardened in the pipe, check for shrinkage. A minimum amount may be expected; however, if the plaster looks cracked and extremely shrunken, something is wrong. Your mixture may have been too thin. If the plaster looks all right, go on to the next step.

10. If you have a kiln, put the piece of pipe, still on end, into the kiln and heat it to about 1200°F. If you do not have a kiln you may try using a Bernz O Matic® torch and playing the flame along the outside of the pipe to burn the wax away. The kiln method is far more satisfactory as you obtain a more uniform and exact heat that way.

11. Once the pipe has cooled, remove and examine it. You will find that all the wax has burned away leaving an exact imprint in the enclosed plaster. Now take your scrap lead and melt it in a ladle with your torch. Pour the molten lead into the pipe through the stem hole. It will harden in about twenty minutes. Run cold water through the pipe to fragment and wash out the plaster while the lead is still hot. You will then have the lead casting together with its stem and a small button of lead at the end. Cut away the stem and you are left with your ornamental lead piece—which should be the exact duplicate of the wax.

When we make these, we do a number of them at one time and put them all in the kiln together. We burn the wax out in an evening firing and by morning the casts are cooled and ready for the lead. (Figs. 8.14 to 8.25.)

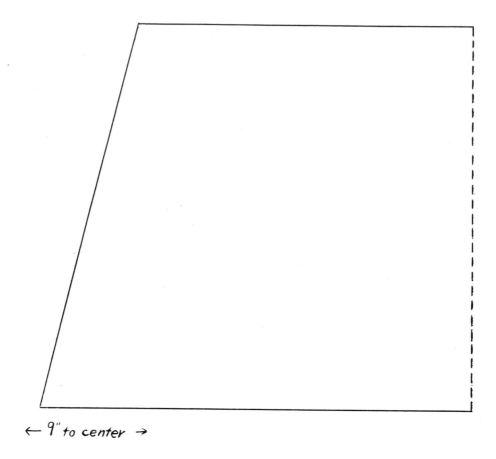

← 9" to center →

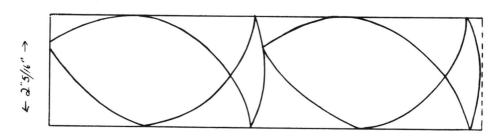

Fig. 8.14   Side panel of basic rectangular lamp with skirt.

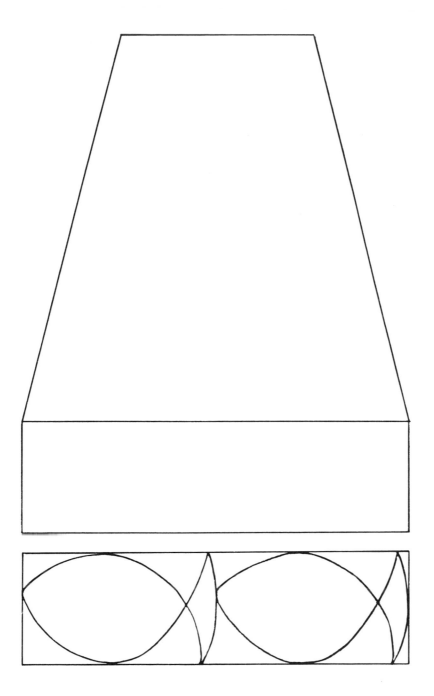

Fig. 8.15 The front panel, half
view showing relationship and
measurement to the skirt.

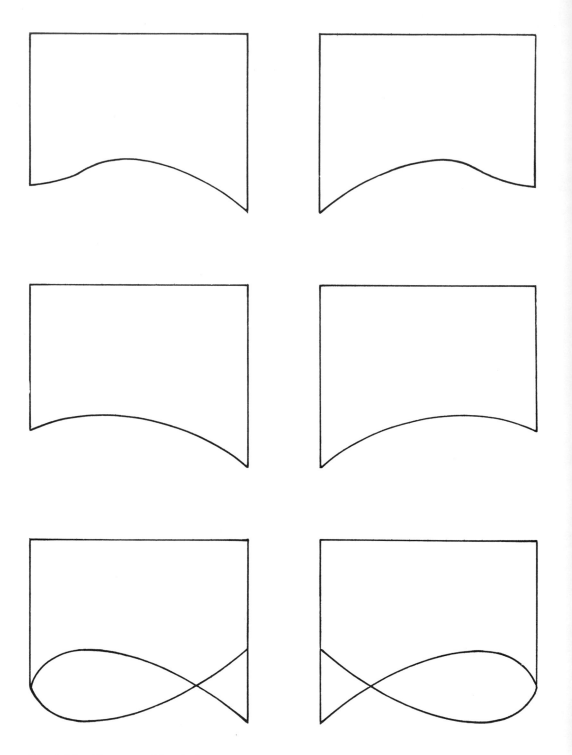

Fig. 8.16   Alternate skirt designs.

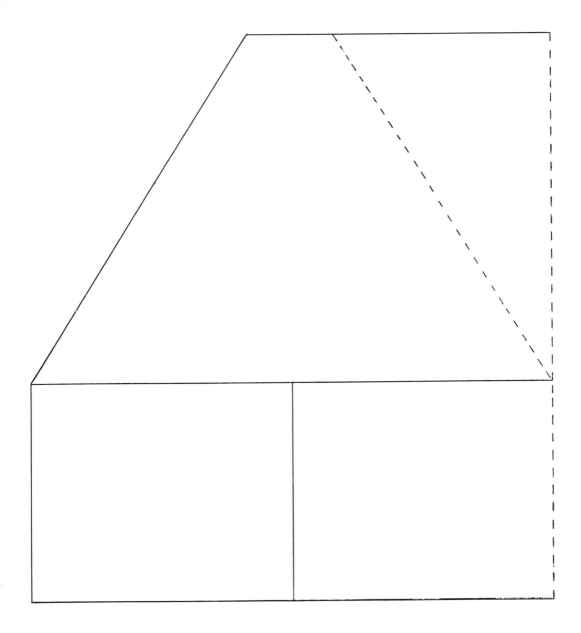

Fig. 8.17 Size of side panel in relation to half the front panel (base of side is half the base of the whole front panel). Skirt is wide and simple in design. The color will carry it.

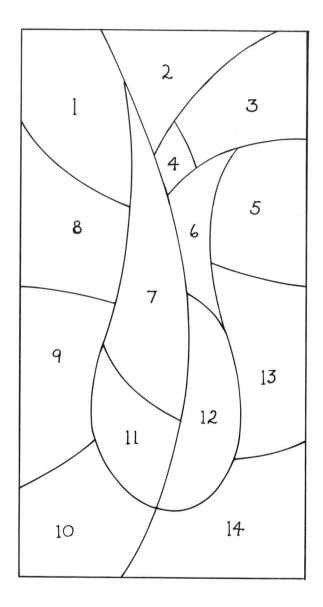

Fig. 8.18 A square panel lamp.
Background and foreground
should be distinctly separated.

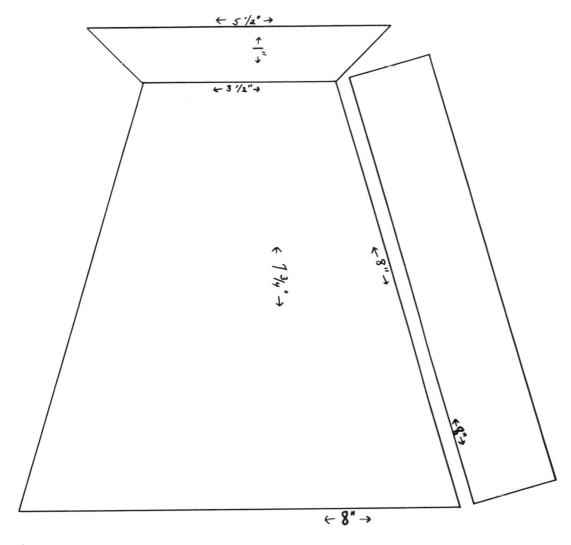

Fig. 8.19 A square shade with four "lead in" panels. Measurements are given, though, of course, you can alter these to suit yourself.

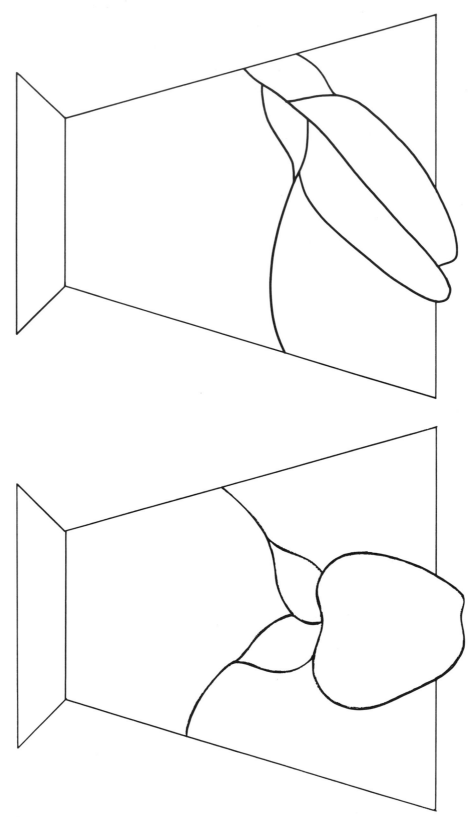

Fig. 8.20   The four panels of the Fig. 8.19 shade.

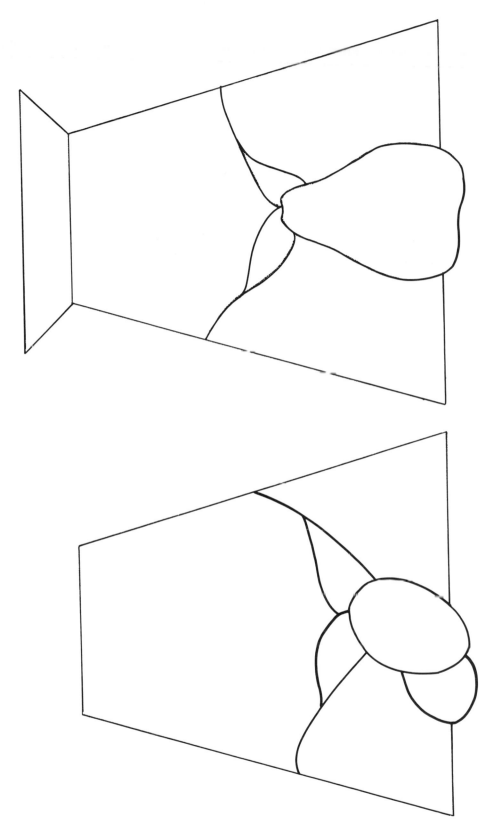

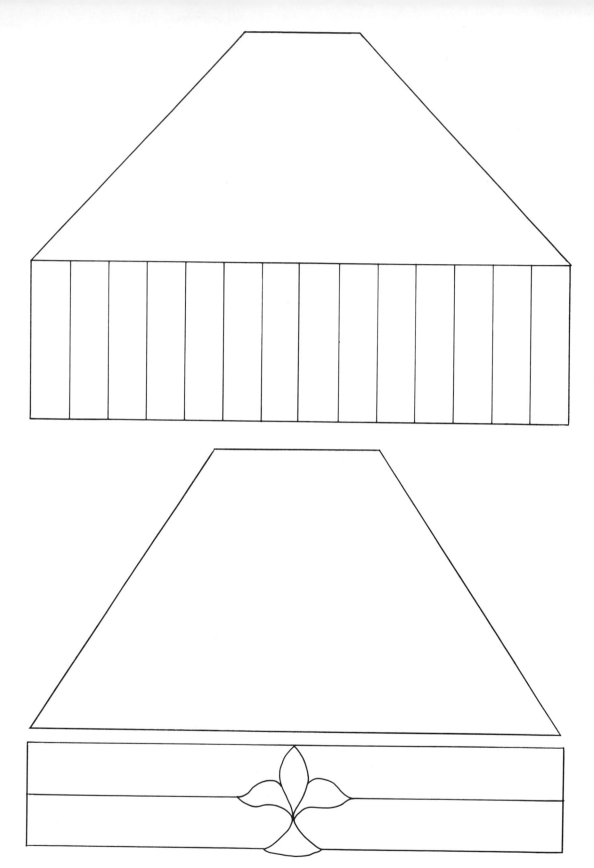

Figs. 8.21–8.25   Designs for rectangular shades.

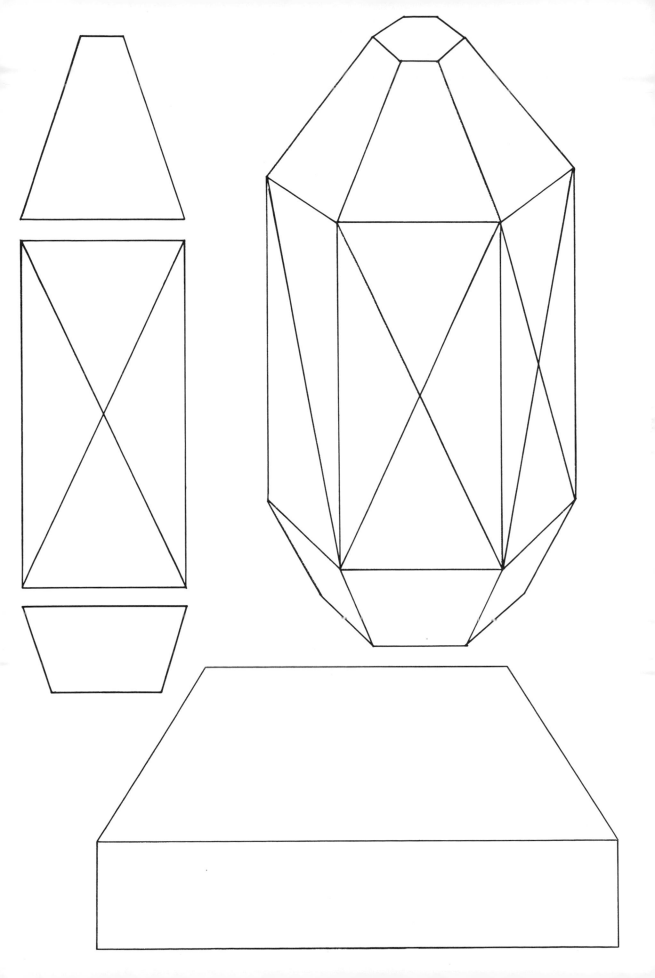

Chapter 9

The Globe Shade

MAKING THE GLOBE FROM A FORM

One of the most difficult shades to design and the most intriguing from the standpoint of creativity is the globe shade. Almost any design may be used in this category so long as it fits a circle of sorts. The sides may be flat—enough flat sides can still encompass a globe shape.

There are a few basic points to keep in mind concerning this type of lamp. Its use is almost unlimited; it is one of the few patterns that look well in any

Fig. 9.1 A globe shade. You open the hinged bottom to change the bulb.

134

Fig. 9.2 A typical form for a globe light showing lines for tiered pieces.

Fig. 9.3 On the left: the globe light. On the right: its mold. (See color section)

room. However, it is rarely a truly functional lamp but more often a designed element in its precincts. Globe shades can become rather complex. No matter how complicated the design, if you are going to make your globe shade from scratch, you must still follow a pattern and lay it out in the flat. Failure to do this will drive you around in circles, and you'll probably steer clear of globe shades for a long time thereafter. These shapes can be a lot of fun, but they can also be frustrating. If your pieces do not go together accurately there is no way you can cheat them in; tolerances in this shape are minute.

We don't want to scare you away from globe shapes; on the contrary, we wrote this chapter to help you do them. However, if you have been remiss in your standards in other shades, it would be a good idea to approach these shades with some wariness (Figs. 9.1 and 9.2). Sliding panels, swinging flaps and hinged sides all abound in globe shades, and they won't work well if their boundaries are insecure. All globe shades, other than those making use of an existing globe, depend on a form. This form must be planned out as though it were, itself, a shade (Figs. 9.3 and 9.4). Spend time on your form; if it is off all future work will be a waste of time. (See Figs. 9.5 through 9.8.)

Fig. 9.4 One-half a globe light atop its mold. Top and bottom can be made in this fashion so they separate, the top lifting right off as this one would from the lower cardboard.

Fig. 9.5 A globe light using leaded triangles.

136

Fig. 9.6 Globe light made from "chunk" glass—dalle-de-verre—either glued and grouted or foiled together.

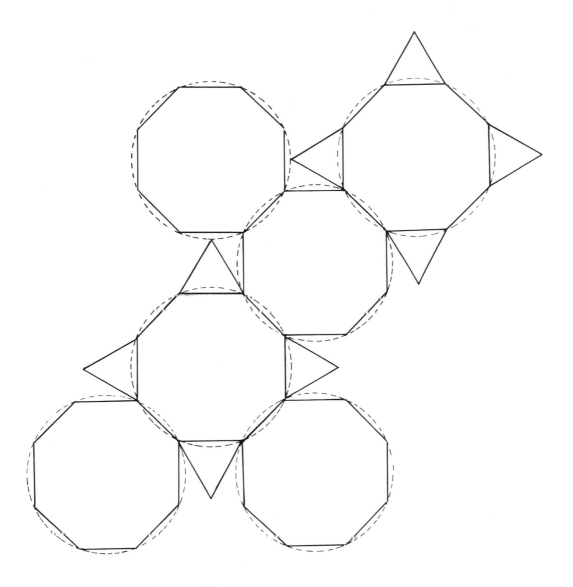

Fig. 9.7 Pattern for a globe shade. The dotted lines show how the individual polygons were arrived at. Fold at the straight lines and affix with masking tape or Scotch tape to achieve the form.

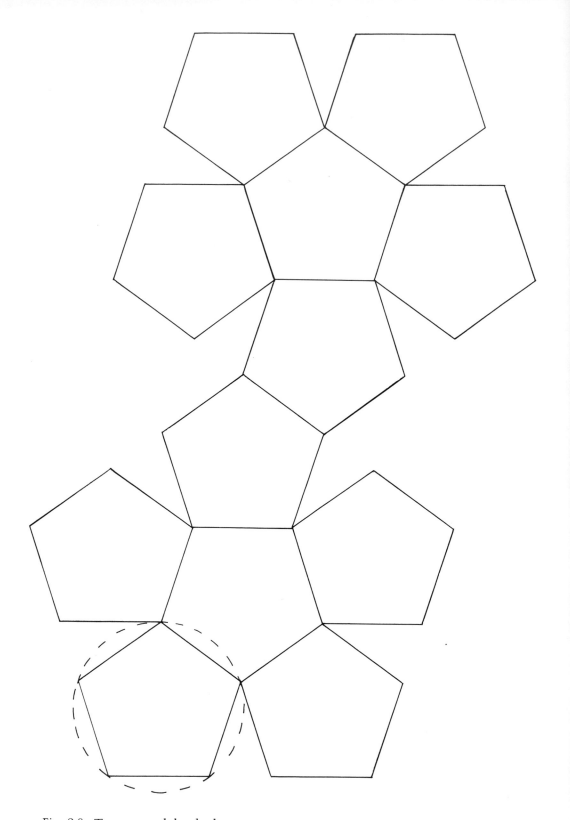

Fig. 9.8 Two more globe shades.

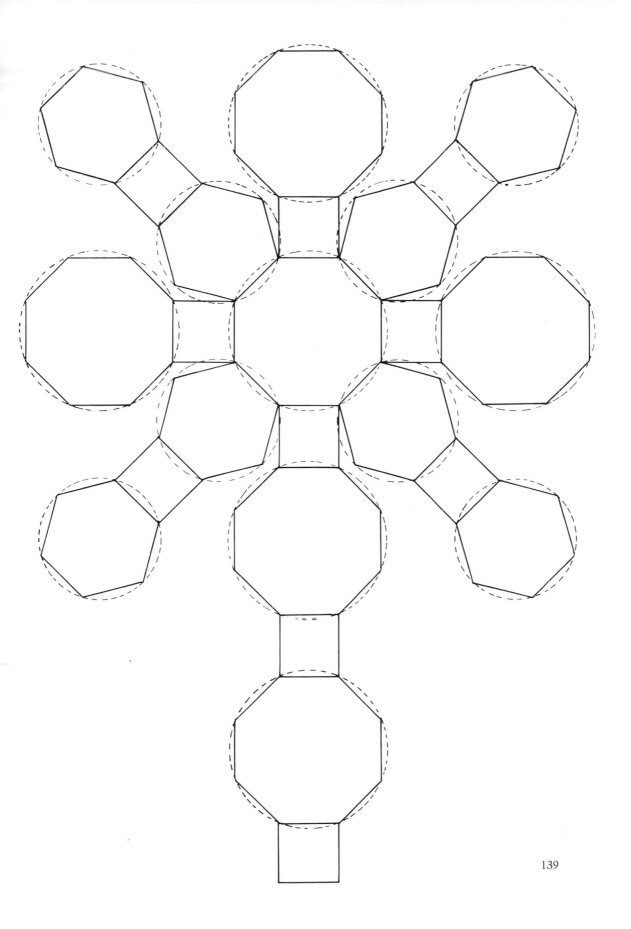

139

Having stated the difficulties inherent in globe shades, we can now turn around to state that a shade made from an existing globe is the simplest shade to make. Get hold of a globe—whatever size you like—and decorate it. It is as simple as that. We have started children off in the lamp field using this method. You can use either copper wires wound around the collar of the globe for stability, or copper foil, in strips down the sides of the globe. This metal then forms a sort of net over the surface to which may be soldered foiled pieces of glass of your choice. The evenness of this background net is up to you. Lovely effects can be achieved by just producing bunches of grapes out of glass globs which hang down the globe and perhaps curl slightly around the bottom.

If you don't want to solder your pieces to the globe, you can forego the entire net production and use epoxy to glue your decorative material directly to the sides of the globe. Naturally, your pieces must be small enough to take the bend of the globe where you want to follow such a bend. While you are somewhat more dependent on the actual shape of the globe with epoxy than you are with solder, you can get a certain amount of the material to stand away from the sides of your form even here. The gluing process, if you want to do it effectively, still takes a little practice. Be sure you use a quick, clear-drying epoxy and one that is not too runny. Remember that you are not going to be working on flat surfaces. Don't worry about the heat of the bulb melting your glue; we have never found this to happen with any of the good epoxies on the market. Once your pieces are affixed to the globe, you can grout or liquid lead between them to allow the light to escape only through your colored surfaces. A "chunk glass" globe lamp (Figs. 9.9 and 9.10) can be done this way quite effectively.

These globe lamps can be hung and wired directly from the globe holder which also comes in fancy, decorative shapes the better to provide functional hanger and finishing cap. Used with a provocative, handmade chain, swagged in proper order, the final ensemble, done without even having to cut a piece of glass, is a perfect first project for someone beginning in the craft.

Fig. 9.9 Materials necessary for working with "chunk" glass to make the chunk glass globe shade. The dalle hammer and the anvil are shown. We imbedded the anvil in lead (we had a few old cames around) and added a block of wood to provide a sturdy base. The heavy dalle is held against the wedged anvil and tapped from above with the dalle hammer along the line of cleavage desired.

Fig. 9.10 A foiled globe lamp. *(Courtesy of Clemence Stanley)*

Chapter 10

The Story Lamps

WHAT IS A STORY LAMP?

Story lamps are those which project along their circumference a picture pattern which provides a name for the lamp itself. They are usually small-pieced, Tiffany-type lamps. By their story you will know them—they are the "windmill" lamp, the "bamboo" lamp, the "swan" lamp and so forth. These identifying tags impart a grandeur and a sense of workmanship that distinguish such projects as being out of the ordinary. To call a shade "pyramidal" seems to classify rather than style it. To distinguish it as a "windmill" lamp gives it a specificity that implies uniqueness. And, in a sense, this is proper, for there are far more pyramidal lamps being made than story lamps of any nature. Story lamps are more difficult and more time-consuming; more than any standard pyramidal shape, they belong in the province of the experienced lampmaker. All the same, the pyramidal styling can be imparted to a story skirt or to the straight panels themselves—though this is not something we ordinarily advise until you are pretty good at design, for the two anatomical parts of the lamp can clash pretty badly here (Fig. 10.1).

Fig. 10.1 A foiled, antique Tiffany-type shade for a base lamp.

142

Fig. 10.2 Large panel lamp with a small-pieced foiled skirt.

Keep in mind that when we speak of "story," we are talking not of an abstract but of a specific pictorial design. Abstract designs done on forms in Tiffany-type technique are not story lamps, though they are made the same way. We are making the distinction within these pages as a guide. Abstract designs can certainly be done by any worker using the techniques we will discuss; we feel abstracts are modifications of story lamps, being the same in all but design, but we personally prefer to distinguish between the two. We refer to the latter as a Tiffany-type shade, or one done in the "small-pieced" method.

STRAIGHT PANEL LAMP WITH A STORY SKIRT

This is our old friend, the pyramidal shade, with an extremely ornate skirt done in small, foiled pieces of glass in story fashion (Fig. 10.2). The delicate balance between skirt and panels is a factor here. The panels should not be of a size to compete with or overmatch the skirt; on the other hand, the skirt does not exist alone and should tie in with the panels.

Such a tie in is automatically accomplished by the angles the pieces of skirt form with one another, and of course, these follow the panel folds. Another way to tie in is by color. Skirt color and panel color should have some common basis. Picking up a color or two from the panel and reflecting it in the skirt, even by just a touch, will provide a logical basis for the tie in. Design should not be used as a tie in; that is, straight panels with an ornate skirt attached should be panels only—be they square, rectangular or pyramidal—and should not be broken up. You will already have enough breaks in the skirt.

You may well find it easier to sell this type of lamp than a complete Tiffany-type globe, which of necessity you would have to price much higher (see Chapter 12). The main work involved in the straight panel lamp with a story skirt is the skirt—make certain that you don't get so ornate that the skirted procedure takes as long as an entire globe. Once the skirt is completed, it is a simple matter to attach it to the body of the lamp via the procedures discussed in previous chapters (see Chapters 3 & 6), and there you have it. Just make sure that the skirt fits the associated panels. If you stick to your dimensions on the small pieces and make certain you keep checking your underlying cartoon (you do have an underlying cartoon, we hope), then your dimensions will stay just as you planned them. If you are lazy in your cutting and start forcing pieces together figuring you will make up the difference as you go along, you will probably have problems later on. You can solder all the internal pieces in each skirt panel, but solder only the strutted joints of those supports that face you. You still will have to bend the skirt around to fit the panels, and it won't bend with all the joints soldered.

There are even simpler straight panel story skirt lamps. These shades rely on their framework to provide distinguishing features of design as well as support, while the glass, clipped behind in straight pieces, provides color only. If you are fortunate enough to discover such frames in good condition in an antique shop, buy them. It is a simple matter to cut and place glass within them.

THE FRUITED SKIRT

The commonest story skirts are those containing fruited designs. In many instances the fruits—apples, pears—are curved away from the plane of the skirt and toward the viewer. They are actually hollow, half pieces of fruit concave from within. Grapes may hang down in bunches from the skirt; these are either small purple "globs," glass jewels (which have a uniform shape, having been pressed from a mold) or half marbles.

It is, as you may imagine, difficult to design such a skirt. The main thing to keep in mind is that you cannot calculate the size of your bent fruit until you actually make it (Fig. 10.3). Leave enough space for it, and then mold your fruit to the size space you leave; the outward bend doesn't matter as far as the plane of the circle of the skirt is concerned. It is a good idea when designing bent fruit (see Chapter 11) to make the fruit slightly larger than the space you have provided. It is easier to trim the glass later than to end up with a piece of fruit that has withered from the bending and now wobbles in the shade with an abyss to either side. Building up with foil and solder looks horrible here; a graceful flow of line in contour is the reason for the insert in the first place (Figs. 10.4 and 10.5). Our advice is to stay away from bent fruit until you have had a considerable amount of experience in making small-pieced skirts in two dimensions.

As far as grapes are concerned, these should be placed exactly when the design is being laid out. Take the actual pieces of glass you intend to use and arrange them as they will fall. Then, with a sharp pencil, trace the outline of the mass. This will let you know how much space you must leave for them. Be careful when you foil or lead your grapes that you stick to the same arrangement you have laid out on your cartoon. We make it a practice to number all small pieces which are to be put together as a unit away from the main design (indeed, somebody else may even be doing them). Then we take a picture of them which will accompany the unit until it goes into the major production. We also transfer a copy of the outline with any such unit. There are a lot fewer whines coming from grapes processed in this manner. (See Figs. 10.6 through 10.9.)

Rectangular shade with offset designs.

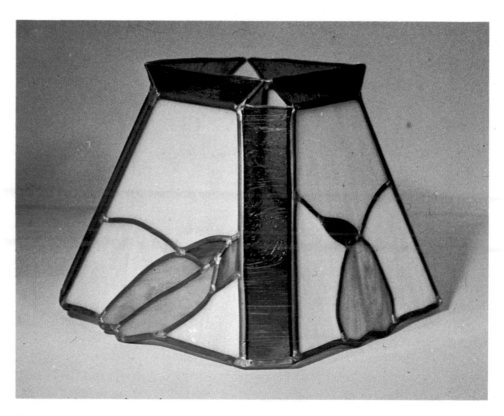

Kitchen lamp—large panel with broken design.

Globe shade.

Tiered pyramidal lamp with grape border.

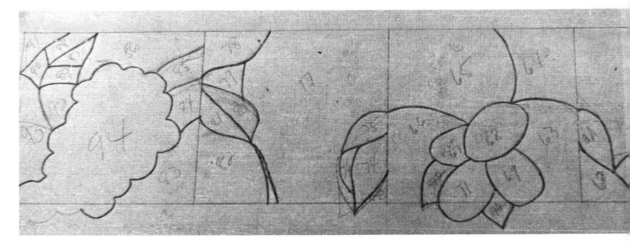

Fig. 10.3 Planning the skirt: the work drawing or cartoon.

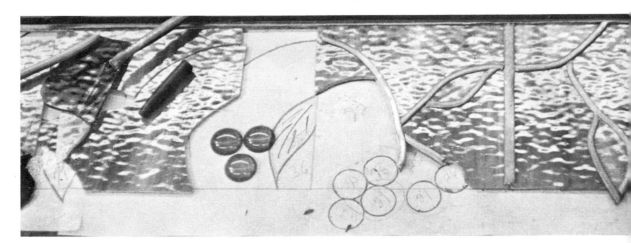

Fig. 10.4 The glass is filled in, and the leading is started.

Fig. 10.5 The leading completed, the soldering is begun.

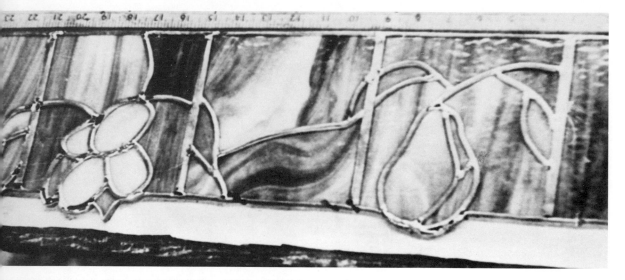

Fig. 10.6 The skirt leaded and soldered.

Fig. 10.7 Closing the circle on a round, small-pieced skirt.

Fig. 10.8 Placing the skirt on the lamp proper.

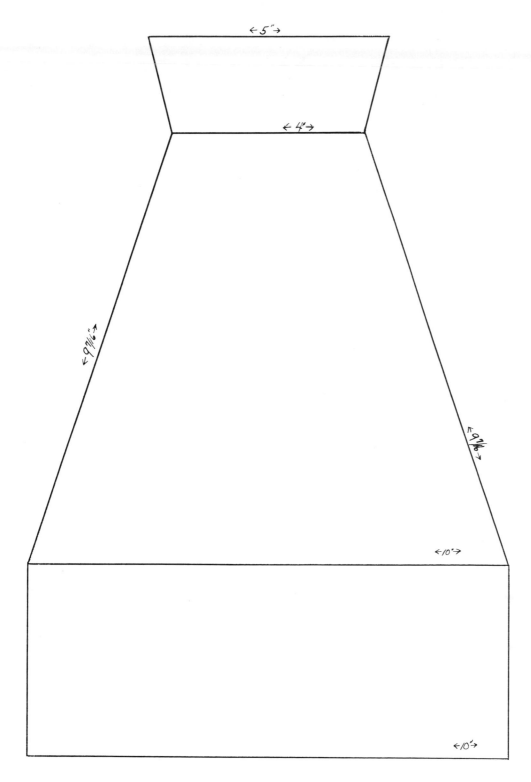

Fig. 10.9 Basic rectangular
shade with alternative fruited
skirt designs.

The Bent Panel Lamp with a Story Skirt

While we will be discussing bent panel lamps in the following chapter, a word or two about their story skirts may well be added here. Bent panel lamps, unlike pyramidal, square or rectangular shades, form a true circle at their base. No longer, then, are we dealing with a skirt divided into panels. This is an important consideration because we can no longer depend on an external geometric division of the skirt to guide us. Nonetheless, it is important to make such a division for purposes of designing. Your division won't be explicit in the finished shade, but it will help you retain your original intent during construction.

Where you place these designer's breaks is up to you. The diameter of the lamp dictates the number of repetitions of the story. The story and the background—complete to the last piece of glass—will thus alternate in measured beats around the skirt. Designer's breaks should occur at these divisions. If you are unsure of yourself, make them more often—you can divide each repetition in half—but there is really no need for this. It does no harm, except that it will probably go right through a piece of bent fruit. Remember: it doesn't matter if such breaks go through pieces of glass; they are not actual breaks.

Even so, measurements must be exact. The rhythm of the story and the diameter of the skirt demand precise measurements. No play whatsoever is allowable in dealing with bent panels; they either fall true or look terrible. Just an eighth of an inch off on the skirt will throw the whole lamp out of alignment.

Bent panel lamp skirts must be made on a form (Fig. 10.10). Whether the form be wood, metal, plaster or plastic makes little difference except in the manner in which the pieces are held onto it. Since the same technique is applicable in its entirety to the Tiffany style small-pieced lamp we will defer discussion of it for the moment (see Chapter 11).

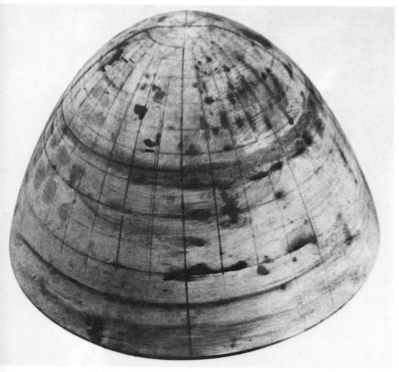

Fig. 10.10 One style of rock maple mold on which to build a Tiffany-type shade.

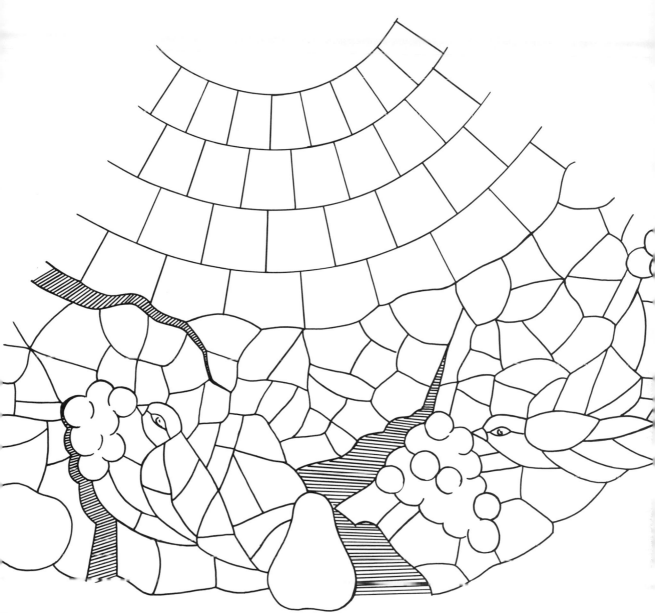

Fig. 10.11 Pattern of one complete section of Tiffany style mul-
tiple-pieced shade. The hatched
areas are closed when the lamp is
in three-dimensional form.

THE TIFFANY STYLE SMALL-PIECED LAMP

This is the style that Tiffany made famous—a shade consisting of small pieces of
glass arranged in staggering tiers and convolutions of color (Fig. 10.11). Such lamps
may or may not tell a story, that is, have a pictorial design. They may or may not
have a straight border. Almost without exception they are foiled. Without exception they are made on some sort of mold or form. (See Figs. 10.12 and 10.13.)

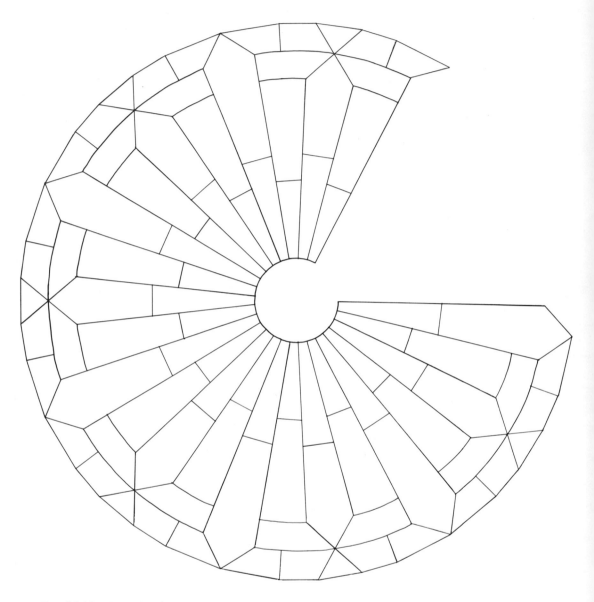

Fig. 10.12 Pattern for an even border small-pieced shade. The open space determines the height the top of the shade will rise from the flat plane.

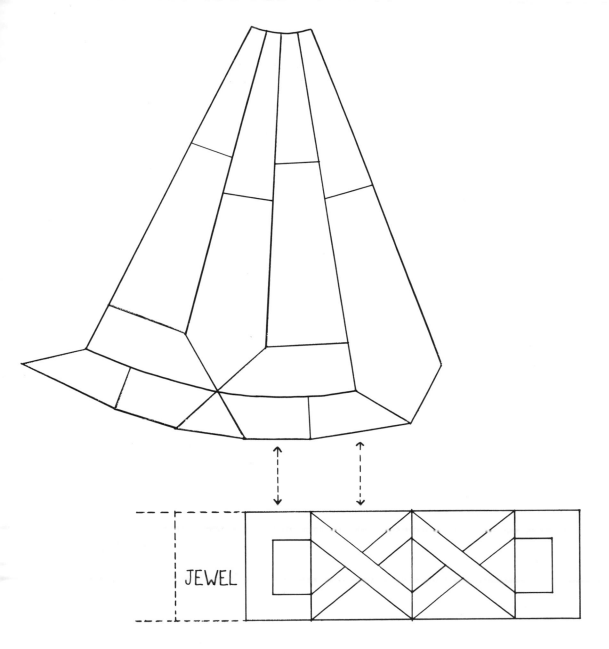

JEWEL

Fig. 10.13 One repeated section of Fig. 10.12 with the cartoon of the skirt to show the relationship of both.

Any circular object may be used for a form. Upturned salad bowls, chopping bowls of wood or plastic, plastic domes or Styrofoam globes all have their place depending on their shape and dimensions. Since a number of manufacturers have begun to put plastic domes on the market, the hobbyist can now select a shape more closely approximating the shape he wishes to create in glass. Years ago you made do with the salad bowl you could pry loose from the kitchen; today the selection of available forms is more gratifying, but even with this expanded choice, alas, you still may not find just the shape you want. If this is the case, you might desire to have a mold made to your own specifications or, better still, to make it yourself.

The average mold turned out of rock maple by a mill will cost several hundred dollars. If this doesn't faze you, you may have all your specifications satisfied and acquire a mold that will pay for itself many times over—if you can sell a great many shades of that same shape. Unfortunately, whether for sale or your own decor, what you will probably want are different shapes not available in hobby shops. Since it is impractical to get a rock maple mold turned for each shape you desire, you are much better off making your own mold and disposing of it when you are done. The following outline will help you to make your own mold.

1. Let's suppose you have seen a Tiffany shade you would like to have.

2. You decide to rival the master and build it yourself.

3. You need a mold or form to work on.

4. Assemble the ingredients and take a deep breath.

5. The shade you like is twenty inches in diameter across the skirt and twelve inches from the bottom of the skirt to the base of the crown.

6. Get a piece of plywood at least twenty-one inches square for a platform on which to build. While you're at it, make a six-inch plywood circle. This is the top, or crest. Also get a twelve-inch dowel stick for the backbone (a broomstick handle will do).

7. Assemble as shown in Figure 10.14.

8. You should have the outer shape of the lamp drawn on paper. This may be your own design or a copy made from an antique. The latter is best gotten while the antique dealer is busy with another customer.

9. Bend a heavy wire to follow the contour of the sides. A straightened and rebent coat hanger will do. Make sixteen of these.

10. Fasten the wire shapes to the form as shown in Figures 10.15 and 10.16.

11. The assembled skeleton frame is covered with screen wire in strips as shown in Figs. 10.17 and 10.18.

12. You now have a wire form ready to be covered. Here your individuality comes into play. We like to cover ours with plaster-impregnated cloth strips and rolls like those used by your doctor to make arm or leg casts. Having a doctor friend helps here. Otherwise you can get both splints and roller gauze plaster bandages in any surgical supply house—they are quite reasonable in price. Simply soak the entire roll in warm water until the bubbles stop rising and then give it a brief squeeze. Remove it from the water and start covering your frame, unrolling as you go. As you go along, wet your hand from time to time and pass it

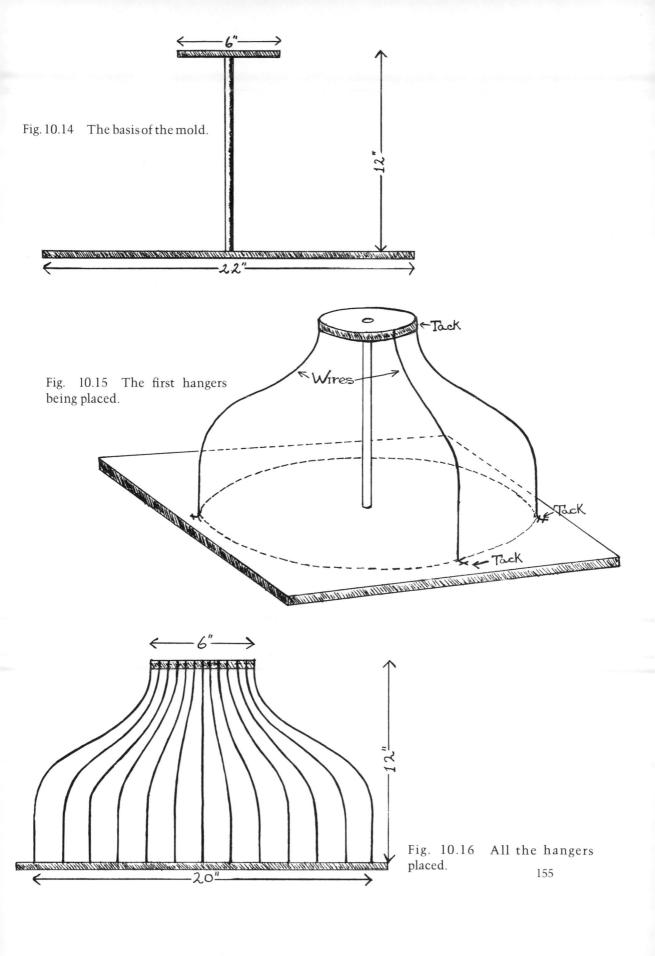

Fig. 10.14   The basis of the mold.

Fig. 10.15   The first hangers being placed.

Fig. 10.16   All the hangers placed.

155

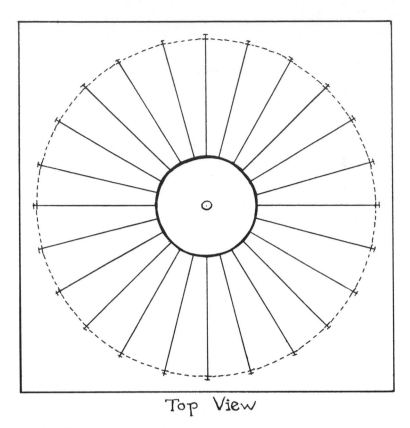

Top View

Fig. 10.17 Top view of the mold
skeleton.

Fig. 10.18 The wire screen
being placed.

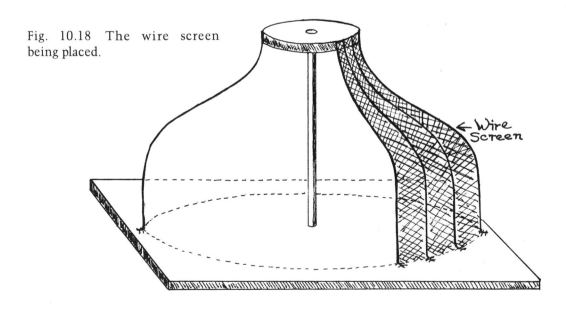

← Wire
Screen

over the plaster to be sure of a smooth finish, but don't overdo this as too much water will leach away the plaster from the underlying linen. Be careful not to get folds in the material as one fold will produce a bulge through many layers of plaster and make your mold's finished surface uneven.

13. After it has been covered and allowed to dry—allow forty-eight hours for this—the mold can be painted white. Be sure all the water is out of the plaster at this point. If the pores of the surface are covered too soon, your mold will never dry, and it will start to crumble. The plaster surfaces give off heat as the plaster "cures." The mold is ready for painting when cool to the touch. Painting the mold white gives you a base on which to draw your pattern (also taken from the antique store original, if you wish).

14. There is really nothing left to do. We just felt it was tempting fate to stop at thirteen steps.

GETTING YOUR DESIGN ON THE MOLD*

Suppose you have decided that your next project will be a stained glass shade for a table lamp. Your first step would be to choose a base, since the shape and size of the shade will be governed by the proportions and design of the base.

The base used in this project suggested a dome-shaped shade to be done in the Tiffany method, that is, to be done with small pieces of glass foiled together. We used a plastic dome with a bottom circumference of 34¼ inches as a basis for the design.

At this point, the creative urge asserted itself. We had a framework on which to try our technical and artistic abilities. We did not want to make a reproduction but an original. Here indecision can take place. The choices are wide open. Should the shade be of a color and design suitable for the plush decor of the turn of the century, or should it be ultramodern? After many tentative decisions, after having considered the glass on hand or readily available, a design was conceived and preliminary sketches were made.

To insure the proper placement of each glass piece, the plastic dome is marked off with a magic marker (Fig. 10.19). Divide the bottom circumference

*Project Courtesy Marvin Riddle

Fig. 10.19 The surface of the plastic dome mold is evenly divided vertically. The string is held taut, and a pen traces its vertical line.

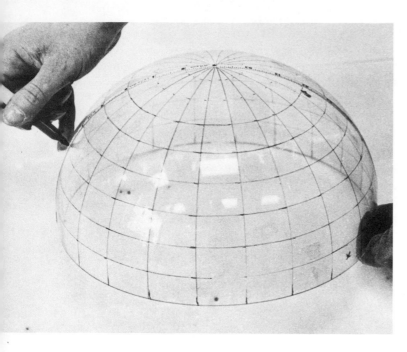

Fig. 10.20 The flexible ruler method of placing the lines.

of the dome by the widest dimension you intend to cut, bearing in mind that if it is too wide, the shade will appear too angular, and if too narrow, the pieces at the top will be too small to cut and foil effectively. For this shade we made 1¼-inch divisions. Since the circumference could not be evenly divided by this, we made twenty divisions of 1½ inches and two (on opposite sides of the dome) of 2⅛ inches. After these divisions have been marked, take a ¼-inch flexible steel rule with a catch on the end, hook it on the bottom on one side, run it across the exact apex of the dome to the mark on the opposite side. Hold the rule securely in place and draw the line with the magic marker. Mark each of the vertical lines at one-inch intervals up from the bottom. When all are properly marked, draw the horizontal lines around the dome. A flexible curve will be helpful in doing this (Figs. 10.20 and 10.21).

This network is then transferred to ⅛-inch graph paper for further development of the design. To insure accuracy of the transfer, use an artist's compass to check the juncture on the model with that on the drawing.

Each piece of the pattern must be numbered. This number must be indicated on the cartoon, as well as on the working drawing and on each glass piece. While the pieces may appear identical, slight differences could distort the shade if care were not taken in this respect.

A flower pattern was drawn flat and then superimposed on the drawing, two opposing flowers near the bottom and two nearer the top (Fig. 10.22). It is necessary to adjust the pattern to compensate for the dome shape being used—which shape is not, of course, a true circle. This compensation is done by positioning the outer edge of the flower pattern on the appropriate lines of the master pattern. You will find that a perpendicular wedge of the flower will overlap the edge of the master pattern. The wedge must be carefully cut away. A new flower pattern can now be cut. This new pattern will be used in cutting the glass.

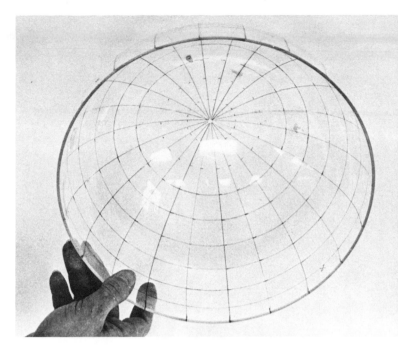

Fig. 10.21 The mold with all lines in place spaced as accurately as possible for the background pieces.

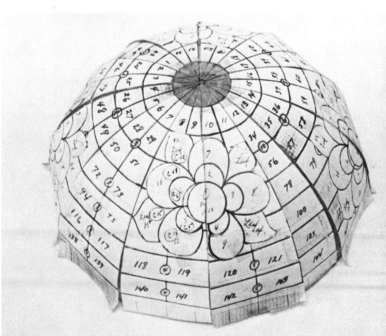

Fig. 10.22 The flower pattern is now placed as a paper overlay and positioned.

CUTTING THE GLASS TO FIT YOUR PATTERN

When you are satisfied with the pattern, have checked it for glass cuts that are impossible to make and made the corrections required, you are ready for the next step. Lay a piece of pattern paper large enough to accommodate the entire pattern on your drawing board or table, carbon paper on top, then brown kraft paper on top of this, then more carbon paper and your cartoon on top (Fig.

Fig. 10.23 The paper pattern in the flat is transferred to kraft paper and a cartoon is made. Here the lines are being darkened while at the same time a pattern is being made through carbon paper (see text).

10.23). Hold all three in place with thumbtacks in at least the four corners. With a ball point pen, press firmly and trace all lines of the cartoon. When finished, lift one corner carefully and check to see if the tracing has penetrated clearly to the pattern paper on the bottom (Fig. 10.24). If it has, separate the copies and retrace each with a fine point felt pen. This is done so that the carbon will not smudge and create an indistinct pattern which would cause problems.

With a regular shears, cut each piece of the pattern exactly on the line. When all the pieces are cut, trim about 1/16 of an inch from all sides to allow for the copper foil. We did not use the pattern shears in this case because it takes too wide a cut for our purpose.

On the back of each pattern piece put a piece of two-sided adhesive tape. You are now ready to cut the glass. Stick each pattern piece to the glass you have selected, one at a time, and cut carefully. As each piece of glass is cut, lay it on the kraft paper working drawing and make sure that it fits. (Fig. 10.25.)

USING COPPER FOIL

A brief review of the foiling process might well be in order at this time since the very existence of small-pieced lamps depends on the foiling process (see Chapter 3).

Copper is easily soldered if, like lead came, there is no interference from an oxide coating. Unlike lead, it is impossible to burn copper with the heat from any soldering iron used for working in stained glass. At the same time, copper by itself is much weaker than lead came. Accordingly, it is not sufficient to solder "joints" of copper foil. The entire seam between pieces must not only be soldered front and back but "beaded" as well. This process entails raising a smooth ridge of solder over the seam for strength as well as looks.

Each piece of glass rimmed with copper should be "tinned." Once this process of flowing solder over the metal is accomplished, a rigidity and strength is

160   THE STORY LAMPS

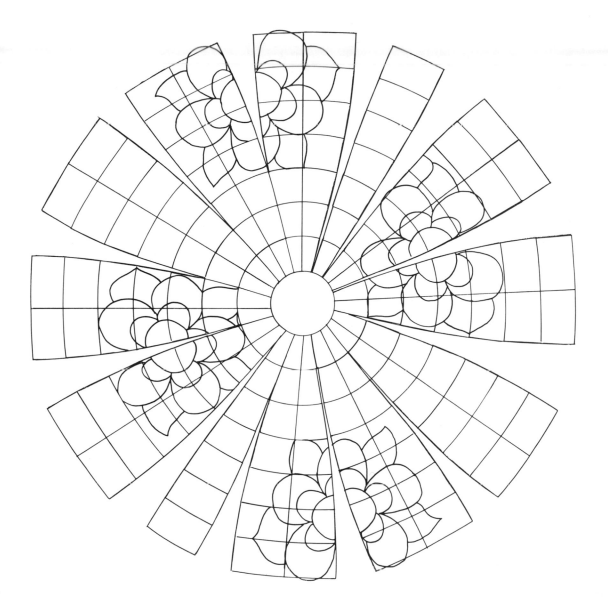

Fig. 10.24   The pattern cartoon.

Fig. 10.25 To avoid confusion as each piece of glass is cut to pattern, its pattern is fixed to it with tape and the glass and pattern are placed back on the work drawing. Each piece of pattern is used for only one piece of glass.

imparted to it that it would not have otherwise. This should be done before the pieces of glass are put together on the form. (See Figs. 10.26 through 10.30.) Some individuals feel this is a waste of time; we advise you to do it. Aside from the firm grip on the glass that tinning provides, you will find soldering is done more readily between previously soldered surfaces than between glass pieces bound by the raw metal (Fig. 10.31). This is not affectation, but a practical necessity, when dealing with borders that must be soldered together along the vertical curve provided by a form. If you have not tinned your copper rims and the metal is dirty, oxidized or just temperamental, you will find the solder rolling off as fast as you apply it down the length of the curve. Struggling with one hand to maintain the piece's place on the form while trying to manipulate the iron

Fig. 10.26 A Tiffany-type shade on a mold. The top row of pieces is being added. The pieces are foiled and in place but not yet soldered together.

Fig. 10.27 The top row is completed, and the pieces are spaced to fit.

Fig. 10.28 The tiers of the above lamp seen from within. The lamp is upside down on the table to allow for soldering the interior surfaces.

Fig. 10.29 A possible crown is fitted.

Fig. 10.30 The crown in Fig. 10.29 is decided against in favor of a filigree crown arrangement. Note the space (lower right) where a piece of bent fruit is yet to be fitted. (See color section.)

with the other should convince you of the necessity of tinning. Although the copper won't, you may well burn up.

If you want to save time by tinning your pieces as rapidly as possible, get a soldering pot. This item allows you to melt and maintain measured amounts of solder in a molten state. Instead of bringing your iron and solder to the glass rim and running the solder around it front and rear, you bring your copper-rimmed glass pieces to the solder and roll their edges through it. It's really quite simple, provided that you don't break the glass by moving it too slowly. The rotation of the glass edges through the molten solder must also be accomplished without burning your fingers. Since copper is an excellent heat conductor, hold the glass in the center and pivot it round from there. You will find, once you get used to it, that a soldering pot can be a great help even though you may have to smooth off a few pieces with the iron anyway at first. Do not try the soldering pot for large panels of glass; you will almost surely break them. When you are through using the pot, you needn't empty out the unused solder; let it harden right in the pot until you are ready to use it again. A word of caution here: if some time elapses between uses of the pot, be sure to clean out any dust that may have collected before you reheat it. Debris from the air will form a scum on the working surface of the alloy and hamper and pit any future soldering. We place a plastic bag over our soldering pot when it is not in use; it saves a lot of cleaning later on.

SOLDERING THE PIECES ON THE MOLD

With each piece of glass now foiled and tinned, you are ready to put them into place on the form. Guidelines on the form should already have been established, and you are anxious to see how your pieces will fit together.

We suggest you commence at the top of your form and work your way

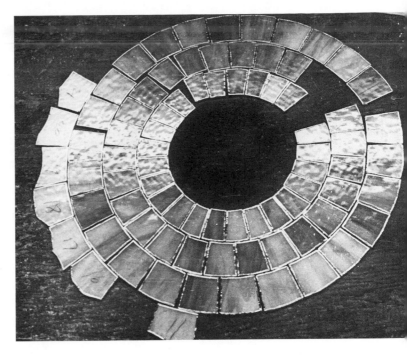

Fig. 10.31 The circles of the top three tiers of the previously seen Tiffany-type shade and the beginning of the fourth and final body tier. These are laid out in the flat before they are placed on the mold so that an idea is gotten as to how the pieces will go together. The alternating line panel was decided upon at this stage. We felt the body of the lamp was more effective broken up than in straight lines.

around and down the sides. Your first pieces should form the guideline for your top hole, through which the wiring will run and against which your crown (if any) will be affixed. As each piece is applied to the form, check the guidelines to make sure there is no overlapping. If you have cut your pattern well and checked it carefully, there should be no trouble here other than in correctly placing the piece. Each piece of glass must now be held in place while the next one is being placed. As these multiply, you cannot keep holding them with your fingers; indeed, even if you can keep four or five steady with finger pressure against the mold while you solder them, it is extremely awkward. Here is where nails, pushpins or clay come in handy. Whether you employ one or another depends on your mold.

Leading nails may be tapped gently into the sides of a rock maple form to brace the pieces. Do not hammer the nails, as the holes they leave will not help the next lamp to be done on that mold and you can actually crack the wood if you get enough deep holes in it. If you have a plastic mold or dome, naturally you cannot nail into it. Use small pieces of clay here—Plasticine® will do—against the back of each piece of glass. The clay will stick the piece to the mold, and you will continue to have an even surface on your formative lamp provided that you don't use so much clay that one piece of glass sticks out from another. A little practice will quickly give you an idea of how much to use. Keep the clay from drying out as you use it or you will find that you have to use more and more per piece of glass as you go along. The clay will yield readily to the pressure of your fingers, and the glass should slide nicely into position.

Pushpins are used for Styrofoam molds—the most fleeting of all the molds. If you can use a Styrofoam mold more than once, that is a lot. The pushpins do no damage, but the heat from the iron melts away parts of the mold and leaves an irregular surface. All the same, Styrofoam is an excellent material for a mold, and pushpins drive into it with ease. Get the long, metal handled pushpins rather than the stubby, multicolored plastic-handled ones; they last longer and hold better. The plastic handles will melt in places from the soldering iron and soon will not hold the pieces of glass well.

Tack all joints lightly with solder first. Do not attempt to do the final soldering until the project is "tacked" together. When this step is finished, you may finish the soldering.

One advantage of the Styrofoam mold is that it can be dug out from behind the completed lineup of glass pieces. This is especially helpful if you are making a Tiffany-type "ball" lamp. The two halves of the ball would have to be made separately and joined together off the mold if a wooden or plastic form were used. With Styrofoam, almost the entire ball may be completed on the form, the form dug out, and the few remaining pieces of glass soldered in by hand.

When the outside is done, remove the shade from its form and solder the inside. Then attach the hardware to the open circle at the top to accommodate the finial to hold the shade to the base.

Clean the shade immediately with cleaning compound and then glass cleaner.

THE GROZING PLIERS

Because of their picture-puzzle arrangement, the small pieces of the Tiffany-type shade with their multiple, irregular surfaces must be cut so that one fits closely into another. The more ill-cut these pieces are, the wider will be the gulf that separates them which must be filled with solder. An ideal small-pieced lamp provides a delicate, lacy effect best achieved by a maximum area of glass held with a minimum amount of solder. The more this ratio is reversed, the more ill-kempt your lamp will appear. The grozing pliers is essential in cutting glass pieces which cannot be cut to their proper area by the glass cutter alone. The grozing pliers is really a carving tool; nowhere in stained glass is its function so well demonstrated as in carving pieces for the small-pieced shade.

When we speak of grozing pliers we are talking of the German made, imported item, not of the unfortunate substitute made domestically. A true grozer has a flat upper jaw and a slightly curved under jaw. Both jaws are equipped with fine horizontal "teeth" that are sharp and deep. The small grozer is 5¼ inches long with a jaw length of about 1 inch and a jaw width of ¼ inch. A medium grozer measures 6¼ inches in length and has a jaw length of 1¼ inches, jaw width ¼ inch. Large grozers can be imported, but they are more difficult to use. Their measurements are: overall length, 7¾ inches; jaw length, 1½ inches; jaw width ⅞ inch.

The mobility of the grozer is due to its low slung, armed under jaw, the width of both jaws and its fit in the hand. It can follow curves and cut around bends and circles; with it you can chip and file through great amounts of "waste" glass to obtain the exact shape you want. These pliers can groze (file) either upwards or downwards depending on the edge you want to smooth or the type of glass you are using. Filing is done with the teeth of the instrument; carving is done by nibbling away at the glass using the nipping action of the jaws and filing with the teeth. This entire action may be termed "grozing," but grozing also refers to just the filing part. The word itself may be used rather carelessly, the pliers may not. It takes a certain amount of experience to learn how to use grozing pliers well, but once the technique is acquired, the worker has a valuable tool when a Tiffany-type lamp is in progress, or indeed, when any fine work in stained glass is to be done. (See Figs. 10.32 through 10.34.)

Fig. 10.32 Pattern for small-pieced tulip skirt showing imaginary borders (dotted lines) when this pattern is used with a pyramidal-type lamp.This versatile pattern can also be employed with a bent panel shade.

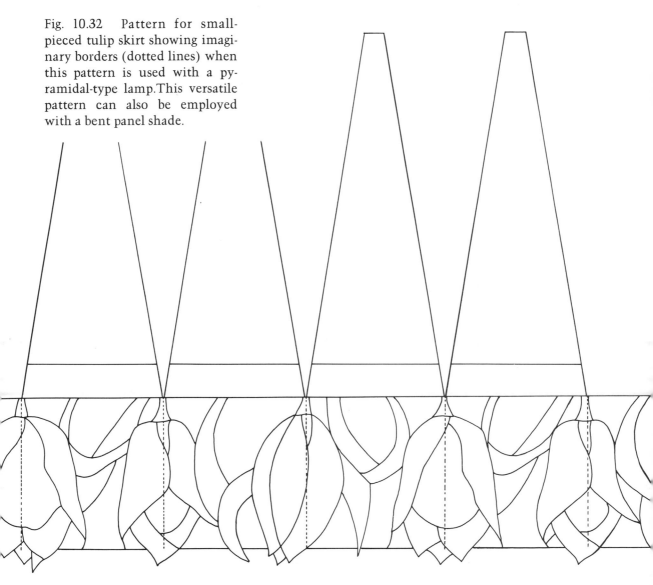

Fig. 10.33 Pattern for a small-pieced shade, large panel style.

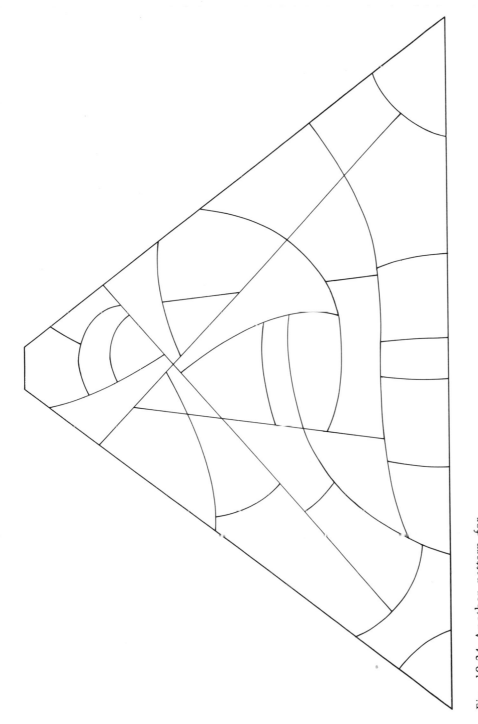

Fig. 10.34 Another pattern for the small-pieced shade in Fig. 10.33, second and fourth of above shade panels.

Chapter 11

The Bent Panel Lamp

By a bent panel lamp we mean a shade composed of panels which are molded by heat into a curve. (Fig. 11.1.) This curve can have a greater or lesser depth; it may have undercut surfaces or develop into an S bend—in reality, two curves within the same panel. The techniques used to form such curves may also be employed for bending small pieces of glass into decorative shapes—such as fruits or animals or birds—which can be used as internal designs within the panels of straight sided lamps or in skirts of either straight or bent panels.

CALCULATING THE DIMENSIONS

The curve of the panels determines the width of a bent panel lamp. Bent panels are almost always curved in two directions—length and width. Where they are a simple C shape curved only in length, little difficulty is found in planning them out as the curve they form will be the actual circle of the lamp. This is not necessarily so in panels that are curved not only top and bottom but side to side as well. This factor must be taken into consideration when deciding how these panels are going to come together. It is this outward, side to side curvature that determines how much of each panel will touch the neighboring one, for the edges of such panels form a slight dip as the circle progresses (Figs. 11.2, 11.3 and 11.4). Where a skirt is to be added, this dip must not become too extreme as a

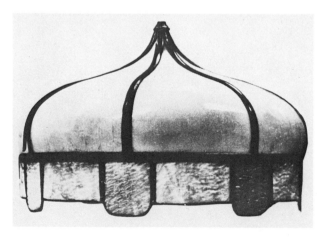

Fig. 11.1   A typical bent panel lamp. The juncture of each panel is hidden by a bent strut of brass.

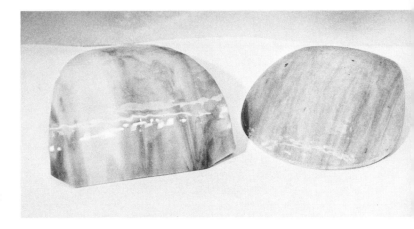

Fig. 11.2 Two types of bent panels.

Fig. 11.3 Bent panel lamp with straight, flared crown. Diamonds form a break between the panels.

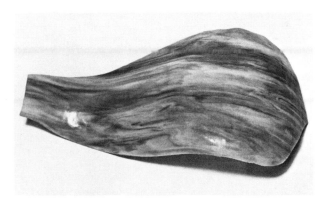

Fig. 11.4 S shape bent panel from Fig. 11.3.

circular base line is necessary to form the top line of the skirt. The slight dip of the panels can be compensated for in the leading. If you wish a more scalloped circumference, make your dips more acute but do not plan on a skirt—carry your panel lengths all the way down and let them be skirt and body all in one.

It is a good idea when calculating the dimension of any bent panel lamp to draw three circles to scale on graph paper (Fig. 11.5) as though you were looking at the lamp from the top. The smallest, inner circle would then represent the top hole; the next circle would represent the crown curving upwards; and the widest, outermost circle would show the bellies of the panels. This will give you an idea of the proportions of the space taken up by the crown and the panels. Your next step is to add a circle between the "belly" and "crown" circles which corresponds to the inward curve of the panels and shows the edges of these bowed pieces. Note that now, if you draw a curved line between each of these circles to represent a panel in cross section, you will have an idea of the depth of its curve. Go around the circle and fill in the number of panels you intend to place in the lamp. The slight curve of the panels will run into and follow arcs of the outer circle. Erase those portions of the outer line that are not under the curve of the panels, and a scalloped edge will appear around the circle. This is how your lamp will look; if the scallop is not to your liking, modify it. Since you are doing this on graph paper which you have previously calibrated, you will know just how deep your panels must bow out.

The length of the panel is a simpler matter. Cut a form out of pattern paper and decide how long you want it to be in its bent condition. Dealing only with this curvature, bend the pattern paper to follow. If it comes out too small, cut a larger form and rebend it. Once you are satisfied, measure the flat length of pattern paper and you will know how long a piece of copper you must cut to make this particular bend for the mold.

All of this is greatly simplified if you are not involved in making a bent panel lamp from its inception. If you have picked up a bent panel or two and want to make more of them to produce a lamp, you already know the type bend and the size of the panel; all you have to do is make the mold. However, we are assuming you have not managed to be that lucky and, anyway, you want to be able to say you have done all the work yourself.

Once you have calibrated your bend from side to side, formulated your up and down bend and decided upon your lamp's diameter, you may determine the circumference by pi times the diameter. Knowing the circumference would seem to allow you to figure out the width of each panel—but it doesn't. Remember: your panels are going to dip in slightly away from the true circumference, and so they must be slightly larger than will appear mathematically. However, the mathematical average that you get will allow you to calculate the widest point of the bent panel. If you were satisfied that this was the true measurement, bent your prototype panel inward and made the others from it, you would end up with a lamp smaller in diameter than you had originally calculated. The proper procedure is to bend your prototype panel to the predetermined curvature (at least from side to side) and then to measure it. Knowing how much of it is going to bend away from the circular circumference—what we refer to as the true circumference—will now allow you to make your next prototype panel that much larger. Bend your second prototype and check its measurements. If it is satisfactory, this is the one you will use to make your form.

All prototype panels should be made of a heavy, flexible metal (Fig. 11.6).

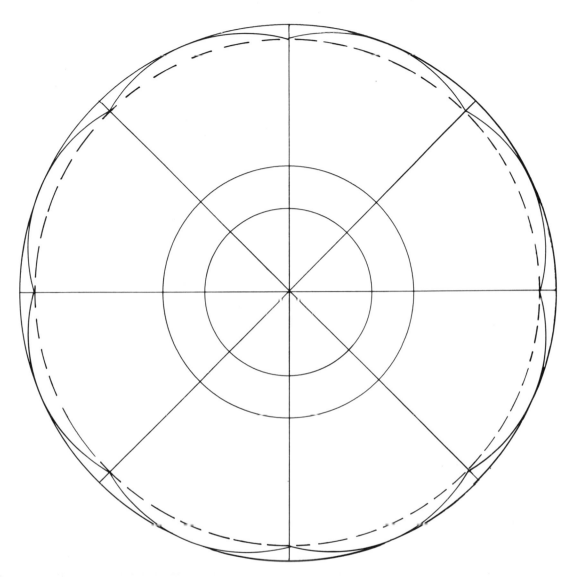

Fig. 11.5 Looking down on a
bent panel shade we see the inner (top) hole, the circle representing the crown, and the
bellies of the bent panels as they
meet the outer (true) circumference of the lamp. The inward
dips taken by each panel will
vary from one lamp to another.

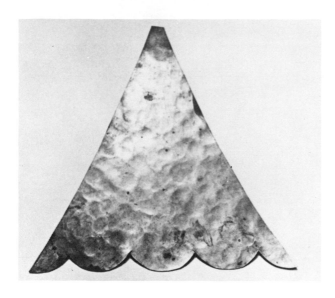

Fig. 11.6 Prototype metal panel.

We consistently use 1/32 inch copper sheeting. This sheeting is flexible enough to take the bends we want to impress upon it, strong enough to hold them, easy enough to cut with tinsnips to an exact size and firm enough to take the pressure against the mold material. The prototype panel must be made freehand. At least the bend is placed freehand on a panel formed from the pattern paper outline. Play with the bend and check all its measurements until you are sure you have it the way you want it. Check it against your original circle on graph paper by dropping perpendiculars from the widest section onto the scalloped circle to make sure it fits. Once you are satisfied that it does fit the predetermined circle of your lamp, put it aside and start making your mold.

DESIGNING THE MOLD

Our molds are not made to last. At the most we can get from twelve to fifteen firings from them before cracks develop and the mold falls to pieces. By that time we are either done with the panels or ready to make another mold.

For lamps with many panels—from twelve to sixteen—which have S shaped bends, we prefer to use red terra cotta for the mold material. Roll the terra cotta out to a flat sheet about one inch thick. Take the prototype copper panel and shape the clay by pressing it against the panel from the inside. Remove all waste clay as the form takes shape being careful not to push the prototype out of shape with the pressure used to mold the clay. Be careful when handling the clay that "thin spots" do not develop; thumbs are especially likely to dig into the clay. Try to maintain an inch of thickness between clay and copper. When the clay appears to be molded accurately to the inside copper surface, roll some more terra cotta into a ball, rough hew the top to approximate the shape of the panel and turn the prototype panel, with the clay attached, over onto this base. This base will help to prevent sagging of the raised underbelly of the panel. Tack the clay form to the base with slips of clay and, once it is secure, lift the copper form from the top. This should leave you with an exact duplicate of the inside measurements of the prototype panel.

This whole complex, base and panel mold, is placed in the kiln and either kiln wash or Kay Kinney's Mold Coat® is painted over it. We use the kiln wash wet and paint it on with a camel's hair brush. Once it is dry we fire the kiln to 1200°F and allow it to cool overnight (Figs. 11.7, 11.8 and 11.9). Without disturbing the humped mold beneath the wash, we fire the glass blanks which have been cut to the same form as the mold from the original pattern paper outline.

Fig. 11.7 Mold of terra cotta for a crown.

Fig. 11.8 The glass slumped into the mold.

Fig. 11.9 The final glass piece removed from the mold, which now can be reused.

We also use the plaster mixture Hydroperm® for making molds. This is mixed in that same useful rubber bowl we mentioned earlier, and a glob of it is placed on a piece of plywood. The copper prototype panel is forced into it so as to leave an outline of its shape; the plaster hardens and is placed in the kiln with the glass blank atop it. Hydroperm has less shrinkage than regular plaster. It is a good idea when using either this material or regular plaster to coat the inside of the copper prototype with a small amount of Vaseline® so that it doesn't stick to the plaster.

For firings requiring no more than two or three panels, we use regular casting plaster. This develops hairline cracks, usually from the first firing; these cracks become deeper with each successive firing until the mold becomes distorted and must be discarded.

HEATING THE MOLD

Glass blanks are fired as follows: The blank is measured by eye against the mold. The far edge of the blank is placed directly against the far edge of the mold—gently, so as not to disturb the kiln wash—and the rest of the blank is pivoted downward from that point until the whole shape lies atop the mold. The kiln is then fired.

The kiln is turned to medium with the top ajar for about fifteen minutes

Hanging Tiffany shade.

Standing Tiffany shade.
(Courtesy of Greta Vardi)

Mushroom lamp.
(Courtesy of Mike Rutler)

Figured Japanese night light.

for venting. The top is then closed and the kiln is turned to high. Watch the pyrometer closely; it is better not to be guided by cones in this regard. At about 1200°F check the panel—it should bend between 1200 and 1250°F. S curves take a higher heat than C curves.

This type of "draping" procedure for firing panels can go awry if the panel is not placed exactly on the mold. Because you are dealing with a curved mold and a straight panel, you may find that what looked like a good lie when you started results in an offset panel in the end. One way to hedge your bet here is to give the panel as much room to sag as possible. The sides of the mold may prevent it from sagging—being even a tiny bit off the mark may hang up one side of the panel and prevent its slumping onto the mold. Before removing the copper prototype, flatten out three sides of the clay with your finger to the level of the impressed copper. This will make new sides for the mold and extend the curve of the mold so that if the panel is just a little crooked on the mold, it will still slump 99 percent properly. This is probably more than enough to fit most shapes, but if you have trouble with an improperly slumped panel, do not attempt to redo it. More than likely, the second firing will crack it. Better to throw it away and try another blank.

Remember to reshape only three sides of a mold. You will need the fourth side—we prefer the side uppermost—to guide the panel to a proper seating. It is easier for it to fall onto a wide surface than into a slot; even so, without one side to position it by, there is no way to tell how it should be placed. Not all panels are balanced atop their mold. Some are decidedly top-heavy, depending on their shape. This does not mean they will not slump correctly. Follow the side you left as a guide and however the panel lies, let it alone. It may happen that the panel appears crooked and you let it alone with misgivings only to find a perfect slump occurring. You can't tell by eye how the panel should lie on the mold.

It is more difficult to make smaller bent objects in the kiln via the drape method. The panel, obviously, being heavier is more responsive to gravity and will fold better than a smaller, lighter piece of glass. Bent fruit such as apples, pears, bananas, and plums may be produced (Fig. 11.10) though you may have to go higher with your heat to do so. Don't attempt strawberries, however.

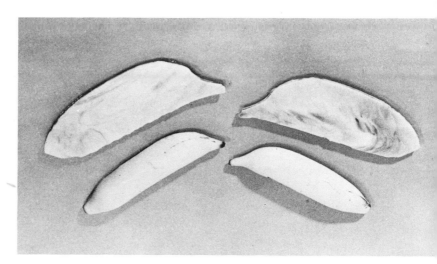

Fig. 11.10 Bananas, before and after being curved and painted.

Another method of bending small pieces of glass to shape—crowns of lamps, for example—is by carving out a piece of firebrick and sagging the glass into it. Sagging works better than draping for small pieces as more of the weight of the glass comes into play. Firebrick molds can last a long time.

There are also molds that you can purchase, rather than make, for glass bending and specifically for lamps. Kay Kinney offers curver molds to fit glass globe lights which can be leaded or attached with heat resistant cement. Such globes come with instructions. Butterfly and floral patterns are available, and these shapes may also be used in the skirts of lamps.

Never use anything other than a kiln to bend large pieces of glass—from strawberry to panel size. We are continually amazed by the number of people who are under the impression that a blowtorch can be employed to make such bends. Not only is this idea erroneous, it is dangerous. Using a blowtorch to bend a panel would explode the glass, since glass is a very poor conductor of heat. If you don't have a kiln, you don't bend glass. It's that simple.

If you do have a kiln, however, you can also make your own glass globs. This is not only fun, it's expensive—it's cheaper to buy them. However, you can get combinations of colors that you just can't buy, and you may just like to say you've done it. Part of the fun is not knowing what you are going to come up with. Certain clear streakies will become lovely opaque rivers of color in no way matching the hues you started with. Add these to your lamp panels and you will have an item distinctly your own. Glass globs are made by cutting scrap glass into small squares and laying them in the kiln shelves which are covered by sheet carbon (Fig. 11.11). This latter item is essential so that the molten globs can "crawl" together. We have tried almost everything else—including steel sheeting—and nothing worked like the carbon. Sheet carbon is not cheap, and it lasts only about four firings since each firing diminishes it. So to get the most out of it, cut up some of your prettiest cathedral glass—opalescents will not melt well—and try them in the kiln. Again, no blowtorch. Kiln heat here is 2400°F.

USING THE KILN

We recommend a top-loading kiln 18 by 18 inches and a foot deep. These dimensions give you the room you need to bend panels, and the top door allows

Fig. 11.11 Carbon sheeting for making glass globs. The sheet on the left has been through four firings; that on the right, two.

178   THE BENT PANEL LAMP

you the proper approach. If you can fit them in, you can bend several at a time, provided they are the same color.

Not all colors bend at the same temperature. Reds and greens, for instance, take a higher heat. This is unfortunate because if the heat gets too high both of these colors tend to a certain amount of "burn out." With the green opalescent glass, the darker greens may go brownish; reds, both opalescent and cathedral, go orange. The temperature is especially critical with the reds as there is only a small margin of heat allowable before the color change. Greens have a wider margin of safety. Another advantage of the top-loading kiln, therefore, is that one can pick up the door in midfiring and check the panel's color and shape. Caramel opalescents must also be watched, as the brown color tends to burn out at temperatures approaching 1350°F.

If you have a red panel that is rather complicated in shape, for example, an S curve with a severe lower end undercut, you had better watch it closely, because the heat needed to bend this particular shape may be too much for the color. We try to handle undercut shapes by taking the panel up to 1200 or 1250°F and using a long, flat steel rod to push the glass of the undercut against the mold. Needless to say, it is a good idea to wear a pair of heavy mitts while doing this. As soon as that top door is open, the kiln begins losing heat at an alarming rate, so you don't have much time to get the glass in shape. If you push too hard in the center, the ends will flare; a subtle nudging of the overall rim is best. You may have to do this in several stages, opening the door and closing it again to allow the panel to come back up to heat. It sounds like a rather brutal treatment of the panel, but it is sometimes the only way to get the shape. Surprisingly enough we have never had a panel break from this treatment. As long as the glass is moldable, it will respond to being tickled a little. It also helps, if you are dealing with a severely undercut panel, to tilt the mold so gravity is allowed to play as much as possible to your advantage. With the undercut end uppermost, the glass tends to fall against it more readily.

If you intend doing any number of bent panels, get yourself a kiln sitter. This mechanical device (not your spouse) will automatically turn the kiln off when the proper temperature is reached. Before we got one, we were constantly having panels ruined from overfiring. No matter how you try to watch them, you get involved doing something else—and then there is that scamper back to the kiln to find shards of melted glass all over and the mold in pieces. To add insult to injury, you have to wait twice as long for the kiln to cool enough to refire. Of course you can, if you get back before the glass melts to rivulets, get some interesting shapes from overfiring—nothing you can use in your lamp, but intriguing pieces, nonetheless. But only three or four degrees can turn a lot of work and effort into a disaster.

Although we prefer an electric kiln for convenience, glass bending can certainly be done in a gas kiln—or even a wood-burning kiln for that matter—providing you have enough depth so that the heat approaches the panel from all sides at once. This applies as well to the mold. You must be careful when making your mold that you don't trap any air within it. If you do, your mold will probably blow up in the kiln. This does your panel no good. (See Fig. 11.12.)

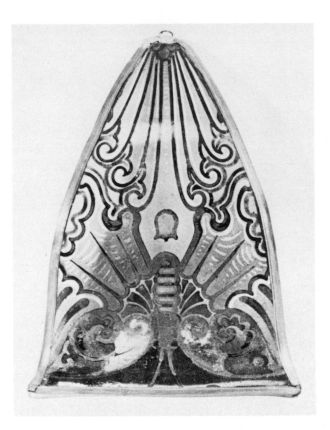

Fig. 11.12 Some panels are curved and painted at the same time.

Once the glass bend, inspected by eye through the top of the kiln, is seen to be satisfactory, the kiln is shut off. We cool the kiln as quickly as possible contrary to what many authorities say. We have experimented with slow cooling by keeping the door shut until the pyrometer reads zero, with medium slow cooling by opening the door from 1000 to 300 degrees and closing it again to zero, and with rapid cooling by just opening the door as soon as the kiln is shut off and allowing it to go to zero. We have noticed absolutely no difference in the glass—except, of course, that it cools faster so we can pop in another piece quicker. The molds take the thermal shock less well, but even they hold up much better than one might think. Whatever shortening of their lifespan is involved, to our minds at least, what is saved in time by rapid cooling is worth it. By rapid cooling, we are not speaking of "cracking" the kiln—opening the door a small amount. We open it all the way. Just keep your face out of the way when you do; the hot air rising will singe your eyebrows.

PUTTING THE LAMP TOGETHER

Once all your panels are done, check to make certain they are pretty much the same. You may have to cut some of them down, here and there. Don't worry about it; it isn't difficult. When we make bent fruit, we generally make the pieces larger than necessary just to be on the safe side and then trim them to fit.

Trimming bent panels, while not difficult, is tricky. The glass is under a strain from the bending, and the wrong type of pressure may well fracture it.

Since it is bent, it is impractical (though not impossible) to use a glass cutter on it. We do all our trimming with the grozing pliers and then smooth off the grozed surfaces with an electric wet belt. You don't have to own an electric wet belt; wetted pieces of Carborundum paper can be used by hand. If you are using any electrical glass-sanding device do not hold the glass stationary against it no matter how much water you are using; the glass will chip and crack. Keep the glass moving and don't exert much pressure. Don't attempt to take off large amounts of glass with any electric grinding machine; sooner or later the whole panel will crack. The wet belt, either power-driven or used by hand, is meant only for finishing off edges of either straight or bent glass pieces where the surfaces are ragged.

If we have to trim a piece of bent glass, we first mark the excess with a red glass-marking pencil or crayon. Some marking is imperative as you cannot tell by eye alone how much is to be removed from any area. If you are going to put the glass back in the kiln for reheating, be sure the red pencil marks are thoroughly removed or they will bake into the surface. Acetone is a good solvent for cleaning these marks off. With the red line as a guide we take our grozing pliers and begin gently taking off the excess glass by either an upwards or downwards motion of the pliers depending on the slant of the involved edge. The tendency to become impatient and take off too much must be overcome as a large bite will probably split the panel. Make certain as you go that no small crumbs of glass are caught in the jaws of your pliers. Glass splinters in the teeth will act as small levers against the surface, and again, a broken panel will result. Blow into the grozing teeth to clean them as you go along and tap the jaws against the tabletop to knock the larger pieces of glass out of them. Use the teeth in a filing motion as the jaws grab and break. When you get down to your red line, recheck the size of the panel to make certain that you will not be going too far by taking the line away. Sometimes the thickness of your pencil point can mean the difference between a panel that fits and one that doesn't. Don't check these panels for size by placing them one atop the next, or you will end up with a short panel. None, or few, of the panels bent according to our instructions will measure up this way, for you are really measuring the inside width of one against the outside width of the next. Measure instead your bent panels edge to edge by rolling the side of one, starting at a specified point, against the side of the next. We say "roll" because the sides are curved, and you must compensate for this. You can then tell if you are short or long on the sides; it really isn't that critical along the curve. You can do only one panel at a time this way. Measure all the panels against the same panel. Try to arrange the two panels as part of their natural circle when you compare them.

Let us assume all your panels are correctly fired, grozed to size, belted smooth and ready to be put together (Fig. 11.13). Rim each with the lead or foil you intend to use. (If foil, each rim of this material must be heavily tinned before the panels are put together.) Place two panels together along their natural curve and tack them with solder top, middle and bottom. Place another alongside them and tack it. Depending on the curve, these three may be able to stand. If so, keep adding panels and tacking them until you have the circle completed.

Fig. 11.13 Start of a bent panel shade—the panels arranged in a circle.

Each panel, tacked, should have enough play in it to allow you to maneuver it so that the circle will close. Be careful, when manipulating them, that the panels do not come away from their copper rims. Each panel should support the next to provide strength to the lamp; if the copper rims come away from the sides of any particular panel, there is a strain pattern developing which must be corrected immediately. More than likely there is a problem with the design somewhere. Do not attempt to force the panels into their rims. If worse comes to worst you may have to unhook them all and start over, but that's why you only tacked them to begin with.

If your panels are so designed that they will not stand until a lot of them are tacked together, you might use a stand of some sort for each panel. Some Plasticine clay makes a good base, but don't use so much that it gets in the way. Your panels will stand upright and you will be able to work on them with both hands. You will probably need both hands.

If you intend to disguise the seam between panels by employing a filigree of brass from crown to base along the curvature of the shade, the brass can be prebent to this curvature by the following method (Fig. 11.14):

1. Acquire a small sheet of Styrofoam at least an inch thick.

2. Take one of your bent panels and place it on edge over the Styrofoam.

3. Cut into the Styrofoam to either side along the bottom edge of the panel.

4. Take away the glass and remove the sliver of Styrofoam between the cuts. You now have a curved slot in the styrofoam corresponding to the curvature of the lamp.

5. Cut your brass to size and bend it into the Styrofoam slot. Make your bends emphatic as brass is flexible and does not always retain an impressed shape well.

6. Solder the brass strip to the shade top and bottom. If there is a space between panels due to their curvature anywhere along their edge, use this space to solder the brass to the panel rims from behind. Do not hold the brass with your bare hands during soldering; brass, like copper, gets hot.

Fig. 11.14 An old bent panel tulip shade. Note the filigree work between panels and the thin, outer edge of brass. These panels are hard to replace; there is absolutely no margin for error because of this edging.

Some lamps are hard to assemble on the worktable because of their size or because they are fragile until fully formed. Their own weight cannot be supported until enough solder is applied, and they will undergo a process of gradual deflation on the worktable. This may take the wind out of your sails as well and lead you to brace pieces with excess solder that you will only have to get rid of later. This difficulty is found not only with bent panel lamps but also with small-pieced lamps. The constant tipping and turning that may well be necessary for both of these types of production may best be alleviated by getting the lamp off the worktable altogether and hanging it on a chain from the ceiling. Now you can tip it any way you want and work on one side without the opposing side giving way. The nuisance here is that the lamp bumps and swings away from you and you may need to keep steadying it. However, this is still less frustrating than keeping the lamp on the worktable. The best way to support such lamps is by an oversize vase cap under the center hole. This will allow the lamp to tip in any direction you wish. Naturally you had best make sure it is well supported from the ceiling.

The glass from which you make your bent panels may appear to have lost its sheen after firing. This gloss is easily burnt away and easily replaced, but do not try to replace it until your lamp is all finished and cleaned. Then spray the panels (never paint them) with a clear lacquer (we use Bond's Mirror Clear Glaze® which is quick drying and requires only one application).

Some of these larger, more complicated shades can be worked on comfortably by two people—indeed, some of them all but call for two people. If you have been occupying yourself with your lamp-making hobby, perhaps now is the time to get a friend into the act—your wife or husband may qualify as such. He or she may have been quietly sitting by all this time waiting for a summons. Generate your own electricity and make your lamps a family affair!

THE BENT PANEL LAMP   183

PART III

Postscript

Chapter 12

Selling Your Work

There may come a time when making objects is not enough. For a variety of reasons, the hobbyist may wish to sell some of his lamps. The sad truth is that one is not going to make a killing selling lamps. You will never make a great deal of money from any craft—unless you are very lucky (not necessarily very good—just very lucky). Many hobbyists wouldn't sell their wares regardless of how much they were offered; if you are one of them, you may as well skip this chapter; but if you wish to make your hobby pay its own way, you should have no aversion to parting with a lamp now and then. And if you belong to the latter group, this chapter may guide you.

ADVERTISING

If you are interested in making lamps for sale, you are basically interested in obtaining clients who will give you commissions. It is unlikely that people will seek you out if they have not heard of you. They will hear of you in only one way: advertising.

To become known in your chosen field, spread the word around that you are willing, able and available. It is not enough to be only one of those three possibilities; you must be all of them. Have enough of your completed projects around so that people can see you are able; tailor-make projects for specific precincts so they reflect your willingness; and keep prices reasonable enough to classify you as available. That's the whole secret. Well, perhaps there are a few other things you can do.

TALKING TO GROUPS

You may be invited to speak at various functions of hospital auxiliaries, garden clubs, PTAs, civic leagues, Rotary Clubs, library luncheons. In all these meetings, the business completed, that moment comes when the guest speaker is announced. Anybody in the area doing anything interesting may be asked to fill this slot. It may well be you. If you have never spoken to a group before and are nervous about speaking in public, bring a prepared set of notes and don't worry about consulting them from time to time. Don't bring a prepared speech and read from it. No matter how interesting the content, nothing is more boring than listening to someone read a talk. You might as well just send copies to the audience and stay home. You can bring examples of your work, but be sure to bring an extension cord as well so you can show how your lamps look when lit. People love to see things, and it is much more effective to show the lamps than just to tell about them.

Before accepting an invitation to such a gathering it would behoove you to make certain of the time. Some thoughtless groups might tell you to show up at nine o'clock, for instance, and you will find, on arriving at that hour, that the business part of the meeting is in full swing with little sign of slowing down. You can fiddle around in the background for half an hour or so until you actually get to the podium. You should explain to the chairman that you wish to arrive at the time you are scheduled to start the talk.

Make certain of the interest. It is disconcerting to be announced and watch most of the audience leave. They may not give a hang about lamps. We always ask how large a group is going to be present and then divide the number we are given by half so we know whether the trip is going to be worthwhile. Sheer number, of course, doesn't always make the difference. We have spoken to audiences of ten and to groups of several hundred, and we sometimes get more response from the lesser crowd. If you are really interested in selling your work, however, it is a pretty good bet that the more people you can reach at one time, the better your chances of picking up a client or two.

Make sure you are given at least a token payment for your talk. A token payment is better than nothing at all for several reasons. First, what is paid for is valued more than what is gotten for free. If you are free, anybody can afford you, and you really do not need this type of group. If they are too stingy to offer you anything for your time and information, they are surely going to harbor few, if any, individuals who are likely sources of commissions. Even more important is the feeling you will get of being "had." This feeling is not good either for your self-esteem or your reputation. Second, being a paid speaker, and therefore an authority, can only help your reputation. Third, if you are being paid, you will put more time and effort into your presentation. Most groups have a "kitty" from which they deduct the costs of their various social events. Don't be afraid to ask them to tap it for you. The more important groups will ask if there is a fee for your talk—unless they are so important that just speaking before them is reward enough. This is for you to decide.

Keep your talk within its allotted time span. If you don't, you may have to leave out the most important parts because of stirrings among the audience. If that doesn't warn you to end it, the chairman will.

Your talk should be informal and friendly. Permit your audience to relate to as much of it as possible. Don't speak over their heads or down to them or you will lose them. Every audience wants to give its speaker every chance—at first. Once you lose them, however, you will have a very difficult time getting them back.

CRAFT MAGAZINE DISPLAYS

Placing your name in a display ad in one of the many craft magazines now available is also good advertisement. This serves more of a purpose if you are selling items through the mail than if you are selling locally. Lamp kits, for example, can be sold this way. Of course, someone from your area may see your ad and come to you, but this is more likely to happen through ads in the local paper. If you are selling lamps on a mail-order basis, draw up a tasteful ad and find out the magazine rates for placing it in the various sizes offered. You don't have to take up a whole page to be noticed. One-eighth page ads of the display variety will be quite noticeable to anyone who is interested; for those who are not interested, a full page ad is not enough. Remember that many hobbyists read the ads in craft magazines with care looking for suppliers. The first place they look is in the display ads; the last place they look, if they look there at all, is in the classified section, and they look there only if they have found nothing to their liking among the displays. If you can afford an ad at all, it should be a display ad; but if you really can't afford a display ad, try a classified.

How do you choose a magazine in which to place an ad? It's a good idea to study past issues to find out what level of the market the magazine is aimed at. Is it a specialty magazine, and if so, is it your specialty? There is little use advertising stained glass in a journal devoted to bottle collectors, or precut kits in a journal going to professional studios. Ceramics magazines, on the other hand, are good choices for advertising stained glass kits as many ceramists are familiar enough with the glass field to want to try it but afraid to cut the glass themselves. Your best bet, however, is probably the general crafts magazine, and among these you have to choose the tone of the one that suits you.

Circulation figures alone can be misleading. We would rather have our ad seen by three hundred interested readers than by three thousand readers who couldn't care less. Find out which of the general crafts magazines run articles about stained glass. The interest of their readers has already been aroused; an ad here is more likely to bring results.

Study the other ads as you go through various publications. Are there other stained glass places advertising? What is good for them may be good for you—or is there too much competition? Maybe you will not all be advertising the same things. If you are, you must arrange your ad to call the most attention to itself. Can you outface the ads already placed? If not, you had better go elsewhere.

We never advertise in a crafts magazine that does not have an index of advertisers. This useful listing, generally in the back of the book, is the first thing many readers turn to in order to see as quickly as possible what is available. Even if the reader goes through the pages first, he will often check this back listing to make certain he has missed nothing. This is a big advantage these magazines have over newspaper advertising. Lack of such a roll call can mean that your ad will be skipped over.

The last consideration is the rate. If all else looks good, the rate is worth it, providing it fits your budget; if all else does not look good, the rate is too expensive no matter how cheap.

Remember that no advertising can be judged by one submission. You can only judge accurately how much an ad is helping your business by maintaining it for a period of time—three or four issues of the magazine, at least. You may pull the ad at the fifth issue just as it is starting to show results. We get responses to ads in magazines months, sometimes years, after that particular issue came out. People don't throw magazines away rapidly—another advantage they have over newspapers—and libraries keep magazines for a considerable time, so your ad stays alive much longer than you may think.

DEALING WITH CLIENTS

The client's responsibility toward you begins with a conception—hazy or concrete—and ends with the payment for that conception's fruition. Your responsibility toward the client is to give him exactly what he wants—no less and, certainly, no more—to the best of your ability. Striving to overplease the client, to give him even more than he has asked for, can bring even those workers who should know better to grief. Artistic ad libbing might be fine for a lamp to be hung in your own home; not everyone, however, shares your exalted tastes, and unfortunately, the client may be one who does not. It is surprising the number of commissions we have seen rejected because the worker was trying to give the client more than he wanted. The client is certainly within his rights to refuse such an offering or to accept it but refuse to pay the extra charges. Remember that you are working for someone else; don't think you know better than he what is good for him, or you will more than likely be unpleasantly surprised.

On the other hand, once the client has decided, he must allow you to do the job without changing his mind in midstream. Fluctuations of purpose on his part may seriously hamper your giving him what he asked for originally. You are entitled to be protected against this. The client must understand that once he has decided on design, colors and dimension, the lamp will be delivered to him just that way. A down payment which is not returnable should close this agreement. If he moves to another apartment, gets a new rug or changes the color of his wallpaper while you are at work on his lamp, you are not obliged to change his lamp accordingly. For you to do so would involve you in the creation of an entirely different lamp with, most likely, an entirely different fee.

It is imperative that a written agreement be made between artist and client describing what is to be done. If you are being commissioned by friends, it is even more important that such an agreement be drawn up. You may lose both friends and fee otherwise.

LAMP KITS

As far as we are concerned, the only way to send lamps by any carrier is in kit form. When we were making lamps for gift shops and department stores, our breakage ratio was seventy percent. This ratio applied whether the lamp went via UPS, Railway Express, the postal service or even registered, insured mail. We got a lot of returns despite the special boxes we had made. We used every packing material we could think of—including popcorn. The lamps didn't always break in the same places. Sometimes it was in the panels, sometimes the skirts. Your profits (such as they are to begin with) can vanish pretty swiftly this way.

Kits are not subject to this problem. First of all, they are packed flat and can take more rough handling than the three-dimensional finished product. Then too, even if a panel or two does break, that much can be easily replaced without any real labor.

If you intend to go into the lamp kit business—and there is a crying need for this sort of thing—get an attractive brochure made up, in color if you can afford it, showing what your finished kit lamps look like. List the specific colors that are available, but be sure to insist that potential buyers make an alternate choice to cover yourself. The way the glass field is today, colors are not always available when you want them. Have pertinent instructions drawn for the construction of each style lamp. All glass should be cut and wet belted so that no rough edges are left. All leads should be cut to fit. If foil is to be used, that should be included in the kit with instructions as to its use. Wrap everything well and label it. It is a good idea to include all the electrical material as well. The customer should not have to buy any material at a store to supplement what your kit provides. The one place you can skimp is in the labeling. Unlike kits sold in stores, mail-order kits need not attract customers by their colorful packaging, so a simple label can be affixed. This allows you to provide more on the inside than on the outside—a reversal of the customary store kit.

Each item in your kit must be well wrapped and the kit enclosed in a sturdy box. It is then ready to go. Even the most well-wrapped kit is subject to breakage. Have a time limit as to how long the customer has to apply for replacements; otherwise, if he is inept in putting the kit together, you may end up paying for his own breakages. You could end up sending several lamp kits free without a time limit clause.

Insure all your kits. If you have a tendency to lose individual pieces of paper, get a "firm mailing book" from your local post office. This book is for use in acceptance of insured, C.O.D. and certified mail. It provides a daily listing of what you send, the date and the insurance number. This way you can keep all your mailings in one place and always on tap.

CONSIGNMENTS

We do not feel that lamps should be put in any gift store—and certainly not in any department store—on a consignment basis. We would not think of putting our product in a home on such a basis; why allow it to dress up someone else's precincts for free? The same rule applies to places of business. Most stores know whether or not they can sell a particular product. If they can, they will have no qualms about buying something outright for resale, if they can't, and they can get something like a stained glass lamp on consignment, what have they got to lose? Your lamp can sit in their store indefinitely as part of the decor, and you aren't even getting a rental fee. You have probably put a lot of time and effort into your lamp, but someone else is reaping the profit. We feel that if a store wants one of our lamps, they should pay for it. We couldn't get one of their items on consignment; why should they get one of ours?

All the same, circumstances may provide opportunities for brief consignments. Art or ceramic exhibitions may be held in local gift shops, and stained glass lamps may well serve to dress up the background. Here, used as part of the display, they serve as free advertising for the creator and may well be loaned on that basis. If you have gotten your products into one of these displays, make sure your card is on them. You may end up getting more out of the show than the primary displayer.

Chapter 13

Teaching

ADVANTAGES OF TEACHING

The old saw, if you can't do, teach, has gotten pretty rusty over the years. The fact of the matter is that, in the craft field at least, some of the best doers are also teachers. The fascination of teaching is closely intertwined with an enjoyment of what one does and an unselfish desire to spread the technique to others who may join you in such enjoyment. Teaching is also a very good way of advertising yourself and your products. Being associated with a school or a college will not hurt your reputation in the least, and though the pay is not overwhelming, it can come in handy.

The entire stained glass field is so new that in most institutions the demand for teachers far exceeds the supply. Instructors, rather than teachers, are hired on an emergency basis, and many of these really know very little more about the subject than their students. Unless such individuals are pretty adept at staying ahead of the class, they will soon be overcome. A book such as this may provide some extra distance, but even if your own knowledge of teaching is extensive, you may find that teaching workers in stained glass poses particular teaching problems. We will get to that, shortly.

WHERE TO TEACH

Colleges are the best places to teach, and a number of community colleges are now offering stained glass as an elective within the arts curriculum. Colleges pay the best and usually have the best working conditions and the most serious students. Next in line are the high schools with evening extension courses. Both in suburbia and in the large cities, an increase in those persons suddenly hungering for knowledge about things they were never taught in school—or never taught well—has formed a respectable body calling for information.

High schools accommodate a large number of these individuals, and if the school is comparatively new and really interested, it can be a pleasant situation for both teachers and students. If the school is run-down and interested only in the tuition, the entire course can be a disaster. We have taught in both types of institutions, and where the first maintained spanking-clean classrooms, proper heating and lighting and courtesy to all, the second gave us drafty prefabs with cola puddles and wadded up newspapers on the floor. Nine times out of ten the latter forgot a class was to be held and had the door locked in our face. A good part of our teaching program was spent hunting the custodian to open up the door. Then we would have to locate him again to fix the lights.

It's a good idea to take a long look at any school you are going to be teaching in. Don't look for a proper setup for stained glass—none of them have that—but at least make sure the room you are to teach in is comfortable and has running water and a reasonable amount of baseboard sockets. Also, check the lighting. If you do not find the room satisfactory, let the school know. They may have a better one and be unaware of your requirements. It's also a good idea to check for parking, since you will probably be carrying supplies to class to demonstrate with. If you have to walk three blocks on a cold winter evening panting under your load just to get in the door, it will take a lot of the sparkle out of your instruction.

Before you sign a contract, find out how many students you will be teaching. Partly because they may not know themselves, partly because they may have to cancel out the course if the requisite registration is not forthcoming and they don't want to lose you as a teacher, schools are not apt to give you this information much before the actual start of the class. Some schools don't base their courses on any specific number of applicants; be wary of these. The dropout rate in any evening course is at least twenty-five percent (or so we have been informed by instructors in other subjects) and you may find yourself, at the halfway mark, giving all but individual instruction. This may not be what you have signed up to do. It is one thing to teach, quite another to tutor. The more in your class, the merrier, up to a point, of course. It is nice to be popular, but it can also be pretty exhausting. Try to get the school to limit the number of applicants, but on the other hand, insist on a minimum enrollment if the school does not already do so.

A BASIC CURRICULUM

If we had our way, no beginning class project would be designed to fit a specific area in the student's home. For one thing, this initial attempt is basically to familiarize the student with materials and techniques new to him, and his executed finished product will reflect that fact. More than likely it will be the worst thing he ever turns out from the standpoint of design. His all-thumbs approach to cutting and leading the rigid boundaries of such a fixed spatial projection as a lampshade will, in most instances, force the teacher to take over and salvage what he can from the mess. This mixed bag of tricks is then proudly hung before the student's front door as an example of what he did in stained glass class—with, he hastens to add fairly, teacher's help. The wretched teacher, thus made an unwilling collaborator, is trapped between the devil of his student's unwarranted ambition and the deep blue sea of his own sinking professional pride. His only recourse is to stand outside the house and throw rocks. Why so many individuals come to class determined that their initial endeavor will be the lampshade of their dreams eludes us. They end up with a compromised product and a halting knowledge of the craft. The latter doesn't seem to bother them; what bothers us is their complacent acceptance of the former as a valid reason for taking the class. It is, we suppose, a cheap way of acquiring a lamp, but then, it's a pretty cheap lamp so acquired.

Ever since our first attempt at teaching stained glass, we have insisted that all students start with a simple panel unless they have had considerable prior experience. Only then can they start with a lamp, and a simple one at that. It is not easy to put the artistic brakes on individuals who want to start right in making lamps, but experience has taught us it is by far the best way. If they can design, cut and lead a rectangular or square panel, they have acquired some familiarity with the alphabet of stained glass. They will need it.

ACQUIRING SELF-CONFIDENCE

You must take control of your class at the very beginning. It is easy for the neophyte to be daunted by his students. Evening classes, especially, contain a good percentage of fairly substantial members of the middle class, and you may tend to feel uncomfortably grateful to them for coming to be taught by you. Don't let them know it. There is usually a leader or two among the students who has read a book or cut himself on a piece of glass and who now considers himself an authority on the subject. If you don't let him know his place immediately, members of the class will start going to *him* for instruction. If such a person exists in your class, it is probably the best thing that could happen to you; your ego, being threatened, will respond, and you'll be surprised at how fast your self-confidence expands once you find how much more you know than he does. Even without this stimulus, however, you will find your students in general a friendly lot, there to enjoy themselves and learn what you have to teach them. You probably will not realize just how much you do know until you find how little they do. Once this comes home to you, you will find yourself enjoying the luxury of elaborating on a subject you revel in to eager listeners.

OUTLINING YOUR COURSE

Start the first class with a brief history of stained glass, explain what glass is and how to handle it without being injured. Since most people are afraid of glass, it is necessary to allay their fears without at the same time minimizing the results of carelessness. Don't overwhelm your students with a lot of detail, but get right into the technique of using the glass cutter. It is best if you bring scrap window glass to this first meeting. If you have extra glass cutters, bring them and pass them out with the scrap glass so each student can follow you as you demonstrate. Classes should never be longer than two hours; attention seems to flag after this period of time. Between the introductory remarks and the practice session, the initial class will be pretty full.

In the week between the first and the second meetings, the student should sketch and design a simple panel to bring to the next class. Once this is checked to make sure it can be accommodated to the medium, the student may begin to select, cut and lead his stained glass. He will now travel at his own rate through the succeeding classes under your guidance. The products he accumulates along the way, for good or bad, will testify to both your ability to teach and his to learn.

HOW NOT TO TEACH A CLASS

A pyrotechnic display of economic genius was produced in one of our early classes by an individual who suggested that everybody share tools instead of buying them individually. Before we knew it, a precedent had been established which led to more than a little bickering as the semester wore on. There never seemed to be enough of any one tool to go around, and pilgrimages through the room of individuals clutching unfinished pieces and looking for instruments became common. It was interesting to note that the group leader who had started all this had yet to present a single tool to the cooperative, though most of them—even leading nails—seemed to accumulate at his working area. He finally took a soldering iron to work with at home and somehow never remembered to bring it back. Then he took a few more tools home to work with and never came back himself. There was considerable skittishness and dark undertones among the class members after this, a good deal of which seemed to be directed at the instructors.

We have since made it a standing suggestion that only two students could share tools. It also helps if each student carves his name on his tools; these items have a habit of walking off. We ourselves, if we lend things, make sure we know where they are. Even as a teacher, you are entitled to leave for home with what you brought. If you lend one of your tools to a student and he lends it to someone else, you are likely not to see it again. Any student to whom we lend a tool is responsible for it. If you tell this to the class at the first meeting, no misunderstandings will occur. It is much better to get these facts out in the open immediately than to have them creep nastily into the atmosphere later on.

It was in this class, as well, that we had our first experience of students who were totally unprepared to do so making lamps. Despite our warnings, they plunged ahead until, overcome by technical difficulties, they went back to the training panel we had suggested initially. Only two persevered with their lamps. One went through two full sheets of opalescent glass without coming up with a single usable lampshade panel. She ended up gluing her scrap pieces into a free-form design to a piece of plate glass and muttering to herself. The other fabricated a truly formidable looking object which she proudly declared was going to be mounted over her kitchen table. "I'll never have coffee at her house," one pessimistic pupil was heard to remark. And indeed, the lamp, when she held it up for all to see, rattled alarmingly. The artist, herself, was disconcerted enough to put it quickly back on the table. It was well she did so, for three panels fell right out, and after a moment, two more followed. This lamp did little for anybody's morale, least of all the creator's. She ran screaming from the room.

HELPFUL TEACHING TECHNIQUES

1. Describe your course as fully as possible in the school brochure. This will give potential students an idea of what you are going to be doing over the course of the term so they can plan accordingly.

2. Describe your qualifications for teaching the subject. A name with no background is eminently forgettable.

3. Type out a list of supplies each student is to provide himself with and

distribute this list at the first class. If possible, add to this list several suppliers who will have the material in stock.

4. The recommendation of books on stained glass to be used as textbooks may help. Make certain, if you recommend a book, that it is not out of print. Needless to say, it is a good idea to have read such books yourself.

5. Do not encourage your students to help one another even if one has more experience than another. If someone in the class has a question, he should turn to you for help. Otherwise, he may just pick up his neighbor's bad habits.

6. At the same time, don't get trapped into a situation where, out of sympathy or disgust, you end up virtually doing a student's entire project for him. He will not learn anything that way.

7. Do not let anyone cut stained glass until he is thoroughly proficient at using a glass cutter on scrap window glass. That includes straight lines and curves.

8. No student should proceed with work at home until all steps have been checked in class.

9. Don't be afraid to make people take things apart. Solder works both ways—it can come unstuck, too. If you allow shoddy work to pass, your name will always be associated with it.

10. Cleanup time in any class should be announced fifteen minutes before the period is over. To avoid accidents, you should stay until all the students have left. If you don't start them cleaning up at this time you will be putting in a lot of extra time for nothing.

11. You must allow a certain leeway as far as tools are concerned. Tools are expensive, and if the students want to try to make do with what they have at home—within reason—let them. Certain items, such as glass cutter, glass pliers and grozing pliers, cannot be replaced. The approximate cost and absolute necessity for such tools should be stated in the initial description of your course in the school catalogue.

12. Keep bandages available. A good teacher will always know what the glass will do; he will never know what the class will do. Students tend to get careless, and despite the fact that glass, if handled correctly, is not a dangerous material, familiarity can breed contempt among some individuals. We do not keep our bandages on display, but if the occasion arises, they are always at hand. Glass cuts, no matter how tiny, bleed vehemently and look pretty scary. If someone gets cut in class, take them out of the room immediately. Most halls in schools have a water fountain. Wash the cut and apply pressure. Bleeding should stop in a matter of seconds. Apply a bandage and get the individual back into class as soon as possible so everyone can see the incident was not serious.

13. Be prepared for that individual who is not really in class to learn but to socialize, comment on and steal everybody else's ideas. This person invariably tells one and all how much work he is accomplishing at home. In fact this home project is usually so big that he cannot bring it to class. If this individual persists in annoying everyone after a couple of warnings, it would be best to get him out of your class. Otherwise, he will disrupt each session by his presence.

14. Finally, be prepared to answer the same question in multiple shapes and forms, over and over. But then, that's what teaching is.

Chapter 14

Repairs

A QUICK SURVEY

Any stained glass object can be repaired, including lamps. The question always is: is it worth it? (Fig. 14.1.) Lamps tend to get dropped more than other glass items, and the fractures and amputations thus acquired are usually terminal. It is a difficult job in many instances to convince a customer that what he really needs is an entirely new shade rather than a repair of the old. People tend to think you are trying to boost the cost of your job in this fashion, when actually, it would cost them far more for the repair than for a new lamp. Sentimental preoccupation with a ruin may be all very well, but time marches on and all our yesterdays eventually fragment. Even stained glass lamps do not last forever, and where euthanasia is required, that should be your diagnosis no matter how emphatically the customer wants a repair. If you give in to him on a total wreck, neither one of you will end up being happy—he because you will never be able to get it exactly the way it may have been (he may not even remember exactly

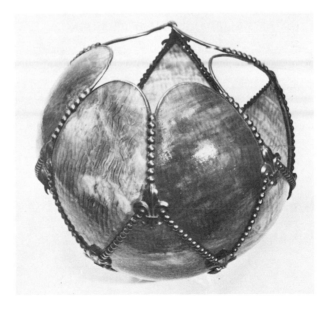

Fig. 14.1 A difficult repair job. The thin brass edging hides few discrepancies. Many of these bent panel shades are not worth repairing for this reason, especially if, as here, the brass edging is bent out of shape.

195

the way it was) and you because, no matter how much you may charge for a hopeless case, you'll find as you go along that it is never enough. Old brass doesn't solder well; old white metal tends to burn and bend; colors of very old glass often cannot be matched exactly. On top of that, such jobs are tedious and one always tends to put them at the bottom of the pile and to think about them "later." Unfortunately, the owner always wants them "now."

Repair work other than the type described above can be fun and financially rewarding, provided that you always remember to tell your customer that the item will not be in as perfect a condition as it was before it was broken. If you do not say that, no matter how small the difference may be after you repair it, you have left yourself wide open for complaints. Even if we know we can repair a lamp perfectly, we never promise. People are unpredictable, and we have found that if we warn them in advance of possible discrepancies in the workmanship they will be pleasantly surprised at finding none. Even if minor discrepancies exist, the customer will find none because he really doesn't want to see them. If you tell the customer that everything in your repair will be a perfect match, he will bring a magnifying glass with him when he comes to pick up his item, and even if the match is perfect, he will locate discrepancies. Don't look for trouble by claiming to be perfect; you are only challenging people to find your flaws.

STRAIGHT PANEL LAMPS

Cracks in any panels mean the entire panel must be removed and remade. This goes for all lamps except small-pieced ones. We do not glue broken panels for the same reason we do not disguise any lamp's deformity by turning its bad side toward the wall or by replacing it with cardboard or plastic (Fig. 14.2). We have been asked to do these things by individuals who don't want to pay the price for a true repair. "Just put any old thing in to fill the space," they say. "We'll turn that part to the wall." We do not do that sort of work even for "a couple of bucks," and we advise you not to; it is bad for the self-esteem.

On the other hand, we do try to save the customer money where we can. If the crack is so hairline that it cannot be seen except on very close observation

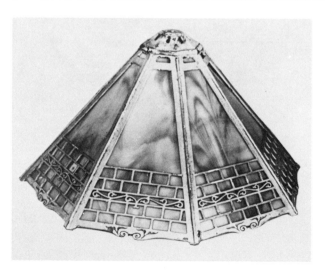

Fig. 14.2   On the other hand, this type of straight panel, clip in variety is quite easy to repair and requires only the cutting and fitting of the panels. The clips hold them in place and there is a wide margin of brass covering them. Take as many of these as you can get.

and there is no movement of the pieces despite repeated testing, we generally advise that such a panel be left alone. You may be fooled, however, if other panels are badly cracked or missing. The lamp, being off balance, may be weighing down this side, thus holding the pieces together pretty firmly. Test this panel again after the lamp has been repaired to make certain the pieces don't move. They well may, and then a repair here is also necessary.

Pyramidal lamps may be repaired as follows. Disassemble the lamp until you have left only the leaded shade. With a sharp lead knife, slice away the front portion of the lead cames holding the afflicted panel. Slice away, as well, the top U lead. In many instances, this portion need only be cut to either side of the panel and flipped upwards. You can now remove the broken pieces of glass, if any remain. You can make a new pattern from the old panel if it is cracked but intact or broken but with all the pieces present. If neither of these is the case, trace your pattern from one of the panels still in the lamp. The remainder of the cut lead cames will present the back surface and the "heart" or in-between wall of the lead. A good panel may be resting on half the caming to either side. If you can manage to cut the front of the caming in one piece without crumpling it too much, you can save it, stretch it slightly and reuse it.

Once the new panel is cut, it should slip neatly back atop the two supporting back portions of came. You can then run a little epoxy cement over the cut "heart." Then reapply the cut strip, or a new-cut strip from a fresh came directly over it. Make sure the new strip is cut as flat as possible so it does not stand away from the glass. Let the epoxy bind it; then solder it top and bottom and the panel has been replaced. The top U lead can then be pressed down again and resoldered.

This same process can be applied to crown or skirt, though here, since one end is open, the entire affected piece can be taken out and replaced without much ado. It is usually in the panels that trouble in repair arises.

For square or rectangular shades, this process is not so easily accomplished. Here the corner leads must be opened along one channel, the flap of the channel pried upwards, and the glass sneaked in and out. This is not always possible, and you may end up having to take a good portion of the lamp apart and even replacing beat up brass channels. Another problem is that even if you do get those corner brass or lead channels bent upwards, you may not get them down again smoothly. In this case you are worse off than when you started. You had better make sure you can replace the brass channels before you start disassembling anything.

Try working from the bottom, rather than from the top, of a square or rectangular lamp so you do not get involved with the wiring, metal top plates and crown pieces. It is easier to take the skirt apart since you can sometimes remove it as a unit. A lot of ad libbing is required to repair these lamps, and if you aren't sure you can do it, pass the job by. In terms of time, effort and worry, it may just not be worth it.

If any lamp looks a lot worse after the repair than before, you may find yourself buying a lampshade you really had not counted on, nor really wanted—especially if the repair job is terrible. On the other hand, we have acquired a number of beautiful shades quite inexpensively from people who originally brought them in for repair, didn't want to pay the price and sold them to us instead. Unfortunately, you cannot count on this happening as often as you might like.

BENT PANEL LAMPS

The panels of bent panel shades are held in place by any one or a combination of three methods. The manner in which the panels are held should be your primary consideration when taking in a bent panel shade for repair because, not only do you have to replace the panels that are broken, you must also remove a good panel to use as a prototype from which to make your mold. This is not always as easy as it sounds.

1. *The Clip In Type.* In Figs. 14.3, 14.4 and 14.5 the bent panels are held by metal clips attached to the frame. To remove a panel, bend the clips which hold it and pry the glass loose. In very old lamps, one bend may be all such a clip will take; it may then come away in your hand with the panel. Soldering such clips back on can be exasperating. A lot of flux and sweat can go into the job. You should keep a sheet of brass or copper handy on your worktable whenever such lamps come into view, since you'll probably be cutting out a lot of new clips. The frames of these shades are also pretty well oxidized, and you have to scrape all this off with brush and lead knife before the metal will accept solder. All in all, it is better if you do not have to replace clips. This part of the job alone may take more time than making the panel which is after all the primary concern. Look well at such a shade when it comes in, count the number of missing clips, add a few more that will probably be missing before you are done, and add all this to the price (Fig. 14.6).

Some of these lamps will arrive with broken frames. Don't allow this to develop you into a "while you're at it" situation, where, after you give the customer a price for panel replacement he says, "While you're at it, fix the shade." His tone of voice assumes this is all part of the same price, and if he is quick enough, he may get you to assume so, too. You may even get the idea that if you make a point of charging for this you will lose the whole job. We used to fall into this particular trap regularly. Now, if a customer wants a frame fixed, we charge for the service. Otherwise, we have found it better to lose the job.

Fig. 14.3 A bent panel clip in type shade in for repair.

Fig. 14.4   Fig. 14.3 seen from the bottom.

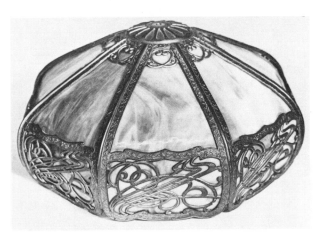

Fig. 14.5   The repaired shade.

Fig. 14.6   A bent panel foiled shade in for repair. Making the panels, as we did, is only half the battle. Putting them into the same channeled struts they came out of is something else again. Often we have to refoil and replace them—a risky business since the frames of these old lamps are hardly ever true anymore and each panel no longer takes up the same amount of space. You can get a lot of practice making panels when these shades present themselves.

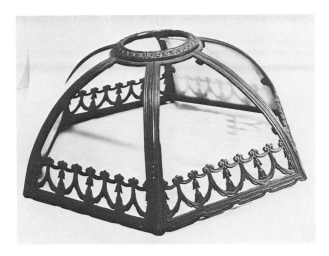

Fig. 14.7 A bent panel frame with no panels at all. We had to make the prototype as well as the final panels.

2. *The Channeled Type.* These bent panels are held in place by channels in the framework as well as by straps of metal running down the sides (Fig. 14.7). Sometimes there are clips along the sides to add to the channel support if the panel is a large one. These channels can be a problem if the glass has been seated in the lower one and the rest of the lamp built up from there with the entire top placed as a unit. You may have quite a bit of trouble getting a panel out. The only thing you can do is attempt to pry up one of the channels and slip the glass out while pulling down from below. If you slip, you will have still another panel to replace. We have had such lamps in for repair where we ended up doing more

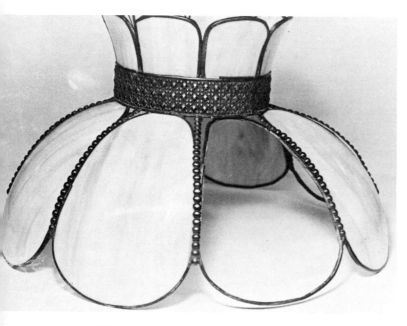

Fig. 14.8 A bent panel shade with one panel out. Look how thin that edging is.

panels for free than we ever got to charge for. Some channeled type lamps are more amenable. One outside channel bends up as readily as a flap, the panel comes out easily enough, and the flange then bends down again to hold the new panel in place. We don't suggest bending this channel back and forth too often, however, or you may get to keep it.

3. *The Foiled Type.* This is usually the worst of all the bent panel lamps from the standpoints both of getting panels out and replacing them. The rim of metal that surrounds each panel may prove a formidable barrier to the removal of a prototype bend. (Figs. 14.8, 14.9 and 14.10.) You may have to use a metal

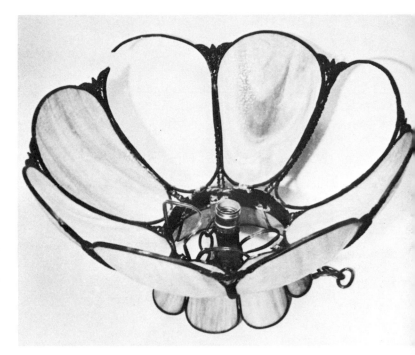

Fig. 14.9 We removed the panel upper left to use as a prototype by cutting the brass edging. This will then be soldered together. The solder will be colored to match the metal once the panel has been replaced.

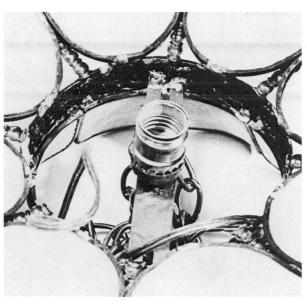

Fig. 14.10 Interior of that same lamp demonstrating how the panels are hooked to the frame. Sometimes it is necessary to break (melt) these joints to get a panel out. It may not be as easy to replace them later so the lamp assumes the original shape.

clippers or even a hacksaw to get a panel loose. Both of these tools must be used gently or you can break the glass. Once you have gotten through this outer rim, your troubles are still not over. You may have to break solder joints to get the framework loose enough to allow the glass to slip free. Worst of all, these panels are generally S shaped and hang up in the frame, half in and half out. Take your time working them loose. (Fig. 14.11.) Needless to say, replacing them and making new ones from the prototype are also problems. Because of their thin metal edging, the matching panels you provide have very little tolerance for error. Attempting to make the metal rim conform to an imperfect shape will throw the whole lamp off. Sometimes the metal edging is concealed behind a framework of brass or white metal which can be maneuvered somewhat to disguise a panel that is not quite up to snuff. Even here, however, the lamp itself does not permit any really shoddy workmanship. Don't attempt this one unless you are really good.

Once you have a panel out of the lamp, you must make a mold from it and fire a flat blank on the mold. The mold is made as previously described (Chapter 11). To make the blank, take a piece of kraft paper and press it around the bent panel with the curves uppermost. Make sure you get an imprint of the edges. Leave slack in the paper where it dips between folds if an S shaped panel is what you are working on. Lift the kraft paper from the panel, and you will find a rough approximation of the panel, in the flat, creased into the paper. Cut along these margins and reapply the template which you have now made to the panel. You may find further trimming is necessary now that it can take the shape better freed of excess paper. Once you are satisfied you have transferred the shape

Fig. 14.11 Seen from within, a channeled and brass-foiled shade presents insuperable problems just to remove a panel to work with. Almost the entire frame would have to be cut apart to get a good panel out here.

as perfectly as possible to the kraft paper, outline it onto pattern paper using the kraft paper for a guide. Cut this out and use it as a standard pattern to cut your glass blank. This is then fired over the mold surface and should, when completed, match the other lamp panels perfectly.

SMALL-PIECED LAMPS

Repairs on small-pieced lamps can be made with little trouble if the piece to be replaced is on a bordering edge. (Figs. 14.12, 14.13 and 14.14.) If it is not—and

Fig. 14.12 Repair begins on a small-pieced Tiffany shade. First the broken piece (fortunately a border piece) is removed by cutting the bottom metal with a snippers.

Fig. 14.13 With the metal cut and swung back, the pear is easily removed.

Fig. 14.14 A new pear is made and foiled into the existing space.

Fig. 14.15 Where the bottom metal cannot be cut away—as in nonbordering pieces (second row, left)—a paper pattern is made, and a new piece of glass is cut and foiled to fill the space. The end result, as seen in the bottom row of this Handel shade, is a somewhat thickened border around the replaced piece. Here the bottom metal was too thick to cut and bend away and get back again without a problem. When it is colored with hydrochloric acid and sulfur and overlaid with copper sulfate, the resulting hue will pretty well match the rest of the frame. The thickened border will then be less noticeable.

somehow it usually is not—then you must use a replacement method which will compromise the lamp somewhat, but is the only way you can fix it.

First you must remove the broken glass. The best way to do this is to take a Phillips® screwdriver, and using it as a punch, hold it against the glass to be removed and hit it a short, sharp blow with a hammer. This will literally blast the broken pieces out of the copper-bound space and yet not bend the copper rim inward and off the surrounding glass pieces. Whatever small pieces of glass remain should be removed by gentle wriggling with the fingers, so that the channels in which they were placed remain open. We are not going to reuse these channels—an almost impossible task—but we don't want to disturb the adhesion of the copper to the glass pieces around the fault.

Now heat your soldering iron and melt away as much of the old solder as you can, working within the open space provided. Go around all the edges so they flatten out as closely as possible to the borders of the surrounding glass (Fig. 14.15). You want to get the copper as thin as possible here.

Take a rubbing of the open space with a piece of paper and cut it out with a pair of scissors. You should obtain the exact dimensions of the piece of glass that will fill it. Try your rubbing in the space. If it fits too snugly, trim it down. There should be an edge of open space all around. Transfer this now to pattern paper and, using it as a template, cut it out of glass.

Try the piece of glass in the space. If it is too large, groze it down. Once you have it to the right size, smooth the edges with Carborundum paper and foil it. Tin the foil and place the foiled piece in the space and solder it to the neighboring pieces of glass. You may find a larger border of copper here because of the double amount, but that cannot be helped. Once the piece is soldered into place, you can antique the shiny finish with copper sulfate to make it look just like the rest of the lamp. The inside must be soldered, but it is not necessary to bead it. Clean off all flux residues and your repair is completed.

PRICING

No one can really tell you how to price a repair job. A lot depends on how fast you work and on how many lamps you can do at a time. The price also depends on how many lamps you want to do at one time. You can do three easy ones in the same amount of time as one difficult one and make three times the profit. If you are only interested in seeing how adept you are, this will not make any difference.

You must remember to charge for your time, but you must also remember that you are being paid as an expert and not as a beginner learning by trial and error. In the long run, you will find your own shortcuts to the methods described and possibly even your own methods. There are a lot of lamps waiting for you if you do.

PART IV
Potpourri

Afterword

Making stained glass lamps is a craft. It is not magic; there are no metaphysical overtones. Neither yoga nor encounter groups will make your stained glass creations any more beautiful or technically accurate. If you want to turn out beautiful lamps, become adept at glass cutting and leading, follow the principles of design and use your imagination. You might well do the same by attending yoga classes or going to encounter groups—but only if you have already grounded yourself in the fundamentals. You can then attribute the end result to anything you like.

The joy of the artificer is evident in any handcrafted object. A stained glass lampshade, done to a turn, is an object of which anyone might be proud. It provides its own best reason for being—and perhaps, as well, that of the individual who created it—for, as Cyrano said of his poetry: "When I have made a line that sings itself, I have repaid myself a thousand times."

Magazines Dealing with Stained Glass

The following magazines deal either in toto or in part with stained glass as a craft, hobby or esthetic experience. Almost all of them provide a marketplace for ideas and sales through their advertisements and articles.

Artisan Crafts. Star Route #4, Box 179-F, Reeds Spring, Mo. 65737. Editor, Barbara Brabec.

Country Wide Crafts. Published quarterly by Country Wide Publications, Inc., 222 Park Avenue South, New York, N.Y. 10003.

Craft Horizons. Published bimonthly by the American Crafts Council, 44 West 53rd Street, New York, N.Y. 10020.

Creative Crafts. Published eight times yearly by the Model Craftsman Publishing Corporation, 31 Arch Street, Ramsey, N.J. 07446. Editor, Sybil Harp.

Glass Art Magazine: Published bimonthly, PO Box 7527, Oakland, Ca. 94615. Editor, Albert Lewis.

Glass: The Complete Magazine for the Serious Collector. Published bimonthly by Special Publications, Inc., 5 Lincoln Court, Princeton, N.J. 08540. Editor, G. Gerald Davis.

Leonardo: International Journal of the Contemporary Artist. 17 Rue Emile Dunois, 92 Boulogne sur Seine, France. Editor, Frank J. Malina.

Popular Ceramics. Published monthly by Popular Ceramic Publications, Inc., 6011 Santa Monica Boulevard, Los Angeles, Ca. 90038.

Popular Crafts. Published bimonthly by Challenge Publications, Inc., 7950 Deering Avenue, Canoga Park, Ca. 91304.

Saturday Review of the Arts. Published by Saturday Review Inc., 450 Pacific Avenue, San Francisco, Ca. 94101.

Stained Glass: The Magazine of the Stained Glass Association of America. Editor, William S. Clark, 66 Malin Road, Malvern, Pa. 19355.

The Glass Workshop. Published six times yearly by The Stained Glass Club, 482 Tappan Road, Northvale, N.J. 07647. Editor, Anita De.

The Metropolitan Museum of Art: Bulletins. These bulletins are published bimonthly by The Metropolitan Museum of Art, Fifth Avenue and 82nd Street, New York, N.Y. 10028.

Your Church. Published six times yearly by The Religious Publishing Co., 198 Allendale Road, King of Prussia, Pa. 19406.

Lamp Mathematics

CIRCLES AND DIAMETERS

The diameter of a circle is a line drawn through its center from one side to the other. The radius is half the diameter. The circumference is the distance around a circle. The diameter of a circle being given, the circumference is found by multiplying the diameter by pi (3.1416); the circumference being given, the diameter is found by dividing the circumference by 3.1416.

The following table contains diameters and circumferences in inches and fractions to allow you to concentrate more on glass and less on math.

Diameter (inches)	Circumference (inches)	Diameter (inches)	Circumference (inches)	Diameter (inches)	Circumference (inches)
½	1.57	8½	26.70	16½	51.83
1	3.14	9	28.27	17	53.40
1½	4.71	9½	29.84	17½	54.97
2	6.28	10	31.41	18	56.64
2½	7.85	10½	32.98	18½	58.11
3	9.42	11	34.55	19	59.69
3½	10.99	11½	36.12	19½	61.26
4	12.56	12	37.70	20	62.80
4½	14.13	12½	39.27	20½	64.40
5	15.70	13	40.84	21	65.97
5½	17.28	13½	42.40	21½	67.54
6	18.85	14	43.98	22	69.11
6½	20.42	14½	45.55	22½	70.70
7	21.99	15	47.12	23	72.25
7½	23.56	15½	48.70	23½	73.82
8	25.13	16	50.26	24	75.40

The following shapes are to aid you in the basic planning of a shade. It is imperative that whatever shape you decide on be drawn as accurately as possible. You may combine these shapes or modify them to suit your creation, but until you are thoroughly familiar with them, you will not be certain how to do either. We therefore offer them for your study.

The Pentagon. This is a polygon of five angles and sides (Fig. Ap. 1). It is constructed by first drawing a circle. Draw a diameter AB through its center. Open your compass a bit, and draw two arcs centered at A. Without changing your compass draw two more arcs from B intersecting the first two. The line through these intersections is a radius CD perpendicular to AB. In the same way, bisect line CB with a perpendicular at point E. Place your compass on point E and draw an arc through D crossing AB at point F. Place your compass on D and, opening it to reach F, draw an arc from F to G. Keeping your compass the same, put it on G and draw arc H, and continue from H to I and from I to J. Connect these arcs with straight lines, and you have your pentagon perfectly drawn.

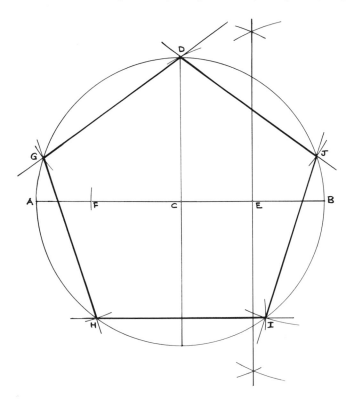

Fig. Ap. 1.

The Hexagon. A hexagon is a polygon with six sides and angles (Fig. Ap. 2). To line one up, first draw a circle with line AB as the diameter. Without changing your compass, put it on A and draw an arc at C, at C draw an arc at D and so forth around the circle. Connect the arcs with straight lines and you have your hexagon.

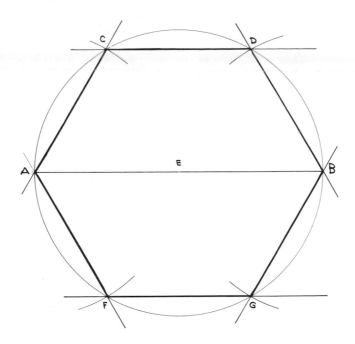

Fig. Ap. 2.

The Octagon. An octagon is a polygon with eight sides and angles (Fig. Ap. 3). You may draw it as follows: on your circle draw the perpendicular diameters AB and CD. Then bisect each of the central right angles thus formed at E. You may do this by setting your compass on A and drawing two arcs to intersect arcs from C and D. Lines from these intersections through the center of the circle will be the bisectors. Connect every point where a line crosses the circle to form your basic shape.

Internal designs—stars, pyramids—can be formed by connecting up different points. Many styles of lanterns can be produced from this shape, and to help you get their walls even, we have provided you with the angle degrees. Most combinations can be made knowing how these lines fall and keeping the angles to the degrees we have indicated.

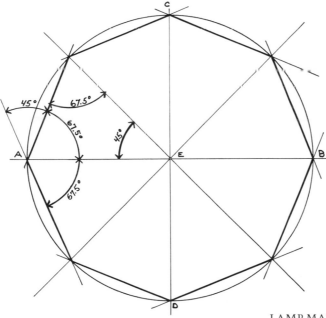

Fig. Ap. 3.

The Sphere. It is possible to design a ball lampshade (or globe shade) by treating it as a sphere. Taking a plane through such a sphere will leave you with a circle. Divide this circle (which we now may think of as a small cylinder) into sections as shown in Fig. Ap. 4. Marking each section with equidistant lines and bending them forward will give you the outside grid of your sphere. Make this first out of cardboard, and then use your cardboard model as a mold.

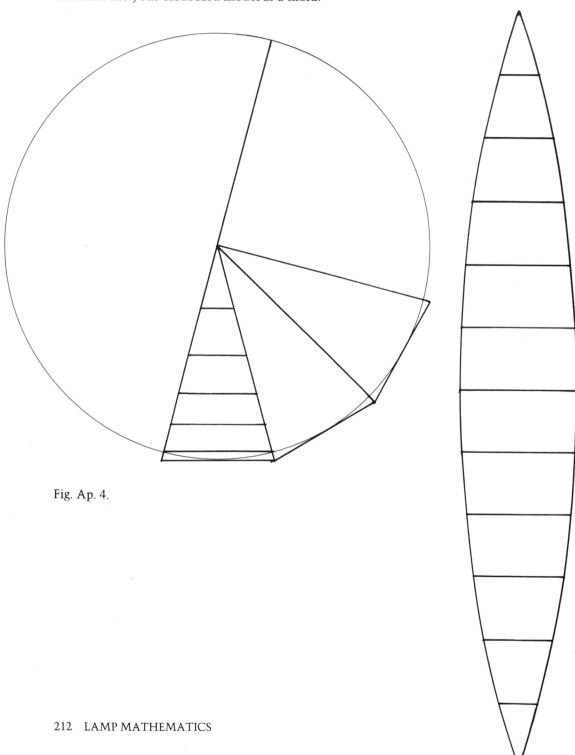

Fig. Ap. 4.

The Square. Constructing a square is done as follows. Measure off the line length you want from A to B and make an arc (Fig. Ap. 5). Do the same from B to D and from A to C. Draw a line tangent to both arcs. Connect the line points. To provide 45 degree angles cross arcs BD and CD and from that point draw a line through the right angle at A.

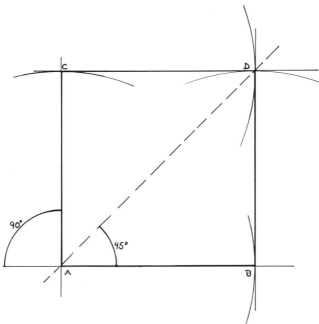

Fig. Ap. 5.

The Triangle. Constructing a triangle is done as follows. With your compass draw AB (Fig. Ap. 6). With the same opening, make an arc at C from A and another at C with the compass point on B. Where the arcs cross is the triangle peak.

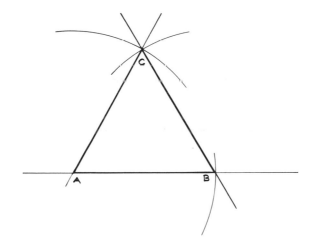

Fig. Ap. 6.

The above review is merely to indicate some basic rules of geometry which might stand the reader in good stead in his lamp designing.

Suppliers

Bottle Cutters

    Fleming Bottle and Jug Cutters
    Seattle, Wash.

Brass and Copper

    Lamart Corp.
    Richmond Street
    Clifton, N.J.

    T.E. Conklin Brass and Copper Co.
    West 23rd Street
    New York, N.Y.

General Supplies

    The Stained Glass Club
    P.O. Box 244
    Norwood, N.J. 07648

Glass

    Blenko Glass Co.
    Milton, West Va.

    Kokomo Opalescent Glass Co.
    Kokomo, Indiana

    The Paul Wissmach Glass Co.
    Paden City, West Va.

Glass Cutters

    The Fletcher-Terry Co.
    Spring Lane
    Farmington, Conn.

Glues

    Bond Adhesives Co.
    Jersey City, N.J.

Kilns and Kiln Materials

    Stewart Clay Co.
    133 Mulberry Street
    New York, N.Y.

Lead Came

    Gardiner Metal Co.
    4820 South Campbell Avenue
    Chicago, Ill.

    National Lead Co.
    Perth Amboy, N.J.

Molds

    Kay Kinney Contoured Glass
    725 Laguna Canyon Road
    Laguna Beach, Calif.

Paints

    Kay Kinney Contoured Glass
    725 Laguna Canyon Road
    Laguna Beach, Calif.

    L. Reusche and Co.
    2 Lister Avenue
    Newark, N.J.

Soldering Irons

    Esico Co.
    Deep River, Conn.

    Weller Co.
    100 Wellco Road
    Easton, Pa.

Glossary

Astrascope® The brand name of an inexpensive, excellent enlarging or reducing projector. Such an instrument will be found extremely helpful in bringing the diagrams in this book up to size. Such projectors may be found in most good artist supply emporiums.

Base The standing support for a table lamp. A base may be made of just about anything so long as it complements its individual shade.

Beading The process of applying additional solder to a seam to provide a rounded rather than a flattened surface. Both beauty and stability are thus increased.

Cartoon This is the working drawing for a stained glass design which contains all the cutlines. Sometimes it contains the paint lines as well, but this varies with the individual studio and with the artist doing the designing. The cartoon is essentially a blueprint of the work.

Chunk Glass Dalle-de-verre and slab glass are two other names. These slabs generally measure 8″ by 12″ by 1″ thick.

Cluster Socket A triple socket with the bulbs at angles to each other. These were quite often used in Tiffany lamps rather than one large globe. They still give more of an art nouveau effect.

Copper sulfate Copper sulfate reacts with the tin in the solder to form a dark, coppery tone on the surface thereby "antiquing" it. This chemical is toxic if ingested and should always be handled with care and kept out of the reach of children.

Crown The top anatomical division of a lampshade which is thus divided: crown, body of panels, skirt. The crown need not be present; its absence can produce potent aesthetic effects. Crowns come in different shapes and heights and may flare from the central vertical line, depending on the designer.

Dalle A thick glass slab which may be employed as is or may be cut to "chunks" with the proper tools. Also called dalle-de-verre. Used with either copper foil or cement, dalles will add texture and dimension to a sheet glass lampshade and can create their own faceted-type shade.

Dalle Hammer A tool for breaking chunk glass which resembles a bricklayer's hammer. It has two chisellike surfaces that allow for exact breaking of the chunk glass.

Double Rolled A term used to define the manufacture of both commercial and stained glass which is not blown. The glass—cathedral glass, mostly—comes out in large sheets between two rollers which gives the sheet a uniform thickness not found in most "antique glass" and which may also impress a texture onto the surface of the glass.

215

Drape Method Placing the glass blank on a mold the surface of which is convex and allowing the glass to settle or "drape" over it—rather than to sag into a mold which has its design indented into the surface. (This latter technique is called "sagging.")

Filigree Brass designs or flat strips used in shades as dividers to hide the seam either between crown and body or body and skirt or between the individual panels. Some styles are quite ornate, and you must avoid the temptation to let such strippings overbalance your shade.

Filigree spears Small, individually discrete strands of filigree.

Finial The small, brass (usually) screw top which holds the shade to a table lamp base. These come as simple or as ornate as one could desire.

Flemish glass A cathedral glass with an impressed design of many channels running every which way through its surface.

Flint A planned, unbalanced break in a geometric window. The purpose of the flint is to give the eye a break from the unqualified sameness of all those parallel lines.

Flux A material used in the soldering process. A good flux is liquid, cleans the material to be soldered, does not affect (pit) the soldering tip, does not release noxious fumes, will not burn the fingers, will flow readily into the pores of the metal to be soldered (thereby allowing the solder to flow just as readily by capillary action) and will not leave residues impossible to clean away. The flux we prefer is oleic acid.

Frame The skeleton (white metal, brass, lead or copper foil) of any shade.

Glass, antique Not of necessity "old" glass, but rather glass made by antique methods, i.e., handblown. Some of the most beautiful glass is made this way.

Glass, opalescent Sheet glass, usually "double rolled" by machine, which diffuses light over its surface rather than permitting it to penetrate through the surface.

Glass, transparent Clear glass, colored though it may be, that permits the passage of light so that objects may be seen through it.

Glass pliers Instruments with wide, toothed jaws that are good for breaking away small edges and rough-grozing score lines. These tools are a necessity for stained glass work.

Globe The milky white balloonlike covering of a bulb. A globe provides the formal effect that some shades need. They must be held in place by globe holders, many sizes of which are available. What is the right size for your lamp? A well placed globe should take up about half the inside diameter of the shade and round out almost at the bottom. Some globes protrude from the bottom; this is up to you.

Globs Rounded, thickened pieces of glass with one flat surface. They provide offset relief for flat surfaces in shades.

Glory hole The name given to the furnace in glass-making plants.

Granite-backed Sheet glass with a very rough texture on one side.

Grozing pliers Small-jawed pliers with an upper flat and a lower curved jaw. This instrument is used for taking off rough edges and specifically for getting into tight, rounded corners.

Heart The heart of the lead is the separation bar of the H in an H lead. It is thus the boundary of either side, or if you want to think of it this way, of each half H.

Hydrochloric acid A strong acid (also called muriatic) with strong fumes. Used with sulfur, it will darken lead came and solder. Use with caution.

Joint The meeting place for two or more lead cames. Soldering takes place here.

Kiln An oven made of firebrick. The heat source can be gas, fire or electric. Electric heat is the most expensive, but it provides the cleanest energy for your money.

Kiln sitter An instrument placed on your kiln to turn it off when the proper temperature is reached, leaving you free to watch TV in peace.

Kraft paper Brown drawing paper of a specific thickness which can be used for project blueprints (work drawings). We like the strength of this paper. Flux can be spilled on it, erasures made on it, hot solder dropped on it—it won't disintegrate.

Lantern A portable, narrow lamp, usually with a peaked top.

Lathkin An instrument made of wood, bone, plastic or metal which is used for opening the channel of lead came.

Lead came Lengths of lead (usually six feet) extruded with channeling for use in stained glass.

Lead knife A weighted, sharp, generally curved knife used to cut, mold, bevel, place, fit, size and basically cope with lead came in any manner, shape or angle you can come up with.

Lead stretcher Essentially a small vise, a lead stretcher holds one end of a piece of lead came while you stretch it and then lets go when you are done without your having to drop, kink or curl the piece you have just stretched.

Mold We use the words "mold" and "form" interchangeably. Actually a mold is a heated template, either curved or hollowed out to allow glass either to slump over or drape into it. A form is a basic cardboard or paper shape put together either to get an idea of the finished glass product or for use as a guide in the shaping of the primary material.

Mosaic Glass Sheet glass with definite, regular square patterns that resemble mosaic tiles.

Moss-backed A modification of the granite-backed design in which the backing is not quite as rough. Here again, we are talking about sheet glass.

Navettes Specific glass jewels as opposed to globs. All glass jewels are stamped from molds; globs are allowed to "crawl" together haphazardly. Navettes are sharp ovals.

Oaktag A heavy paper used for patterns in stained glass work.

Pantograph An instrument for enlarging or reducing a primary drawing.

Plate In lamp work, the top support of the lamp by which it hangs, if it is a hanging lamp, or is braced, if it is a table lamp. Plates may be complete coverings or partial coverings such as straps. Straps may be crisscross or single depending on the weight of the lamp and the designer's choice.

Pyrometer The temperature gauge on a kiln. It is best to fire stained glass using such a gauge rather than with cones, as ceramics are fired.

Rondelite A type of glass that has circular whorls representing rondels imprinted on its surface. It can be a good lamp glass as the texture breaks up light passing through it and hides the bulb.

Runing pliers A tool for breaking out long, thin scores. This instrument is especially useful in making tubular shades where long, thin pieces of glass so often play a part.

Sconce A modified lantern, usually protruding from a wall rather than hanging from a ceiling.

Score The scratch on the surface of a piece of glass left by a glass cutter. Scores can be "breakable" or "nonbreakable" depending on their depth, amount of wobble and incisiveness.

Solder An amalgam of tin and lead. The best solder for stained glass work is sixty percent tin and forty percent lead. Soldered lead joints are extremely strong, stable and, if done correctly, inconspicuous. Solder does not stick to glass.

Soldering gun A soldering tool held like a pistol. We do not recommend such a gun as it really does not allow for proper joints, but if it is all you have and you are a beginner, use it.

Soldering iron You should have an iron from 80 to 120 watts with a set screw barrel. We prefer bores of ⅜ inch for this work. Put an off-on switch on the cord as eventually your iron will get so hot it will burn the lead came. (Esico and Weller both make good irons in this wattage.)

Sketch Your idea transferred to paper with all deformities, flashes of genius and vagaries laid bare.

Skirt The bottom anatomical portion of a shade providing, when necessary, a finishing touch to the project.

Story skirt Our own term for a small-pieced lamp skirt which is pictorial in nature rather than abstract.

Strapping Decorative filigree or lead came that has been flattened. Strapping is used to hide a seam without obstructing the general design.

Streaky Most opalescent glass contains whorls and streaks of colors—in some instances, three or four different hues. We reserve the word "streaky," however, for antique or cathedral glass with such whorls and streaks.

Swagging What you are entitled to do for yourself as well as your lamp if you are proud of the job. With your shade it is done with chain in loops from the outlet over the ceiling to the socket.

Template A pattern for individual pieces of glass. We make these from a special paper.

Tinning The act of coating lead with solder all along its length. The action also applies to copper or any other metal which is being so treated.

Vase Cap Decorative or plain brass cylinders which are used to finish off the tops of lamps and also to provide a method of supporting them.

Bibliography

ABBATE, FRANCESCO: *Art Nouveau, The Style of the 1890s*, Octopus Books, London, 1972.

AMAYA, MARIO: *Tiffany Glass*, Walker and Co., New York, 1967.

ANDERSON, HARRIETTE: *Kiln Fired Glass*, Chilton, Pennsylvania, 1970.

BATTERSBY, MARTIN: *Art Nouveau*, Hamlyn Publishing, London, 1969.

BURTON, JOHN: *Glass, Philosophy and Method*, Chilton, Pennsylvania, 1967.

HALL, NATHANIEL (Ed.) *Metal Finishing*, Metals and Plastics Publications Inc., New Jersey, 1969.

HORNUNG, CLARENCE P.: *Designs and Devices*, Dover, New York, 1932.

ISENBERG, ANITA and SEYMOUR: *How To Work In Stained Glass*, Chilton, Pennsylvania, 1972.

JOHNSON, VIRGIL: *Millville Glass*, Delaware Bay Trading Co., New Jersey, 1971.

KINNEY, KAY: *Glass Craft*, Chilton, Pennsylvania, 1962.

KOCH, ROBERT: *Louis C. Tiffany: Rebel in Glass*, Crown, New York, 1964.

———: *Louis C. Tiffany's Glass, Bronzes, Lamps*, Crown, New York, 1971.

KRONQUIST, EMIL F.: *Metalwork for Craftsmen*, Dover, New York, 1972.

LETHABY, W. R.: *Leadwork*, Macmillan, London, 1893.

NEUSTADT, EGON: *The Lamps of Tiffany*, Fairfield Press, New York, 1970.

QUICK, LELANDE and HUGH LEIPER: *Gemcraft*, Chilton, Pennsylvania, 1959.

Index

Page numbers referring to illustrations are set in **bold.**

advertising, 185–188
angle, 73, **78**

bandages, 154
base, 52, 53, **54**
   ceramic, **58**
   flat, 53
   harp, 53
   pipe, 53
beading, 38
bending brake, **62,** 78
borders, 31
bottles, **82**
brass came, 52, 120
brass, decorative, **47,** 118
brass edging, **195**
brush, flux, 12
   wire, 13
bulbholders, 53
bulbs, 79

candleholders, 80, **82**
canopies, 48
capping, 49
carbon, 178
cartoon, 20, **83,** 110, 144, 158
carving, 123
chains, 47
chandelier, **82**
charcoal, 13
check ring, 46
circumference, **173**
clamp, 79
classes, 192
clay, 165
clients, 188

consignments, 189
contract, 191
copper foil, **37,** 39, 81, 160–164
copper sheeting, 75, 172
crown, 3, 25, **26,** 44, 93, 95
   curved, **27**
curriculum, 191

design, 23, 43, 52, 78, 87, 143
   inlay, 118
diameter, 22, 33, 86, 150, 209
display advertisement, 186
dome, plastic, 158
drape method, 177
drilling, 113
Dura Lite, 51

enlarging projector, vii
epoxy, 140, 197
eraser, 13
extension cord, 186

filigree, 27, 113, **181**
   spear, **121**
flanges, 96
Fletcher, 5
flexible curve, 158
   ruler, **188**
flint, **17**
flux, 12
   residues, 92
form, 150, 154
   cardboard, **35,** 154
   geometric, 210
   wire, 154
fruit, 144

glass, 12
    antique, 6
    blanks, 176
    cathedral, 6
    chunk, **136**
    cleaning, 15
    cutter, 10, **11**
    cutting, 13
    Flemish, 6
    frosting, 5
    globs, 118, 144, 178
    mixing of, 41
    opalescent, 4
    photographing, viii
    rondolite, 6
    scoring, 15
    scrap, 9, 66
    storage bins, 8
    transparent, 5
globe, 29, 50
    holder, **47**
grapes, 144
grouting, **136**

hammer, 13
hinge, **134**
hot spot, 5
hexagon, 210
hydrochloric acid, **204**
hydrofluoric acid, 5
Hydroperm, 176

inlays, 117

jewels, 118

kerosene, 15
kiln, 123, 177–179
    wood, 179
Kinney, Kay, 178
knife, lead, 12, 90, 95

lamp kits, 186, 188
lampshade, 48
    bent panel, 150, 170, 198
    globe, 134
    pyramidal, 21, 86
    small-pieced, 203
    story, 142
    table, 51
    tiered, **88**
    tiered pyramidal, 92
    tubular, 108

magic marker, 11, 158
metal top, 75
    snippers, 203
mini lamp, **59**
mirror, 6
Mirror Glaze, 183
mold, 36, 157, 174, 177
    plastic, **157**
    rock maple, **150**
Mold Coat, 175
molding, 110

nails, 13, 165
    leading, 89
navettes, **26, 119**
night light, 68
nipples, 48

octagon, 211
offsets, 117
overlay, **159**

packing material, 188
panels, 2, 57
    belted, 181
    bent, **170,** 179
    clip in, **198**
    diamond, 68
    trimming of, 180
pantograph, vii
paper, 11
    carbon, 11
    Carborundum, 22, 78, 204
    graph, 86, 158
    kraft, 45, 48, 109, 159
    pattern, 7, 11, 15, **16,** 20, 88, 158, **160,** 165,
        172
    sketching, 11
pattern knife, 11

scissors, 11
payment, 186
pencils, 11
pentagon, 210
plaster, 123, 154
plastic, 4
pliers
   chain, 49
   glass, 12
   grozing, 11, 166–167
   running, 110
plywood, 11
pricing, 205
prototype, 33
push pins, 111, 165
pyrometer, 180

repairs, 195
rock slabs, **43**
rondel, **61,** 63, 64, 66
rondelite, **40**
ruler, 11

sagging, 178
sandblasting, 5
scallops, 118
sconce, **79-81**
seams, 35, 96, 97
set screw, **51**
sheet metal, 44, 122
shield light, **viii**
sketch, 19, **20**
skirt, 3, 29, 30, 90, 94
   fruit, 31, 144
   scalloped, **86**
   story, 143
   tulip, **169**
slumping, 177
socket, 57, 191

solder, 12, 18, 19, 75, 90, 117, 183
soldering, 44
   iron, 13, 204
solder pot, 164
sphere, 212
square, 213
stained glass
   types, of, 5
strapping material, 47
straps, 46
struts, **199**
Styrofoam, 110, 164–166, 182
swagging, 49

tacking, 92, 166
teaching, 1, 190
template, 114
   paper, **76**
terra cotta, **174**
thumbtacks, 13
Tiffany, 2, 4, 31, 32, 143, 150, 157, **162, 165,**
   166
tinning, **38,** 164
tool caddy, **10**
tools, 10, 193
tops, metal, 70
triangle, 213
tulip shape, **102**

vase caps, 24, 33, 47, 49, 111, 183
Vaseline, 176

wire, lamp, 48
wiring, 56
workspace, 8
worktable, 8

X-ray view box, **9**

About the Authors

Anita Isenberg was born in New York City and attended high school in Tucson, Arizona, and then went on to the University of Tempe in that state. She did graduate work in art and design at the University of Paris and at that time her interest in stained glass came to the fore.

She was an apprentice at William O'Connor's Castle Hill Studio from 1963 to 1966 and after that time she opened her own studio, the Stained Glass Club, to promote the craft of stained glass among hobbyists as well as a commercial art venture.

She has executed commissions for windows, room dividers, lamps and shutters in New York and New Jersey and she repairs antique stained glass for such people as Beatrice Weiss, the noted Tiffany collector, among others. Mrs. Isenberg, under the name "Anita De," is also editor of her own journal of stained glass and the allied arts, *The Glass Workshop*, which enjoys a large circulation in this country and goes to subscribers in such places as Manila, Curaçao, Puerto Rico, France, Mexico and Canada.

Seymour Isenberg is a graduate of Horace Mann School in New York City, Syracuse University, and Kansas City College of Osteopathy and Surgery. Although a practicing physician, he is an active stained glass craftsman and works closely with Anita Isenberg in the Stained Glass Club. He is the author of another book, *How to Multiply Your Real Estate Sales*, and is a contributor to medical, crafts and wildlife journals.

Dr. and Mrs. Isenberg live in Northvale, New Jersey, with their son Arthur.